Partnerships in Educational Development

Partnerships in Educational Development

Edited by
Iffat Farah & Barbara Jaworski

Oxford Studies in Comparative Education
Series Editor: David Phillips

SYMPOSIUM
BOOKS

Symposium Books
PO Box 204 Didcot Oxford OX11 9ZQ United Kingdom
the book publishing division of wwwords Ltd
www.symposium-books.co.uk

Published in the United Kingdom, 2006

ISBN 1 873927 35 5

This publication is also available on a subscription basis
as Volume 15 Number 1 of *Oxford Studies in Comparative Education*
(ISSN 0961-2149)

Typeset by wwwords Ltd
Printed and bound in the United Kingdom by Cambridge University Press

Contents

Preface

This book is about the development of one institution and its developmental work in education in South and Central Asia and in East Africa. It is the Institute for Educational Development (IED) at the Aga Khan University (AKU) in Karachi, Pakistan.

The IED came into being in 1993 and launched its first programme in 1994, an M.Ed. in teacher education. It recruited 20 teachers, carefully selected from schools in Pakistan, East Africa, Tajikistan and Bangladesh. There should have been a teacher from India, but sadly she was not granted a visa to come. These 20 teachers, graduating from the M.Ed. course 18 months later, were the first graduates from the IED. They became the first Professional Development Teachers (PDTs), working with schools and running short courses for other teachers at the IED. After three years of PDT work, some of these graduates were selected for Ph.D. studies overseas, and are now doctoral graduates, and central IED faculty. The wheel has come full circle.

In the meantime the M.Ed. programme has flourished and developed with eight cohorts of selected teachers. The IED programmes have expanded in a variety of ways and in a variety of directions. Some are academic programmes educating teachers and educational managers in a university environment, albeit with school-focused work. Some are professional programmes, located in the field, albeit with theoretical elements perceived as central to the developmental process. The IED has attracted attention both nationally and internationally. In the countries we have listed above, professional programmes have developed to run alongside the central IED operation. The IED's work has become visible to government agencies, who from tentative initial investment are now looking towards the IED to work with them in the developmental field. Other countries have seen the results of the IED's work in the original countries and have asked to join the developmental enterprise. The IED now works with three countries in East Africa, namely, Kenya, Tanzania and Uganda, in Afghanistan, Syria and several central Asia countries including Tajikstan and Kyrgyzstan. There are possibilities of initiating work in other countries in the region.

Perceived in such terms, the IED's growth and influence reads like an educational developmental success story. And of course it is a success. But this is not to say that there are not many issues and problems to face in its day-to-day and decade-to-decade development. In 2003, the IED celebrated 10 years of operation. This was a time to celebrate and also to take stock of its achievements and issues. It has many impact programmes in place, seeking to provide sound research evidence to document processes in learning and growth and issues that have to be addressed. One problem of rapid growth is that it is easy for the institute and its faculty to become overextended, so that in-depth review of programmes and outcomes is never achieved. Despite considerable overextension, the IED is striving to avoid this danger.

This book is a product of the 10 years of development. We hoped to complete it for the 10-year celebrations, but as with other aspects of the IED, it kept on growing. In the volume we have tried to provide an account of development from a number of perspectives, such as historical, chronological, issues-based and honestly critical.

Work at the IED has been based on a theoretical vision of school development through production of a critical mass of knowledgeable, reflective practitioners: teachers, educators and educational managers. Partnerships have been made with schools, school systems, governmental organisations and universities in other countries. Development of partnerships has taken time and there have been many issues to address and problems to overcome. Gradually, other institutions or groups have come to see the IED in practice and to appreciate the nature of educational growth. As the critical mass has developed, along with it has come the beginning of a maturity of perception and confidence in the growth process. Schools and systems have taken on the mantle of responsibility themselves and are running developmental programmes in parallel with the IED and with its continued support. This book documents the paths by which such outcomes have been achieved, and reports from what has been learned in the process.

One of the partnerships has been between the IED and two institutions overseas, its 'Partner Universities' (PU), the Universities of Oxford and Toronto. Academics from these two institutions have worked closely with the IED faculty over the years, and have played a significant role in development. At the same time, all have learned significantly from their involvement. This book, edited jointly by a member of the IED faculty and a member of the Oxford University Department of Educational Studies, is just one product of this partnership.

The chapters in this volume tell a story. In Chapter 1, we present an historical perspective of the origination and early work of the IED. Chapter 2 looks at relationships between IED and its PU, and the issues that arose from early collaboration and negotiation of PU contribution. Chapters 3, 5 and 9 are spinal chapters. Chapter 3 looks at the development of the M.Ed. programme and the education of Professional Development Teachers. Chapter 5 takes this development further looking at how PDTs developed after their M.Ed. programme, and in particular in their work with teachers in the Visiting Teacher Programmes at the IED. Chapter 9 deals with issues in educational management. It was very clear from early days that the IED had to work closely with school principals and other educational leaders if school development was to be achieved.

PDTs were educated to work with teachers in school and at the IED for teachers' professional and academic education. They needed therefore to have an understanding of school subjects and the didactics and pedagogy associated with subject teaching. Chapter 4 looks at the nature of subject studies and the issues it raised in the M.Ed. programme.

Chapters 6-8 and 10-12 take up a range of developmental concerns related to field-based development. Chapter 6 looks at a mentoring programme in the Baluchistan province of Pakistan. Chapter 7 is set in East Africa and reports the development of Visiting Teacher Programmes, later Certificate Programmes, and the beginnings of an East African Professional Development Centre. Chapter 8 is set in Central Asia, focusing particularly on IED-related development in Tajikistan and Kyrgyzstan. Whole school development is the focus of Chapters 10-12. Chapter 10 reports development within one Karachi school which significantly sought its own developmental programme early in its relationships with the IED. Chapter 11 is based in Bangladesh, and similarly reports the development within one school, building on its relationship with IED. Chapter 12 reports on the Whole School Improvement Programme (WISP) in the Northern Areas of Pakistan, where a team of PDTs worked with a widely spread group of schools The final chapters each take up a particular area of activity or concern within IED development. Chapter 13 looks at the problems faced by teachers returning to their schools from an eight-week Visiting Teacher Programme at the IED, and traces some of the issues in putting university-based knowledge into practice in the real world of school and classroom. Chapter 14 is about health education and reports the IED's early work with urban and rural schools in Pakistan. Chapter 15 focuses on research training in the M.Ed. programme, and ways in which future educators gain their first insights into processes and practice of educational research. The last chapter, Chapter 16, written by the editors, brings the story to a close by addressing issues in partnership and teaching development, with particular reference to reflective practice and school improvement. The people writing these chapters are IED and PU faculty and PDTs. A large number of people, change agents themselves, and learners, in the developmental processes reported, have contributed to the story we have told.

As we write now, we are aware that things move on. By the time this book is published there will be further developments, new aspects, people and places in the IED's work, and new issues to address. As we take our final steps in the editing process, we are part of planning for the new Ph.D. programme which is to be launched in the autumn of 2004. There are plans to establish an AKU-IED in Tanzania to serve the countries in Africa. The learning processes are ongoing. Much work is needed in researching the outcomes and impact of existing programmes, so that new activity and initiatives can learn from what has been done so far. We hope that readers will find much that is informative in these pages. Moreover, we hope that what is reported here and the issues it raises will add considerably to the corpus of knowledge about developmental work in education worldwide and highlight particularly the contribution to knowledge that comes from studying educational development in the developing world.

Iffat Farah & Barbara Jaworski

CHAPTER 1

The Establishment of Aga Khan University – Institute for Educational Development

SADRUDIN PARDHAN & DENNIS THIESSEN

Introduction

The Institute for Educational Development at the Aga Khan University (AKU-IED) was established in July 1993 and is located in the school complex of the Sultan Mohamed Shah (SMS) [1], Aga Khan School in Karachi. The AKU-IED operates out of its own Professional Development Centre (PDC) [2], which was inaugurated in November 1994. Speaking on the occasion of the inauguration, His Highness the Aga Khan [3], said:

> The Institute for Educational Development (IED) targets a very important, low status profession: teaching. The very creation of IED highlights the importance of teaching, and the programmes of IED are crafted to amplify that message. The technical work of the Institute is designed to raise the competence of teachers, both in their substantive areas of specialty and in their teaching skills, with the expectation that a truly excellent teacher can inspire others by example. Greater competence may not ensure higher status, but it will make it easier to achieve. Neither publicity nor good training is likely to make much difference, however, unless an environment is created in which good teachers can be more effective. IED is planning to devote much of its work to creating such an environment. By working with school heads, not just individual teachers, IED will try to build a new teaching environment. The leadership of school heads is essential to real reform.

Speaking on the same occasion the first Director of AKU-IED Dr Kazim Bacchus said:

AKU-IED courses focus on in-service training which, in most developing countries has been more effective than pre-service teacher education in raising students' academic performance. This is due to the poor quality of the latter training in these countries often being unrelated to local classroom realities.

Our programmes place great emphasis on school-based training so as to link theory and practice more effectively. This explains the location of this Professional Development Centre within the SMS school complex, thereby allowing our students to try out immediately any new ideas about teaching acquired from their classes or discussion groups.

School improvement is more effective when one works with entire schools – since each school has a culture of its own, which exerts an almost independent influence on the quality of its students' work. Therefore we shall be increasingly involved with key school-related groups to help develop in schools a culture that facilitates a high quality of academic performance.

In addition, our teachers are being prepared to be critically reflective inquirers into their own professional practice.

The above quotations summarize why AKU-IED was established and how it planned to operate. The institute's mission was to become a leader in educational reform and improvement in the developing world. Its focus was (and continues to be) on improvement in the performance of teachers and other stakeholders through professional development leading to overall school improvement. AKU-IED aims to achieve its goals through human resource development, institutional capacity building, research and dissemination and policy analysis and advocacy.

In developing all its programmes the Institute has worked closely with its overseas partners, the Faculty of Education, University of Toronto (and more recently the Ontario Institute for Studies in Education University of Toronto [OISE-UT]) and Oxford University Department of Educational Studies (OUDES).[4]

The remainder of this chapter gives a background to the development of AKU-IED and summarizes its evolution. Subsequent chapters will deal in more detail with its programmatic activities, research, outreach and associated challenges.

Genesis of the Institute for Educational Development

For a number of years, we have been grappling with the issue of declining trends in the quality of education in the countries where we operate schools. The problem is not confined to our schools, nor does it exist only in the developing countries. During the last decade, some alarming reports have come out describing the downwards trend in levels of knowledge, skills and habits in reading, writing, mathematics and science. Declining quality of education has become an international problem.[5]

Concerned about the status of education in general but more specifically in areas where the Aga Khan Development Network (AKDN) [6] operates schools, His Highness the Aga Khan convened a Task Force in December 1988 to consider possible strategic interventions in the realm of teacher education and teacher motivation, curriculum development, school management and performance and educational research. While his primary concern was for the quality of education in AKDN schools, his overall vision was the development of models of high quality education which could impact national education systems.

In the course of its deliberations, the Task Force studied various reports from the UN agencies, UNESCO and UNDP, the World Bank and other Social Sector Organizations on the state of education in developing countries in general and more specifically in areas served by the AKDN. It reviewed educational activities of the Aga Khan Education Services (AKES) and the Aga Khan Foundation (AKF), and discussed successful models of professional development and school improvement in both developed and developing countries. These included the teacher professional development work of the Pittsburgh School District Board at Schenley School in Pittsburgh, the Michigan State University Professional Development Schools model, the Oxford University Department of Educational Studies (OUDES) Internship Programme, and some of AKDN's school improvement programmes.

The western models cited above were based in real schools and involved teachers working with colleagues who were trained as Master Trainers and recognized as experts in contemporary aspects of teacher education. These models demonstrated that schools flourish when they are treated as individual entities and that the same inputs made in different schools do not yield the same results. School management plays a key role for the impact of the inputs and is critical to the reprofessionalization process of teachers in the school. They also suggested that teachers are critical in any school improvement effort and must be empowered and engaged in the process of change.

The Task Force also reviewed some small innovative grass-roots level school improvement programmes in the AKDN institutions in a number of countries in South Asia and East Africa. These included:

(i) The School Improvement Programme (SIP) (1987-89) of the Aga Khan Education Service, Pakistan (AKES,P) which targeted the development of governance structures, school management, teachers and physical facilities in four large school complexes over a period of three years. This initiative followed denationalization of AKES,P schools in 1984-85 by the Government of Pakistan which had nationalized private schools in 1972.

(ii) The Field Based Teacher Development Programme (FBTDP) in Northern Areas of Pakistan which was launched by AKES,P in partnership with the Government in the mid-1980s. This programme provided professional development opportunities for untrained practising teachers at their local primary school over a full academic year under the supervision of Master Trainers. Teachers were selected from a cluster of village schools within walking distance of the school chosen as the training centre. This was particularly beneficial to women teachers for cultural reasons as parents were reluctant to let their daughters (or daughters-in-law) go to larger urban centres to access teacher education and because the number of places available to women in teacher education institutions was limited.

(iii) A School Improvement Programme of AKES, India, in Bombay, which aimed at improving school structures and curriculum content, teaching methodology and language skills of teachers. Increased community involvement was also addressed.

(iv) The School Improvement Programme in Andhra Pradesh, India which aimed at curriculum enrichment, improving teaching methodology, school infrastructure and school management.

(v) The School Improvement Programme of Aga Khan Mzizima Secondary School, Dar es Salaam, Tanzania during the mid-1980s, which focused on the development of teaching and learning resources for specific subjects followed by developing teaching skills and teacher leadership.

All of the above initiatives – school improvement programmes – were focused on specific issues and were one-off time-bound activities. Several of these programmes had a very small professional base, were often dependent for their success on one or two outstanding individuals and were led by expatriates from contexts very different from the one in which the SIPs were launched. Moreover, there was little recognition and professional advancement for teachers undergoing in-service professional development through courses and classroom experiences. The AKDN SIP efforts also suggested that schools do not improve once and for all but need renewed efforts.

Based on their findings, the Task Force believed that a new and imaginative initiative was needed by the AKDN to institutionalize successful school improvement efforts of AKDN in developing countries. A credible base was required which could support ongoing school improvement efforts and which could recognize the efforts of the teachers undergoing professional development. The major contributors to any school improvement efforts were to be cadres of classroom teachers who could be trained to support colleagues and take leadership roles in the process of change. After much discussion the Task Force developed a profile of the teacher educator who would become an effective change agent by initiating school improvement activities. The person would be an exemplary teacher. As resident in-service teacher educator in a school he/she would attempt a variety of approaches including demonstration lessons, opening up his/her classroom to visits by other teachers, offering formal in-service training to other teachers, helping younger inexperienced teachers overcome some of the initial hurdles which they were facing or likely to face in teaching. Mentoring, peer-coaching, reflective practice and other individual change strategies would be used by the teacher educator to help overcome teachers' resistance to the adoption of the new instructional approaches. The Task Force further envisaged that the teacher educator in collaboration with colleagues and faculty at AKU-IED would develop short intensive, eight-week courses at the IED for their fellow teachers in special areas of need such as the teaching of English, Mathematics, Science and Social Studies. It felt that developing persons with such a profile would require intensive professional development and envisaged that this could be achieved by identifying successful practising teachers who would participate in an extensive professional development programme lasting up to two academic years culminating in a Master's degree.

Pakistan was singled out by the Task Force as the most likely country for any intervention. Pakistan has a large AKDN presence including the largest Aga Khan Education Service in the network and is the site of the Aga Khan University.[7] As a country, Pakistan typifies the problems faced by developing countries in the delivery of education. It has some of the poorest indicators for education in the world, both for women and men, such as low public expenditure on education and very low literacy rates (as low as 4% in some rural areas). The mean years of schooling for females is an alarming 0.7 months with 2.9 years for males and 7 million children are out of primary school (Haq, 2000). There are gender and rural-urban imbalances in terms of access and quality. Curricula lack relevance and teaching and learning strategies are shaped by ineffective testing and examination systems. Schools are poorly resourced and educational institutions lack proper physical infrastructure and basic amenities, and are sub-optimally utilised. Exacerbating the problems is the underutilisation and mismanagement of resources, lack of accurate data available and the very low status accorded to teachers. Teacher performance is severely handicapped by an insufficient number of teachers to keep pace with a growing school population. The poor quality of teacher education; poor supervision with little attention to performance in the classroom and high teacher absenteeism are critical impediments to increasing community confidence in the value and relevance of education.

The Task Force recognized that addressing these issues would be a major challenge. But a beginning had to be made. It suggested an innovative intervention at the in-service level and made the following recommendations (AKU-IED, 1991):

- the Aga Khan University should found an institution to be called the Institute for Educational Development (IED);

- at the heart of the IED would be a Professional Development Centre (PDC). This should be based in a 'real' school providing regular education for a full range of school pupils from K-10 [8], thus providing a clinical 'teaching hospital' environment to which practising teachers would be brought to develop their skills in classroom settings under the supervision of clinical teachers.[9]
- in order to ensure high standards, AKU should establish a partnership with a few universities, perhaps three – one in North America, one in the United Kingdom and one in the developing world. The universities selected would have experience in the operation of field-based programmes and provide leadership in educational research, policy studies, evaluation and assessment; since AKU's experience so far had been only in the medical field.
- a Unit for Research and Policy Studies should be established to provide the intellectual linkage for the above project.

The First Years of AKU-IED

Recruitment of Schools and Teachers

The AKU-IED commenced operations in July 1993 in a temporary location in Karachi.[10] The faculty and administrative structure were quickly put into place and in January 1994, AKU-IED launched its initial M.Ed. course to prepare the first group of teacher educators. This first programme was designed to take place over 18 months. A majority of the participants in the first cohort were from Karachi, although taking into account possible future interventions in areas served by AKDN, representatives from Northern Pakistan, Central Asia, Bangladesh and East Africa were also selected to participate in the programme. Thus participants came from diverse cultures and school contexts.

Agreement with funding agencies [11], required that a specific number of candidates should be selected from schools in each of the sectors, i.e. Government, AKES, and private not-for-profit. Therefore, the programme was advertised to schools from the three sectors and detailed discussions were held with their managements. From the schools that expressed interest in participating in the programme, a small number were selected on the basis of their commitment to school improvement and their willingness to support teachers during the programme. Schools were expected to pay their teachers' salaries during the period of study at IED and to support the returning graduates in their role as change agents in the school. They also entered into an agreement to share 50% of the time of the returning graduates with IED over a period of up to five years. These selected schools were designated as *Collaborating Schools*.

A very large number of applications to participate in the M.Ed. programme were received from teachers of the selected schools and those who met the minimum selection criteria were short-listed. The IED faculty visited each of the schools with potential candidates, observed candidates teaching in a real classroom and interviewed them, joined by a representative of the relevant sector.

The above selection process of first identifying schools as 'collaborating schools' and selecting individual teachers from these schools was pertinent to the AKU-IED approach to school improvement through institutional capacity building. Currently there are about 40 collaborating schools in Karachi. These schools work with AKU-IED to allow their teachers to participate in the Institute's courses and they open their schools for the course participants to practise teaching approaches and methodologies studied in various modules. In areas outside Karachi the M.Ed. graduates work with the collaborating systems to conduct professional development courses for teachers of the systems.

The M.Ed. Programme

The programme began with a process of reflection and reconceptualization of existing practices as classroom teachers. The participants were provided with contemporary literature and the opportunity to discuss what constitutes meaningful teaching and learning. This process was integrated with visits to Karachi schools during which the participants observed lessons and wrote critical appraisals of those lessons. They spent a number of days in the school observing the school dynamics, talking to students, parents, staff and school management personnel to get an appreciation of the prevailing school culture.

Action research, journal writing and peer observation of classroom lessons were some of the activities embarked upon to inquire into practice. Throughout the programme the participants were encouraged to extend their reflection and inquiry into the interplay between education and extraneous events related to social, economic, cultural and political issues. In this way the participants were expected to relate classroom teaching to the real world.[12] These combined experiences of critical self-reflection and reflection on others' teaching helped the teachers to appreciate the limitations of their own existing beliefs about the practices in teaching as well as those of others. They were encouraged to use these findings as bases to develop and articulate alternate and defensible personal visions about teaching.

In this first programme, 24 weeks were devoted to upgrading the subject knowledge of the course participants. Four subject areas were covered for this purpose. These were English, Mathematics, Science and Social Studies.[13] The process encouraged participants to reflect critically on their existing knowledge of the subjects and how these are taught and learned. The idea was to shift the teachers' conceptions to a more critical perspective of subject learning and to develop pedagogical content knowledge of their respective subjects. They were introduced to innovative ways of subject teaching so that, as well as learning the content, their students can develop skills and qualities which they need to be able to live and work in everyday contexts. Thus inquiry teaching, classroom discussions, concept building and cooperative learning strategies such as peer learning, pair work and cooperative group work were some of the innovative teaching methods embarked upon at the AKU-IED.[14] The participants were encouraged to develop skills to use the library, information technology and the world around them to locate and process information.

Collaboration and collegial relationships among the participants were encouraged through collaborative assignments, group problem-solving conferences and peer coaching activities. To prepare participants for their roles as mentors and educational change agents, seminars consisting of theoretical discussions on mentoring and managing educational change were held for periods of six weeks each, complemented by print and video materials. The seminars were interwoven with examples from participants' experiences from real classroom-related situations and teachers' needs. These were intended to give the participants some practical experiences of mentoring and implementing change as well as opportunities for reflection and action on issues emerging from their practical experiences.

Seminars were also held on issues related to curriculum, instruction and assessment, educational research and education in general in both the developed and developing countries. These seminars were meant to make the participants aware that classroom practice cannot be separated from research and curriculum issues.

Three additional features of the AKU-IED's programme played an important role in ensuring the success of the programme. These were the field-based component, the involvement of school heads and managers in the professional development of the participants and a research-based dissertation.

The field-based component was meant to address the problem of the divide between theory and practice, which pervades teacher education in both the developed and developing countries. To close this gap and to learn how the knowledge, attitudes and dispositions fostered by the AKU-IED play out in local contexts, the seminars offered at AKU-IED were often followed by classroom practice at some of the collaborating schools in Karachi.[15] Whenever specific needs arose, AKU-IED negotiated with the management of these schools to seek access. Thus whatever was learned in the seminars was tried out in actual classroom situations and its contextual relevance and appropriateness was reflected upon and alternatives were considered.

Change depends as much on the heads and managers of the schools where the change is to be implemented as on the teacher educators being prepared by the AKU-IED. Therefore, AKU-IED involved school heads and managers and other key decision-makers right from the beginning of its school improvement efforts. This involvement was mainly in the form of meetings, seminars and conferences concerning important decisions relating to school improvement where, among other things, the supportive role of the school head and managers in the process of change and school improvement were discussed. While these activities were separate from the M.Ed. programme, whenever it was feasible the course participants of the M.Ed. Programme were invited to interact with their colleagues from the school management to share their experiences.

Learning to conduct research, to understand processes of data collection and analysis, and to become consumers of research was considered important in helping the course participants to inquire into processes and issues in learning and teaching. In the course of conducting research they gained insight into the nature of research and were able to get a first-hand experience of research design, implementation techniques, and the analysis and reporting of results. Every course participant wrote a dissertation (of about 18,000 words) on his or her classroom-based research.

All the participants in the first M.Ed. programme were given an opportunity to experience a western school culture through the two Partner Universities. One group was sent to Toronto in Canada and the other group to Oxford in the United Kingdom. During their nine-week residency, the participants explored different educational systems and school cultures, observed classroom practice modelled on current theories and studies and the concept and practicalities of school-based internships. In the subsequent M.Ed. programmes, this module has been replaced by an 'Alternate Exposure Module'. Through this module, the course participants get an opportunity to work in a rural setting (in an area of Pakistan) where an innovative education intervention is being carried out by local organizations. They become exposed to contextual realities of working in underprivileged areas. The course participants have found this experience rewarding in bringing them into contact with ideas and issues beyond their direct experience.

Upon graduation the participating teachers were designated as Professional Development Teachers (PDTs) charged with the responsibility of training teachers both in their own schools and at AKU-IED. The original title for the M.Ed. graduates was supposed to be 'Clinical Teachers' (CTs) (see note 4). However this term conflicted with a similar description being used at AKU's Medical College. The term 'Master Trainer' (MT) was rejected by AKU-IED faculty because of its behaviouristic connotations which do not fit with the concepts of reflection and inquiry. The faculty preferred the title Professional Development Teachers because it sent a clear message that AKU-IED graduates would be teachers involved in professional development activities.

The Professional Development Teachers in Action

On completion of the M.Ed. programme the participants, now PDTs, returned to their schools to work mainly in the capacity of exemplary teachers and as in-service teacher educators in their own contexts. Negotiations had been held with schools and systems about the return of the PDTs and AKU-IED's expectations that the PDTs would get an opportunity to teach and also assist with the professional development of colleague teachers. However, in reality they went through different kinds of experiences (Halai, 2001). In schools with supportive school heads, the PDTs worked as both exemplary teachers and teacher educators. In some schools their role was restricted to teaching. In others they were promoted to management positions, for example, Education Officers in which no teaching was involved.

Soon after the completion of the M.Ed. programme, AKU-IED planned to embark on its first eight-week Visiting Teacher Programme (VTP) designed initially for teachers from the collaborating schools. The Visiting Teachers (VTs) have been seen, from the outset of AKU-IED planning, as key agents of change in their schools. The intention was that, having attended a VT Programme, they would apply their newly acquired professional knowledge and skills in their own classrooms and through modelling and guidance, help to improve the performance of their colleagues. The assumption was that once a 'critical mass' of VTs had been trained for each cooperating school, a significant impact on the overall quality of teaching could be expected.

After consultation between AKU-IED faculty and heads of cooperating schools it was agreed that whenever possible, two parallel VT programmes would be conducted taking into consideration the school term dates. It was agreed that the first VTPs would focus on the teaching of Social Studies and English (in October-December, 1995). This would be followed by Mathematics and Science VT programmes (early 1996). After negotiations with school management, six PDTs with specialization in English (3) and Social Studies (3) were invited to AKU-IED to plan and conduct the first two Visiting Teacher Programmes. The PDTs worked with AKU-IED faculty and Partner University faculty to develop the framework and the curriculum of the programme. The programme attempted to improve the content knowledge of the teachers, introduced them to a wide range of teaching methodologies and assisted the teachers to gain a better understanding of their own and their students' roles in teaching and learning.

A large component of this intensive programme was based in the classrooms of AKU-IED's co-operating schools where the VTs observed teaching and learning, applied new approaches and reflected on their experiences. By the middle of 1996 five Visiting Teacher Programmes had been successfully completed. Details are discussed in Chapter 5.

Evolution of AKU-IED

Findings from the First Programme Reviews

After two years of IED operations, both the M.Ed. and the VT programmes went through extensive scrutiny by external reviewers, an independent research team and AKU-IED faculty. There was a general agreement that both the programmes were successful (International Development Research Centre Report 2, 1996; Skarret et al, 1996). The confidence level of the graduates was high. The PDTs performed well in conducting the VT programmes. Their school heads spoke highly about the change they had undergone. Some PDTs were pleased with their achievements in carrying out professional development activities in their schools. However, many issues were identified for the two programmes. For example, the M.Ed. programme had tried to include too much content for the available time. It was suggested that too much time was spent in face to face class activities, there were overlaps between modules and feedback on assignments did not come on time. Moreover it was felt that the area of primary education had been neglected, the English medium was a major challenge for some participants, and the subject content knowledge in all areas needed further strengthening. Keeping these findings in view the M.Ed programme was extended to two full years and mechanisms were introduced to ensure that issues identified were addressed.

The VT programme was also considered to be too comprehensive in scope. It needed more emphasis on content and a specialist focus on either primary or secondary level. Many teachers preferred a bilingual mode of instruction because of weak English language skills. A follow-up to the programme was considered to be essential. It was felt that this could include regular seminars, school-based support and possible networking. Lessons learnt were incorporated in subsequent programmes. A number of alternative models of the Visiting Teacher Programme have evolved since the inception – details can be found in Chapters 5, 6, 7 and 8.

Development through New Programmes and Centres

In the past eight years AKU-IED has continued with its major programmatic activities. However, it has been open to considering new opportunities to test new grounds and other programmes. Some examples of these include:

- Capacity Building in Balochistan.
- Introduction of Advanced Diploma Programmes.
- New models of the VT Programme.
- New Professional Development Centres.
- Development of Professional Associations of Teachers.

Capacity Building in Balochistan

In mid-1996 AKU-IED faced a major challenge when the government of the Pakistan province of Balochistan approached it for assistance with capacity building to improve quality of education across Balochistan. After a number of meetings between representatives of the Government of Balochistan, World Bank consultants and AKU-IED faculty it was agreed by the Government of Balochistan Primary Education Department to develop a sustainable model of professional development which would create capacity for developing contextually relevant programmes. Through this agreement a pool of 12 M.Ed. graduates was developed, 180 teachers went through a modified VT programme which enabled the teachers to work as mentors for colleagues in the field and a series of short management programmes were conducted for education officers [16], who would support the teachers in the field. The mentoring programme was conducted through the Urdu language medium, a first experience for AKU-IED. This intervention proved to be successful and was lauded by both the government and aid agencies. For example, (i) the graduates of the mentoring programme started a process of working with teachers in cluster schools (within a 15 km radius) supported by District Education Officers and the Primary Education Department staff; and (ii) while the first four mentoring programmes (120 participants) were carried out at AKU-IED, subsequent programmes were carried out in Quetta, Balochistan, by PDTs developed by AKU-IED with some support from AKU-IED faculty. For AKU-IED this intervention in the public sector showed a major achievement of its objectives of capacity building for sustainability (see also Chapter 6).

Introduction of Advanced Diploma Programmes

In July 1997 AKU-IED embarked upon two Advanced Diploma Programmes not envisaged originally in the first Task Force proposal although a mention was made of the possibility of this type of intervention. One programme was targeted at the headteachers of AKU-IED's collaborating schools who felt that they needed professional development to become pedagogical leaders. From AKU-IED's viewpoint, this group of school leaders would become better prepared to support their teachers who had gone through AKU-IED programmes. Upon completion of the programme it was found that the participants felt that it had added value to their work. PDTs felt that the heads seemed to appreciate their work better (see Chapter 9). This was the first time that such a programme had been conducted in Pakistan.

The other diploma programme targeted VT graduates of science and mathematics, giving them an opportunity to continue their professional development. From this subject specialization in mathematics and science, the participants felt that their classroom practices had improved and their pedagogical content knowledge had been enhanced. A number of cooperating schools utilized their expertise in professional development activities for other teachers. Many of the graduates of this programme have continued with their professional development (Aman & Macleod, 1999). Both programmes have become a regular feature of AKU-IED's professional programmes.

New Models of the VT Programme

In 1998 AKU-IED tested a modified model of the VT programme in Nairobi, Kenya. Instead of the usual eight-week intensive programme conducted at AKU-IED and its collaborating schools, this model was spread over five months taking advantage of school vacations in August and December when teachers met face to face with the Institute's team. Between September and early December the teachers taught in their own schools with support from the instructional team. During this period a number of weekend seminars were also conducted. The model proved to be contextually appropriate because it addressed some major issues such as releasing teachers during term time (Pardhan & Wheeler, 1998). This model has since been tried out in Karachi, Dhaka (Bangladesh), Gilgit (Northern Areas of Pakistan) and has also been adopted in various centres in East Africa. The model resolved a major problem concerning releasing teachers during the school term for training. Moreover the teachers got an opportunity to improve their skills and classroom practices in their own classrooms. Further details are provided in Chapter 7.

New Professional Development Centres

In December 1998 AKU-IED in collaboration with the Aga Khan Education Service, Pakistan, launched its second Professional Development Centre in Gilgit, Northern Areas of Pakistan. This centre offers a variety of courses and programmes, suitable for the context, aimed primarily at improving the quality of teaching. It is providing formal recognition of these courses of study through the award of AKU certificates and is acting as a regional educational and intellectual resource. A similar initiative also commenced in East Africa in early 2000. In both these centres the programmes are conducted by Professional Development Teachers (M.Ed. graduates of AKU-IED) with assistance from senior faculty of AKU-IED. Chapter 12 discusses the activity of this first PDC.

Development of Professional Associations of Teachers

Right from the outset AKU-IED has been committed to developing follow-up strategies and continuing professional interaction among the graduates from AKU-IED, their colleagues and other teachers. This issue was highlighted by the Second Task Force of the AKU-IED (AKU-IED, 1996). One recommendation of the Task Force was to encourage AKU-IED graduates to form professional associations for educators similar to the one developed in Pakistan in the early 1980s by the Society of Pakistan English Language Teachers, SPELT (Bacchus, 1996). A start was made in 1997 in mathematics education. Encouraged by Partner University faculty, mathematics PDTs, together with a group of teachers attending a mathematics workshop at the AKU-IED, decided to form the Mathematics

Association of Pakistan (MAP). The AKU-IED supported this venture and soon other associations were formed. These include the Science Association of Pakistan (SAP), the Association of Social Studies Educators and Teachers (ASSET), the School Heads Association of Pakistan (SHADE), the Association of Primary Teachers (APT) and the Pakistan Association of Inclusive Education (PAIE). AKU-IED supports these initiatives by providing space for association-related activities, expenses for refreshments and funds for a newsletter. The association members give their time to conduct workshops and to manage other activities [17]. All the associations are very active, conducting at least one workshop per month for teachers (and sometimes for children) in Karachi. For AKU-IED the development of associations has been important because through this it is able to reach out beyond the collaborating schools to teachers more widely.

Striving for International Standards

In all its work AKU-IED has striven for a level of excellence which meets international standards. In developing all its programmes the Institute has worked closely with its partners in Oxford and Toronto and has benefited from contributions from consultants from other universities throughout the world. All programmes have gone through review processes internally, at the level of Partner University Forum (comprising senior faculty from AKU-IED, OUDES and OISE-UT), and through assessment processes involving other external academics.

Challenges Faced by AKU-IED

The AKU-IED has faced many challenges during the past eight years. Most of these relate to human resource availability and high expectations from partners and other stakeholders. Some of the main challenges are expressed below:

- Very early in its existence the AKU-IED management recognized that the kind of faculty members needed to ensure the quality and implementation of the AKU-IED vision were not easily available in Pakistan. The Partner Universities played a crucial role in assisting AKU-IED in conducting the initial programmes. The few national faculty who were selected worked closely with the Partner University faculty. A faculty development process was also put into action. Junior faculty members with the potential for further development were hired and promising graduates of the M.Ed. Programme were identified for future development including doctoral studies. Some of these faculty have completed their Ph.D.s, and others are in the process of completing doctoral studies at the Partner Universities. The AKU-IED is, at the time of writing, developing its own Ph.D. programme for launch in 2004.

- Developing collaboration with schools and systems was a very slow process. As school/university partnership was a new concept in Pakistan, many problems were faced. These included lack of awareness on the part of school heads about their roles in academic leadership, difficulties faced by women (particularly married women) in participating in AKU-IED programmes for family reasons, competing priorities at school level because of the importance given to examinations. The University faculty often found it difficult to recognize the problems faced by the teachers. These issues are regularly visited in various forums and not all problems have yet been resolved.
- The AKU-IED has found it difficult to establish and document with credible data, the impact of its programmes on school improvement. In part this is because of difficulties, generic to educational research, which attempt to identify and link outcomes to inputs in complex school environments. It is also premature to ensure measurable outcomes in student learning and achievement. To do this appropriate baselines would be required and a longitudinal study needs to be conducted. Such activities require sufficient suitably qualified members of faculty, and, as in other areas of the AKU-IED development, building *research* capacity has been an issue. However, AKU-IED has undertaken some case studies of the qualitative impact on teaching and learning practices in schools to which its graduates have returned. Significant positive impact is observable in a number of schools. Chapter 10 documents some of this impact.
- As AKU-IED becomes better known in Pakistan and internationally there is an inevitable tension between wanting to take on ever more interesting, worthwhile and challenging initiatives and yet being concerned not to overstretch the institution to a point where the quality of its work is compromised.

Throughout the short history of AKU-IED support from the Aga Khan University and from the Partner Universities have been crucial in the overcoming of these challenges.

Conclusion

In this chapter we have given a brief overview of the evolution of the AKU-IED's programmatic activities and the associated issues. As His Highness the Aga Khan stated,

> You can build new buildings, but if you cannot find quality men and women to implement the programmes and to give them confidence that their programmes will be able to continue and grow in the future, you have achieved nothing. (His Highness the Aga Khan at the inauguration ceremony of Professional Development Centre, Northern Areas on 19 October 2000)

The AKU-IED has embarked on a journey to develop human resources critical to the improvement in quality of education. A small beginning has been made.

Notes

[1] The SMS school complex consists of a pre-primary school, a primary school with separate sections for girls and boys, a secondary school with separate sections for girls and boys and a coeducational Higher Secondary School. These schools cater to over 4000 students.

[2] Professional Development Centres are organizations for quality improvement in education. They are established by AKU-IED in association with one or more partners or associates for the purposes of: offering a variety of courses and programmes aimed primarily at improving the quality of teaching and learning; providing formal recognition of these courses of study through the award of AKU certification; and acting as a regional or national educational, intellectual and research resource.

[3] His Highness the Aga Khan is one of the World's most prominent philanthropists. In 1956 when he was just 20, he became the leader of 15 million Shia Imami Ismaili Muslims who live in 25 countries in East Africa, North America, Europe, and South and Central Asia.

The Aga Khan's family has followed a tradition of service in international affairs. Under the Aga Khan's leadership, vast development institutions have been created to serve communities where Ismaili Muslims live. A well-defined institutional framework has been created to carry out social, economic and cultural activities. This framework has expanded and evolved into the Aga Khan Development Network (AKDN), a group of institutions working to improve living conditions and opportunities in the developing world (see also note 4).

[4] AKU-IED signed formal partnership agreements with the University of Toronto, Faculty of Education and the Oxford University, Department of Education Studies in 1993. These agreements have continued until the time of writing. A partner university perspective is presented in Chapter 2.

[5] See Mirza Pardhan, Director Education, Secretariat de son Altesse l'Aga Khan, October 1989, Internal Report.

[6] The Aga Khan Development Network consists of a group of agencies set up to help improve living conditions and opportunities in specific regions of the developing world. The individual agency mandates range from education, health and architecture to the promotion of private sector enterprise and rural development. It includes the Aga Khan Education Services, the Aga Khan University, the Aga Khan Health Services and the Aga Khan Foundation.

[7] Inaugurated in the early 1980s in Karachi, Pakistan the Aga Khan University quickly became an institution with growing international reputation as a centre of excellence in the field of medical and health education.

[8] The SMS Aga Khan School catered only for pupils from K-10 at this time. Ideally K-12 was the requirement. While AKU-IED was being planned, the AKES,P Board approved the construction of a Higher Secondary School (grades 11-12) on the campus of the SMS Aga Khan School. The construction of the Higher Secondary School and the PDC became joint projects.

[9] The phrase 'Clinical Teachers' mentioned in earlier AKU-IED related documents was replaced with Professional Development Teachers (PDTs) who are the M.Ed. graduates of AKU-IED.

[10] Construction of the Professional Development Centre commenced in early 1994 within the SMS complex and was ready for occupation in November 1994.

[11] AKU-IED received a grant of US$12.5 million over a period of a little over six years. The main funders were the European Commission (54%), Canadian International Development Agency (26%), United Nations Development Programme (9%) and the Aga Khan Foundation (11%).

[12] Further details of such activities and issues associated with them are taken up in subsequent chapters.

[13] In subsequent years generic primary education was added to this group.

[14] See also Chapter 4 for further discussion of these practices and related issues.

[15] AKU-IED identified 15 schools in Karachi from the public, private and AKES sectors from which the M.Ed. course participants were drawn. These schools became AKU-IED's initial co-operating schools.

[16] Seventy-four education officers participated in what was described as the Balochistan Education Management Programme.

[17] Recently the associations have networked and developed an umbrella organization called Professional Teacher Associations Network (PTAN). PTAN has been successful in getting external funding through the Canadian International Development Agency and Aga Khan Foundation, Pakistan to support its activities.

References

Aga Khan University – Institute for Educational Development (AKU-IED). (1991) *A Proposal to the AKU Board of Trustees*. Karachi.

AKU-IED (1996) *Second Task Force, Final Report*, p. 24. Karachi.

Aman, A. & MacLeod, G. (1999) *Tracking Study. Subject Specialist Teacher Programme Graduates Report 1*. Unpublished Report, AKU-IED, Karachi.

Bacchus, M.K. (1996) A Suggested Role and Future Programmes of Activities for the Institute for Educational Development. Unpublished paper, Aga Khan University.

Halai, A. (2001) On Becoming a Professional Development Teacher: a case from Pakistan, *Mathematics Education Review, Journal of the Association of Mathematics Education Teachers, UK*, 14, pp. 32-45.

Haq, M. (2000) Human Development in South Asia: the Gender Question. Human Development Centre. Karachi: Oxford University Press.

International Development Research Centre. (1996) Documentation and Evaluation of Programmes and Development, p. 12. Aga Khan University, Institute for Educational Development.

Pardhan, H. & Wheeler, A. (1998) Enhancing Science Teachers' Learning through Pedagogical Content Knowledge, *Science Education International*, 9(4), pp. 1-4.

Skarret, L., Detienne, B. & Zaidi, Y. (1996) European Commission Mid-Term Review Mission of the Institute for Educational Development, Aga Khan University, p. 15.

CHAPTER 2

IED and the University Partnership: the Oxford experience

RICHARD PRING

Introduction

This study gives an account of the role of Partner Universities in the conception, planning and development of the Institute for Educational Development. Since the author was the Director of the University of Oxford Department of Educational Studies, the essay clearly reflects the Oxford story – and, no doubt, both Toronto and the IED would interpret the relationship differently. Indeed, that is one of the main lessons from a partnership between universities coming from different educational and cultural traditions. The partnership has been fruitful for each of the partners in terms of the development of knowledge, understanding, educational practice, and more recently, joint research. However, in achieving this success there were many misunderstandings along the way, which could not easily have been anticipated at the beginning. Suspicions arose from the filtering of communication through preconceived ways of seeing the other partners. It takes a long time to come to see things from the others' points of view – and eventually to reach the positions of mutual respect on which can be built genuine partnership.

Original Conception

The Aiglemont Secretariat of HH the Aga Khan established a Task Force, which, in October 1989, produced a Report on Education in Pakistan (The Aga Khan Institutions and Teachers in Pakistan, 1989). At the heart of the Report was the belief that

> the education of all children in Pakistan depends upon the
> improvement of the performance and the elevation of the dignity

of teachers, and further that such an improvement in turn depends upon the creation of a network of teacher development, dispersed throughout Pakistan but linked with a centre of excellence of international quality. (p. 2)

The Aga Khan University (AKU) with a Faculty of Health Sciences (including a Medical College and a School of Nursing) was already established in Karachi. The Report recommended that there should be, not a second faculty, but an Institute for Educational Development (IED), which would be that 'centre of excellence of international quality' (p. 2).

The key principles governing the work of such a centre (unlike those of a conventional university) were:

1. the engagement of trainers, researchers and other scholars in the real world;
2. the creation of a number (and indeed network) of professional sites;
3. the commitment to standards of quality which would be widely recognised (p. 2).

The Institute would build upon initiatives already started: the field-based teacher development within the Aga Khan Development Network (AKDN) (for example, the Professional Development Center in Gilgit and the Teachers Resource Centre in Karachi) and a number of school improvement initiatives. But it would address the problems of a

> critical shortage of leaders with vision and skills to carry such projects forward, a lack of any professional and intellectual association with a wider community of teachers and scholars ... and ... the absence of recognition and professional advancement for teachers undergoing such courses and experiences. (p. 3)

Therefore, the model was of a *professional base,* rather than a traditional university faculty. Such a base would provide a framework for the recognition of teachers' achievements. Hence, although a *professional* base, it would need to be *within* a university. And it would be a model of professional development, linked with professional development schools which would provide the opportunity for intensive 'clinical experience' of visiting teachers, supported by 'master teachers' or 'mentors', before they returned to their own schools. Subsequently, this has developed into an Institute in Karachi, close to the main university, located within the campus of an established Aga Khan School. There are now several cohorts of Master of Education students who, upon completion, have become professional development teachers for visiting teachers at the IED or in their respective schools. Furthermore, such 'master teachers', known as Professional Development Teachers (PDTs), are increasingly staffing professional development centres in East Africa, Northern Pakistan and countries of Central Asia.

The Task Force argued strongly against a traditional university faculty. This was to be a centre of professional development, albeit one which demonstrated standards equal to anywhere in the world, and supported by a rigorous research tradition and academic scholarship. To achieve this professional base within a university, cooperation with reputable universities with a like-minded 'philosophy' was seen to be crucial for three reasons. First, there was no experience then within the AKU of such professional centres. Second, there was a need for expertise to get this enterprise off the ground. Third, international status and recognition is not easy to come by, and close association with universities which had such recognition would clearly help.

Therefore, the Task Force recommended that the AKU

> should with support from international agencies ..., establish a
> small and closely-knit partnership of universities – one in the
> United States, one in the United Kingdom, and one in the
> developing world....This partnership, an International Consortium
> of Universities (ICU), would jointly operate a programme for the
> exchange of experts, technical bilateral assistance within a
> nationally agreed strategy. (p. 6)

In fact, two universities of international repute were identified: Michigan State University, which was then establishing a number of Professional Development Schools, and the University of Oxford, which had established an 'internship model' of teacher education and training.

Although the Institute was to be essentially a professional centre, it was also recommended that, if supported by the partnership, it should also develop a Unit for Research and Policy Studies with a small number of core faculty. The reconciliation of these two elements – professional development, on the one hand, and policy research, on the other – would be possible, first, through the increased rigour of the evaluation by the research unit of different models of field-based education, second, through the wider international framework it would provide, and, third, through the evidence-based extension of the Institute's professional work into urban settings, rural areas and beyond Pakistan to parts of Central Asia, East Africa and India.

Finally, to 'govern' all this field-based teacher training, professional development schools, a network of professional development centres, and a unit for research, the Trustees were to appoint a Board of Management, which would have about ten members, including representatives of the International Consortium of Universities (subsequently referred to as the Partner Universities). But, as was stated, institutional and intellectual ties would grow and change as the AKU and the IED developed their programmes and missions (p. 6).

That is the end of the beginning. But in anticipating subsequent developments, one should note the following. First, the IED was conceived as a *professional* institute, not a faculty. Indeed, its relationship to the university, though launched as part of the AKU, was referred to as a 'special one' and core members of the Institute would be academic members of the

University. Second, however, as an Institute, it was still to have a unit for research and policy – the kind of unit which normally would have been associated with a university faculty. This could so easily give rise to a certain tension, since those who inherited the work of the Task Force found the distinction between the Institute and, what would normally be regarded as and called a university faculty, increasingly obscure – and possibly untenable.

Furthermore, as the distinction between 'institute' and 'faculty' became increasingly blurred, so did it seem inappropriate to maintain governance by a Board of Management, especially one which could be dominated by 'outsiders' including the Partner Universities (PUs). After all, a university faculty normally enjoys academic autonomy within the statutes and ordinances of a university, and is not beholden to the requirements of those outside the university structure. And, indeed, there is little doubt that the governance of the IED would remain with the Board of Trustees of AKU, and that graduate programmes would go through the University's own Board of Graduate Studies.

Establishment of the Institute

The IED was formally established by a Resolution of the Board of Trustees of the AKU, dated 17 July 1992. But prior to its establishment and the appointment of the Director, the model adopted was much influenced by the practice of the partners within the International Consortium of Universities. The former Director of the Oxford University Department of Educational Studies (OUDES) had drafted several of the reports leading to the establishment of the Institute, drawing upon the Internship experience at Oxford University. That model was of a Professional Development School (PDS) in urban Karachi and a Professional Development Centre (PDC) in a rural area (Gilgit in the Northern Territories). The work of the PDC was to draw upon the example of clinical training in medicine:

> First and foremost it locates the task of teacher training and
> development in the context of real schools (rather than of lecture
> based theory) and exploits the expertise both of practising teachers
> of high quality and of educational researchers and scholars.
> Dominant in the PDS are master teachers (or clinical instructors)
> who are trained to act as mentors to the less experienced teachers
> who attend the PDS for continuous periods of about eight weeks
> ... The intensive work undertaken by those teachers is overseen by
> the IED and, in most cases, contributes to credits for Degrees in
> Education now awarded by the Aga Khan University. (Judge,
> 1991, pp. 5-6)

Initially therefore there was to be appointed a Director and core staff to oversee:

1. establishment of the training function of the PDS (later to be referred to as the Professional Development Centre which would incorporate a school).
2. assurance that the quality of work and study undertaken by the practising teachers was such as to merit awards at the University.
3. mobilisation of support from government and international agencies for both the professional work and the unit for research and policy.
4. cooperation of the Partner Universities in providing training opportunities for Pakistani teachers – with secondments to the Partner Universities' countries.
5. design and implementation of a programme of research. (synopsis from Judge, 1991, p. 7)

Prior to the appointment of a Director with the brief to carry out these tasks, the Chairman of the Task Force approached the suggested Partner Universities, soliciting their support.

> We believe it is essential that this Institute, even though it initially be of modest size, be linked both to the Aga Khan University in Karachi and to two or more universities outside Pakistan with an outstanding reputation regarding professional training for teachers. (Edwards, 1990)

The members for the programme therefore were invited to the planning process in Karachi in April 1990. That planning process would include both the possible input from the Partner Universities in complementing the expertise currently available in Karachi and the possibility of secondments of teachers to Oxford and Michigan universities and schools. From these would be selected the first ten clinical teachers who, obtaining their Master's from the AKU, would then constitute the training team at the Professional Development Centres.

One consequence of the Karachi meeting was the developing idea of the Board of Management (and with it the International Consortium of Universities). The Board was seen to be, because of its size, rather unwieldy and indeed distant from the actual activities of the IED. Furthermore, as has been said, responsibility for the governance of IED had always been seen to be within that of the University, ultimately under the Board of Trustees and working through the Board of Graduate Studies as far as graduate studies were concerned. Hence, the IED would be an Institution (not a Faculty) within the AKU, but with an Academic Advisory Council (AAC) reporting to the University Board of Trustees. On that Council would be representatives of the Partner Universities, who would also serve as advisers and consultants. The Council would (a) provide 'expert advice, sustenance and experienced guidance', and (b) exert quality assurance on behalf of the Board of Trustees (including the scrutiny of budgets).

The 'function and role' of the Partner Universities, therefore, as envisaged in the final proposal for the establishment of the IED, were presented in a paper from the Aga Khan Foundation, 1 May 1992. According to this paper the Partner Universities should:

1. provide international validation of the IED's training programmes and research; and
2. provide a range of specialised services in teacher training.

By 'international validation', it is intended that the PU should confirm that (a) the content of the IED's teacher education programme and research, (b) the quality of the staff implementing them, and (c) the results obtained in terms of the trainees' achievements and the research writing would meet the approbation of the PU's own system of academic awards, staff promotion, research endorsement, etc.

By 'specialised services in teacher education', it is intended that the PU should complement and supplement the skills of the full-time IED staff in (a) designing and deciding course content and teaching style, (b) procedures for recruiting trainees and assessing their progress through and at the end of courses, and (c) actually delivering a variety of teacher education programmes. The process of validation and of providing services will involve:

1. participation by PU faculty over a period of years in meetings of the IED's Academic Advisory Council;
2. secondment to the IED on a short or longer term basis of faculty from the PU or from schools and school boards linked to the PU;
3. training at the PU themselves of IED staff on short study tours or award-bearing courses. (The Aga Khan Foundation, 1992, p. 3)

Furthermore, it was stated that 'partnership' meant that 'all parties would learn from each other' (p. 3). The link, therefore, was envisaged to be qualitatively different from that which often characterises the relationship between universities in the 'developed' world and those in the 'developing' worlds, where the 'learning' is often in practice seen as moving in one direction only. Indeed, from the outset, as the IED became established, so it was envisaged that the partnership would need to evolve.

Moreover, it was made clear at this stage that the IED would reserve the right to enter into linkages with other universities, should that be appropriate for meeting its needs, and indeed the Task Force was to approach other universities for specific responsibilities. For example, in 1994, Sheffield Hallam University was invited to help with the development of the Leadership and Management programme because of Sheffield's expertise in management education.

For this it was estimated that one full-time equivalent post would be required in each of the two Partner Universities, and the cost of this would be incorporated in the proposed budget.

However, partnership was also tied to funding – especially to the source of funding. Towards the end of 1991, it was apparent that, although co-funding was likely to be forthcoming from the Commission of European Communities (CEC) and from the Canadian International Development Agency (CIDA), no such prospect was emerging from the USA. For that reason, it was finally agreed to seek a partnership agreement with the University of Toronto, Faculty of Education, instead of Michigan State University. Toronto was well known for its innovative work in teacher education, and its Dean of Education, renowned for his work on innovation and change.

Very soon, the Partner Universities were playing a part in the development of the framework of the future M.Ed. programme. They took part in the workshop held for this purpose in April 1993, at which were present the Director designate of the IED and others, including senior educators from the Aga Khan Education Services.

In brief, therefore, at this stage of the establishment of the Institute, the role of the Partner Universities was seen to be crucial – in providing teacher support at IED, in advising on field-based teacher education based on experience in their respective countries, and in giving advice, consultancy and quality assurance both directly and through the Academic Advisory Council. In return the Partner Universities would be appropriately compensated for the time which the discharge of such responsibilities would take. However, apart from the expression of hope that this partnership would benefit academically all the partners (in contrast with how the relationship between universities in the developed and developing worlds is normally seen), none of these early papers referred to the benefits, other than financial, which might accrue to the Partner Universities – and in this lay the grounds for subsequent difficulties.

But all this was prior to the appointment of the Director.

Partnership: rewards and difficulties

The undisputed facts of the partnership in practice would be the many visits of faculty from Toronto and Oxford to Karachi to help develop modules on the Master's course, to teach such modules, to support Karachi-based faculty in their teaching of the modules, and to support the students as they prepared their dissertations. Altogether eight members of the Oxford department and over 15 members of the Toronto faculty have, to different degrees, been involved – the Oxford department mainly (but not exclusively) in the teaching of, and mentoring in, mathematics and science; the Toronto faculty mainly in English and the social sciences.

This responsibility soon began to recede – partly due to the success of the partnership. For the M.Ed. class of 1995 (the first M.Ed.), the IED did not have its own mathematics educator. This situation prevailed until 2001-02 when two of that first cohort, having successfully completed their doctorates at Oxford, were appointed. In science and social studies, however, the need for assistance finished after the first M.Ed. cohort, although interest was maintained by the Partner Universities. Similarly, after the M.Ed. class of 1998, the teaching of English required no further assistance.

In some cases the visits of the Partner University faculty were many and prolonged, although clearly (whatever the terms of the contract) there were always limits as to how long visiting faculty could leave their teaching responsibilities in their home universities. And this was an issue at the IED because modules were usually of six weeks' duration. The Partner University faculty, however, were often able to free themselves from their own universities for only two weeks at a time, thereby creating difficulties in the continuity of teaching and in the mentoring of the IED faculty.

In several cases, the Partner Universities were unable to meet some of the demands, and so they arranged for support from other universities, always subject to the agreement of the IED Director. In this way, a wide range of people from several universities have come to be linked with the AKU.

Partnership, therefore, was often seen in terms of the role that the Partner Universities were to have in the development, teaching and quality assurance of the new Institute and its staff. And that role was, at the very least, the delivery of certain modules until such time as the IED was in a position to appoint its own faculty in these areas. But the Partner Universities tended to see their role as going beyond that. They had been chosen initially to help the University establish the Institute. They had been chosen because they themselves had established reputations in the very activities which the Institute was now initiating. Furthermore, having inherited the view of the Institute as portrayed by the First Task Force, namely, as a base for the professional development of teachers, they were wary of developments which seemed to go beyond that more limited vision.

Such different perceptions of that role would understandably give rise to conflict as the Institute developed under its new Director, who had not been part of the original task force or of the subsequent planning meetings or of the choice of Partner Universities. Ultimately, the Director would be held responsible if things went wrong or if the Institute failed to achieve its goals. Partnership could easily be perceived as a constraint rather than an enhancement of the Institute, as that inevitably was to be understood by a new Director. And, indeed, that might be expected where those who are charged with the responsibility of implementing the original plans were in no way part of that planning.

It was felt, however, by the Partner Universities that sometimes the members of the IED did not appreciate the constraints and demands which the Partner Universities were having to face. These were implied in the Oxford Director's letter (2 April 1990), to the chairman of the Task Group. The newly appointed Director of the Oxford University department, who had not been party to the proposals for an Institute or to the proposed involvement of a partner university, wrote:

> The involvement of members of this Department in consultation
> visits would have to be strictly limited because the Department is
> small and hard pressed to meet the teaching and research
> demands upon it. [The previous Director] referred to connections
> in research. These would need to be spelt out more clearly. But
> given the very active group within the Department concerned with
> research into teaching training and into the internship scheme
> particularly, there are interesting possibilities which we would
> want to explore. (Pring, 1990)

The same letter endorsed the attachment for a period of eight weeks per year over a period of three years of 10 IED staff (the 'clinical teachers' in training) to the Oxford University department and its internship schools.

But the quoted section of the letter needs to be enlarged upon, because it reflects an anxiety of the Partner University which seemed not to be recognised by IED – thereby leading to misunderstandings.

Major British universities are under considerable pressure to meet high and demanding standards in the two areas for which they are funded – teaching students who pay fees to be taught and conducting research. Those pressures are increased in a university like Oxford which would want to maintain its position and reputation amongst world-class universities. The Department of Educational Studies had, under the previous Director, pioneered field-based teacher education in the United Kingdom through the highly innovative Internship Scheme, and had justifiably gained an international reputation for this way of delivering teacher education. It had still to achieve similar status in the quality of its research. The question, therefore, that the new Director had to face was how far could the partnership with the IED and Toronto be integrated with main aims of the Department. How could the partnership both complement its teaching and enhance its research programme? What could not be allowed was a partnership, however worthy in itself, which distracted it from its main mission. Of course, the perception of that two-fold mission might itself evolve and be enhanced through the very partnership with the IED and Toronto faculty.

These certainly were the considerations uppermost in the mind of the Oxford Director as the terms of the contract were negotiated leading up to the signing in 1993 and indeed in the re-signing of the contract in 1997 – though neither contract quite reflected this.

The partnership was legally established in a contract between the Partner Universities and the AKU. In Oxford, this was enacted on 16

September 1993, with due ceremony at Green College, signed by the then Warden of Green College, Sir Crispin Tickell, and the Chairman of the AKU Board of Trustees, General Sahabzada Yaqubkhan. The newly appointed Director of the IED, was present and at the celebratory lunch he welcomed the partnership whilst at the same time emphasising the independence of the new Institute. He clearly did not wish to be constrained by any agreements made prior to his appointment.

The contracted agreement (Agreement between Aga Khan University and University of Oxford, 16 September 1993-15 September 1996, Section 5.7, p. 8) reflected the reasons already given for the partnership. It required from each Partner University a minimum of 150 days of academic time, 120 days of which would have to be spent in Karachi, including attendance at the Academic Advisory Council. However, the AKU reserved

> the right to arrange links or any other collaborative arrangement
> or association with other universities or centres of learning or
> engage the services of any consultants to further the objects of
> AKU and/or the Institute (Section 5.8, p. 8)

The partnership was henceforth marked by a certain degree of conflict over the role and function of the Partner Universities. Certainly they had a major part to play in the design and teaching of certain modules on the M.Ed. (Oxford teaching the mathematics and science modules, Toronto the English and Social Studies modules). But the difficulties are reflected in the IED Director's brief document 'Some Observations on Faculty Development Strategies for IED', written in 1995. There he divides the possible contribution of the Partner Universities into three: faculty development, cooperation in research, and preparation and delivery of specific modules. The PU staff should, strictly speaking, be present at the planning stage of different developments; they would need to be more familiar with the actual conditions in the Karachi schools; they would need to engage more with the IED staff in thinking about educational issues: 'professional development in such situations can best come from discussions, etc., on the assumption that the national faculty have important ideas' (Bacchus, 1995a, p. 14).

But that is not easy to achieve where the Partner Universities are so far away and where, therefore, there was not, nor could there be, the presence at much of the planning, the familiarity with the conditions in Karachi schools and the appropriate engagement with IED staff. Already one can see concern over the lack of the collegial relationship which was sought after. There is a hint of sadness in the account: 'For one reason or another, in the majority of cases the teaching of the modules never became a joint enterprise between the IED and PU faculty members' (ibid., p. 14).

One major source of contention with the Director of the IED was clearly the role and constitution of the Advisory Committee – in particular, its assumption that, with the Partner Universities on board, it could and might be fairly directive in the future of the IED.

The latter problem was resolved, to the satisfaction of the IED Director, at the meeting of the Advisory Council in Chantilly in March 1995, when the Council was dissolved and, in its place, a Partner University Forum established. The Forum was to meet twice a year – in Karachi, Toronto or Oxford. When held in Karachi, it would provide an opportunity for the PU representatives to meet the Faculty and to discuss the various ways in which the partnership might progress to the advantage of all.

Also at Chantilly were other members of the IED, Toronto and Oxford, so that, outside the meetings of the Advisory Board, there were important and sometimes intensive discussions about the role and function of the partners. Toronto and Oxford expressed their deep commitment to their work with the IED, but also were anxious to ensure that the partnership addressed together the problems of field-based teacher education. In a letter, dated 21 March 1995, to the former OUDES representative on the Advisory Council, the OUDES Director said: 'I benefited greatly from the Chantilly meeting. I am fully committed to the development of these links but on a much firmer basis of partnership – that is, the partners involved in the conceptualisation of field-based teacher education' (Pring, 1995).

In anticipating the visit to IED in the following June by the Reader in OUDES, who had been the most significant contributor in Britain to the conceptualization of field–based education, the OUDES Director continued:

> I see his role in June much more clearly. It will be (a) to tie up
> research cooperation with clear funding arrangements to be in
> place almost straightaway, (b) to help with the thinking about the
> conceptualisation of field-based teacher education. This latter is
> important because it will be seen much more as part of our central
> departmental research into teacher education. I had never before
> quite seen how AKU could be integrated into mainstream
> departmental interests. Now I can. (Pring, 1995)

Similarly, in a letter to the Director of the IED, the OUDES director again committed Oxford to a partnership 'focused on the development of field-based teacher education – how this might be conceptualised and put into practice'. He reiterated what had been said at Chantilly, namely, that Oxford would not be interested in anything less than that – 'for example, simply providing expertise in mathematics or science where that is lacking at IED'. Thus, Oxford, certainly, did not see itself as simply plugging the gaps in IED staffing. Its own thinking about field-based teacher education was inevitably constantly developing, and it saw that academic and professional collaboration with like-minded people in a very different context would enhance that thinking. And such thinking was as much about conceptualisation of field-based education as it was about practical delivery. For that to happen, the three partners needed to work more closely together – to be (harking back to the IED Director's words) – present at the planning and engaged with each other. But, in fact and inevitably (given the institutional constraints within the Partner Universities and given the distance between all partners), the visits from the Partner Universities tended to be brief (three or four weeks' duration at the very most) with substantial gaps of time in between. Furthermore, a variety of people from other institutions, usually with the agreement of the Partner Universities, were invited to make contributions. All this inevitably made the hoped-for sharing of ideas less easy to achieve and the IED could rightly say that the Partner Universities could not give the time required to consultation in planning and evaluation except at a distance.

This, and the report from the Oxford University Reader, following his June visit, caused a lengthy and at times tense correspondence between Oxford and the IED. The central issues in this correspondence can be pitched at various levels.

At one level, it was simply a matter of how the IED and the Partner Universities respectively saw the PU roles in the partnership – or, at least, saw how the others saw these roles. On the one hand, the PUs did not see themselves simply to be 'supply teachers' – plugging the gaps where there was not the expertise in the IED faculty but rather to be responsible for developing courses with a distinctive philosophy of 'field-based teacher education' On the other hand, the IED Director in particular, and the faculty also, saw the PUs (particularly following a report from Oxford which was critical of the way in which field-based education was developing at the IED) to be overstepping the mark, not fully appreciating the distinctive context of Pakistan (or of the 'developing world'), seeking greater influence than the essentially consultative and advisory role warranted. Indeed, the words 'neo-colonial attitudes' were used twice in subsequent conversations. On the surface, all three partners were pursuing the same agenda which was central to their own distinctive missions – namely, the conceptualization of, research into and development of 'field-based teacher education'. On the other hand, the differences lay deeper in the different perceptions over whose views should prevail and how much Toronto and Oxford should be seen, in practice, as part of the Faculty in taking on specific responsibility for course organization and delivery. Of course, in retrospect such involvement was practically impossible from such distances. And, in any case, institutions develop. The IED could not remain in the same relationship to the Partner Universities as was envisaged at the very beginning.

The first meeting of the Partner Universities in Karachi in November 1995, addressed these issues – with a view to the renewal of the contract in 1997. But the tensions remained, to the extent that Oxford University seriously considered pulling out of the partnership, as was explained in the Oxford Director's letter to the Director of the IED of 1 February 1996. The short-term 'teaching contracts' and the difficulty in arranging research cooperation made it difficult for Oxford to continue – albeit such withdrawal would be 'with the greatest reluctance'.

Clearly, the letters from Oxford and the subsequent replies from the IED Director reflected a very deep division of perception about the significance of what had been achieved, about the role and contribution of the Partner Universities, and about the value of further collaboration.

The proposal of the OUDES withdrawing, however, caused concern at the AKU, for was not one function of the Partner Universities (in the original conception) to validate the quality of the IED's work, and to give credibility on the international stage? Indeed, the Director of the OUDES was suddenly invited to meet the President of the AKU during the Board of Trustees' meeting in Paris in April 1996, to explore what the problems were and to reassure Oxford and Toronto that the partners were integral to the successful development of the IED.

The tensions between IED and the Partner Universities were explored directly or indirectly in two articles. In 'A Study of Cross-national Collaborative Research: reflecting on experience in Pakistan', two of the IED Faculty, and three representatives of the Norwegian Agency for Development Cooperation (NORAD), presented their experience of collaborative research. Writing collaboratively had not been easy; even deciding the appropriate order in which to place the authors of the article was problematic (Penny et al, 2000). Since the fieldwork was necessarily conducted by the 'insiders' (who were experienced and highly qualified researchers),

> it was questionable precisely why the three 'external' persons were involved in any way except to bring to the initiative some vaguely perceived form of 'external' legitimacy as part of the granting of funds to NORAD. As one of the Pakistanis remarked early on: 'Who is the grey haired man coming in telling me what to do?'
> (Penny et al, 2000, p. 447)

An earlier unpublished paper by two AKU-IED faculty members, Iffat Farah and Mehru Ali, presented at the OUDES research seminar in 1998 pointed to the problems of cooperation between the rather imperialistic 'Northern' universities and those within the developing world, even where the faculty in the latter were as experienced and as competent as the faculty in the former. (After all, they had pursued their doctoral training in similar or the same institutions.)

Therefore, the partnership in the first few years went through some stormy periods. Both the Partner Universities and the IED felt deeply committed to their task. And they were always welcomed warmly by the IED faculty, being invited to contribute to seminars when they visited. Indeed, difficulties at the institutional level concerning the exact role of the Partner Universities did not prevent the development of close personal ties. Furthermore, the Partner Universities could be relied on by the AKU to respond to any request for help (for example, informally interviewing prospective members of faculty at the IED or being active members of the Second Task Force). And, indeed, it was generally agreed that (as was stated in the document 'Partner Universities: Memorandum of Understanding', prepared by the IED Director in December 1995, following the first meeting of the Partner Universities Forum, see Bacchus, 1995b):

> The first three years have also affected – and strengthened – the Partner Universities themselves. They have, through their investment of much time and expertise, acquired an understanding and a set of relationships which could be usefully drawn upon so the early achievements of the IED can be consolidated and built upon. (p. 4)

But the Partner Universities saw part of that task, as it had been outlined in the earlier paper, to provide international validation of IED's training programmes and research. And, in so seeing, they felt it their duty to speak frankly of developments in the IED which they thought needed critical examination.

On the other hand, the IED understandably felt that such criticisms often arose from misunderstandings, due to the infrequent visits, or from ignorance of the context in Pakistan schools – or, worse, from what was perceived to be the rather patronizing attitudes of the developed towards the developing world. There was a felt need to assert autonomy, to keep the PUs firmly within an advisory rather than executive capacity.

But as Penny et al (2000) conclude in their article:

> When the intricacies of status, norms, role, equity and authority take centre stage in an international setting which brings together persons from developed and developing contexts, who is 'developed' and who is 'undeveloped' becomes glaringly problematic. Creating, managing, maintaining and sustaining the context for effective partnership and participation was an ever present challenge to us all, but the experience of it was exhilarating and personally and professionally rewarding. (p. 454)

Partnership: research

From the very beginning, research was seen as a main function of the IED and the role of the Partner Universities in cooperating in such research was acknowledged. Indeed, as must be already clear from what has been said, the development of a shared research programme, especially with field-based teacher education, was attractive to both Toronto and Oxford. Furthermore, this was in no way seen by them as their doing research on the IED. Rather they aspired to developing their research knowledge through the partnership with the IED, which was exploring a distinctive model of field-based teacher education in a very different context.

As the IED came to assume greater responsibility for its programmes, the Partner Universities could now refocus on research capacity and cooperation. This research would be supported by successful joint applications for funding. And the cooperation over research would be built into the renewal of the contract.

There were two routes into this research partnership. The first was that of individual links, forged through the shared teaching on the IED Master's modules and through the personal relationships established during the many visits to Karachi. There are several examples of this. The Oxford lecturer, who developed and taught the mathematics modules, worked closely with Professional Development Teachers (PDTs), who were graduates of the first M.Ed. programme, to establish research between teachers and educators. The results showed important relationships developing between mathematics classroom research by PDTs and teachers, and developments in approaches to mathematics teaching and teacher education (Jaworski, 1996, 2001) Furthermore, together they developed the idea of the Mathematics Institute of Pakistan, now a thriving organisation encouraging research into and development of the teaching of mathematics.

The second route was for a more formal development of research proposals between the three institutions. To that end, members of the three universities met in Oxford for a week before Christmas 1998. A lot of work was put into the development of a major research project. But it came to nought. And that, in retrospect, seems inevitable. Good research proposals arise out of a shared idea, a shared problem which calls for solutions. It is not the other way around – a project looking for an idea.

Possibly major and shared research projects of this kind between universities in such diverse settings are necessarily hard to establish. As the article by Penny et al (2000), pointed out, the different perspectives of people in such different contexts make it difficult for one party not to dominate the other – either because one is the 'insider', knowing the context, familiar with the issues, or the other is the' outsider', albeit with greater political and financial clout. On the other hand, the failure of this initiative was a pity. In the shared interest in field-based teacher education, there was the possibility of each partner providing an outside perspective on the distinctive features of each other's conception and implementation of it. Too often the partners in the developing world of a partnership suffer the external, critical and often uncomprehending gaze of the observer from the developed world. Perhaps those in the so-called developed world might themselves benefit from the roles being reversed – especially as the distinction between developing and developed worlds become increasingly blurred.

'Building research capacity' was, of course, one important aspect of the research dimension to the partnership. As early as 1995, at the Faculty Retreat held on 24 October, a Ph.D. programme was being proposed by the IED. One main reason for this was the difficulty in recruiting properly qualified persons to the faculty at the IED. The help of the Partner Universities would be important. This proposal was discussed further at future meetings of the Partner Universities Forum; it received strong advocacy from Partner Universities at a meeting of a subcommittee of the

Board of Trustees meeting in Karachi in 1997. A proposal was put to the Board of Trustees, following a detailed needs analysis and a valuable overview of doctoral courses by Toronto. Initially, members of the PUs would help with the delivery of such a programme.[1]

Meanwhile, however, the building of research capacity had, rather expensively, consisted in successful Professional Development Teachers, having acquired their Master's, undertaking their doctoral studies at the Universities of Toronto or Oxford –'or, in one case, Alberta. Already, having graduated, seven students have returned as members of Faculty (at the time of writing, one from Alberta, four from Toronto, two from Oxford), thereby enhancing the capacity of the Institute, and mitigating the demands upon the PUs for delivering the modules. Mathematics is one interesting case. Two of the original clinical teachers in mathematics education, one of whom had returned as a Professional Development Teacher to a school, the other as a teacher educator with AKES,P (The Aga Khan Education Services, Pakistan), went to Oxford. Now they have returned to enhance the teaching which their tutor at Oxford had previously been responsible for. Furthermore, there are currently further students (future faculty or future leaders of professional development centres) preparing for their doctorates in Toronto and Oxford.

Conclusions: lessons learnt and future direction

One major lesson of the partnership is that it lies ultimately in mutual respect rather than in contractual obligation – although the latter may be an essential step for the former to occur. As the need for the PUs to teach specific modules recedes, so does the relationship change and so does the weight upon a contract recede. Relationships have been established; former suspicions have given way to mutual respect, specific shared tasks have been negotiated freely and reciprocal arrangements have been made in teaching. The IED knows that, at Oxford and Toronto, there are able and well-disposed Faculty who are familiar with and sympathetic to the work of the IED and who can be called upon (in, for example, the development of the Ph.D. programmes). The Partner Universities appreciate the distinctive qualities and expertise within the IED and, in the case of Oxford, has linked key faculty members to its department as research fellows, with invitations to contribute to its courses, particularly in international and comparative education.

Indeed, the suggestion by the (now) former Director of the IED that the PUs did not learn enough from the IED is in retrospect correct. Oxford, for example, has one of the few courses in the United Kingdom at Master's level on international and comparative education, and yet the experience and expertise of the IED hardly had any impact upon it. The experience of frequent visits both to the IED in Karachi and, in some cases, to the Professional Development Centre in Gilgit, has brought to the Partner

Universities experiences and relationships which give rise to new understandings of 'field-based education' in circumstances very different from their own. Indeed, the model established and developed in Karachi shaped the plans for a professional centre in Ramallah, Palestine, funded by the Qattan Foundation and prepared by Oxford. Unfortunately, the renewed 'intifada' has temporarily stopped the research link between that centre, the IED and the Partner Universities, as they addressed together the ideas of field-based teacher education, especially in areas of conflict and deprivation.

Furthermore, the potential benefits are being seen more clearly and urgently, as the Partner Universities themselves seek to deepen their understanding of the multicultural environment in which they exist, especially the education of Muslim children in the United Kingdom, many of whom have come from Pakistan. The potential advantage of the partnership for developments at the Partner Universities, particularly for the units concerned with comparative, international and multi-ethnic education, is only just being realised.

Certainly the PUs are different places, with a range of staff both committed to the development of field-based education with the IED and with individual initiatives flourishing. Partnerships, though established by contracts, ultimately flourish, and continue, on the drive and mutual respect of individuals.

Note

[1] The IED's own PhD programme was launched in 2004 with PU members as part of its advisory board.

References

Bacchus, K. (1995a) Some Observations on Faculty Development Strategies for the Institute for Educational Development. Discussion Paper, Aga Khan University.

Bacchus, K. (1995b) Partner Universities: Memorandum of Understanding. Discussion document prepared December 1995.

Edwards, R.H. (1990) Letter to Dr David Phillips, 16 March.

Jaworski, B. (1996) The Implications of Theory for a New Masters Programme for Teacher Educators in Pakistan, in C. Brock (Ed.) *Global Perspectives on Teacher Education*, pp. 65-76. Wallingford: Triangle.

Jaworski, B. (2001) Developing Mathematics Teaching: teachers, teacher-educators, and researchers as co-learners, in F.-L. Lin & T.J. Cooney (Eds) *Making Sense of Mathematics Teacher Education*, pp. 295-320. Dordrecht: Kluwer.

Judge, H. (1991). The Institute for Educational Development of the Aga Khan University. Notes of the planning meeting held at Michigan State University, April 1991, attended by representatives of Michigan State University, Oxford University, University of Toronto, Aga Khan University, Aga Khan Foundation and the Aga Khan Education Services.

Penny, A.J., Ali, M.A., Farah, I., Ostberg, S. & Smith, R.L. (2000) A Study of Cross-national Collaborative Research: reflecting on experience in Pakistan, *International Journal of Educational Development*, 20, pp. 433-455.

Pring, R. (1990) Letter to Mr Edwards, Chairman of the Task Group, 2 April 1990.

Pring, R. (1995) Letter to Mr Allsop, previously OUDES representative on the Advisory Council, 21st March 1995.

The Aga Khan Foundation (1992) *The Aga Khan University, Institute for Educational Development and its Partner Universities*, 1 May 1992.

The Aga Khan Institution and Teachers in Pakistan (1989) *Report of the Task Force on Education in Pakistan*. Aiglemont.

CHAPTER 3

Developing Professional Development Teachers

FAUZIA SHAMIM & ANJUM HALAI

The Institute for Educational Development (IED) at the Aga Khan University (AKU) in Karachi began its first Master's degree programme, an M.Ed. in Teacher Education, in January 1994. It was designed to prepare Professional Development Teachers (PDTs) through a two-year academic programme that would be school-focused. This chapter will address the M.Ed. programme and the role of the returning graduates as PDTs in their sponsoring institutions. This twofold focus reflects the nature of the programme as part of a wider strategy for improving the quality of education in Pakistan and other developing countries.

The discussion in this chapter begins with a summary of the theoretical principles underlying the programme. The second section provides a description of the nature and length of the programme and a sample of the profile of a Master's cohort. The third section comprises a discussion of the issues and challenges that arose in the course of programme implementation. The final section discusses the impact of the programme.

Principles Underlying the Programme

The M.Ed. in Teacher Education programme at the IED draws its strength from clinical models of Teacher Education of the Pittsburgh school district and Michigan State University in the USA and field-based teacher education programmes in the United Kingdom and Canada (AKU-IED, 1991; Cornbleth & Ellsworth, 1994; McIntyre et al, 1994). According to Cornbeth & Ellsworth (1994), clinical faculty are outstanding experienced elementary and secondary schoolteachers who work with college and university teacher-education programmes. The aim of clinical faculty is to bring the experience of the school setting into the university as well as to work for the university at school sites.

The theoretical position espoused by the M.Ed. programme can be inferred from various reports and documents, for example, course handbooks (1994-2001), several in-house reports (Ali et al, 1995; Mithani, 1996; Khamis, 1997) and from Kanu (1996) and Jaworski (1996). The essential characteristics of the programme can be summarised as follows:

- The focus is on whole school improvement. On return, to the field the graduates are expected to work as change agents in the sponsoring school and/or school system.
- The M.Ed. programme is field focused: throughout the two-year programme participants have opportunities to work with students and teachers in and out of classrooms.
- The M.Ed. programme aims to prepare reflective practitioners and so has an explicit focus on action research, maintaining reflective journals and encouraging a critically questioning stance towards own practice and to all knowledge.
- The M.Ed. programme has a strong emphasis on collaborative processes for teaching and learning.

Description of the M.Ed. Programme

This section outlines briefly the main features of the M.Ed. programme and traces its development over various cohorts of students, or course participants (henceforth CPs). Furthermore, to enable the reader to appreciate the subsequent discussion of issues and challenges, a sample profile of a cohort of the CPs is also presented.

The CPs are seconded by their sponsoring institutions for a period of two years. Upon graduation, the CPs are expected to share their time with AKU-IED and the sponsoring institution for a period ranging from 3-5 years (their 'bond'). This arrangement aims to provide an apprenticeship in teacher education to the graduates following the clinical model of their M.Ed. programme.

Nature and Length of the Programme

The M.Ed. programme at AKU-IED is an intensive full-time course for practising teachers of 84 weeks (including an orientation period at the beginning of the programme) spread over two academic years. At the time of writing it has been delivered to six cohorts of teachers who have graduated from the classes of 1995, 1998, 1999, 2000, 2002 and 2003.[1] Initially, it involved course work planned on a modular structure with ten modules and a dissertation of approximately 15,000 words completed over a period of 15 weeks. Each module was formally assessed as was the dissertation.

Year one of the course included the four curriculum areas, English, Mathematics, Science and Social Studies, taught as four modules that addressed both the primary and lower secondary phases of schooling (see also Chapter 4). In year two, the focus moved from subject areas to teacher learning and school improvement. The CPs were also provided with an alternative experience in an educational context different from their own, usually in one of the areas of Pakistan distant from Karachi.

The theoretical foundations of the programme have remained virtually unchanged over the years, but details have changed, mainly in response to the needs of the schools and school systems which sponsor the CPs and the PDTs and the development of new initiatives at AKU-IED detailed in its Phase Two Proposal [2], (2000-06) (AKU-IED, 2000). The changes can be seen mainly in terms of programme component and structure: for example, the introduction of an elective module focusing on 'new' curriculum areas [3], such as Health Education, Environmental Education, Inclusive Education and Educational Leadership and Management and a four-week module titled 'Research Methods' – the last mainly in preparation for a small-scale investigation for the purpose of the dissertation research (see Chapter 15 for details).

In response to a request from the sponsoring schools and systems, a specialized module in Primary Education was introduced for the Class of 1999 and this was enhanced substantially for the Classes of 2002 and beyond. To allow this time for more detailed work at primary level, the CPs now select just two curriculum areas (from the four available) for study at the lower secondary level. When, in 2001, the course in Educational Leadership and Management was offered as one of the electives, an overwhelming number of the CPs (almost 95%) signed up for this course. Most had been advised to do so by their school or system in the light of their expected future roles as PDTs and/or educational managers. The introduction of this module as a core course of the M.Ed. programme is currently under consideration by the curriculum committee at the AKU-IED. Efforts are also underway to make the programme more flexible both in terms of structure and content through the introduction, for example, of subject specializations and open and distance learning. Earlier, a module entitled *Subject Specialization,* (to become *Enhancement of Pedagogical and Content Knowledge* in future years) was introduced for the second cohort (Class of 1998). The course participants could elect to study one of the four subject areas mentioned above. However, this option was removed in 2000 to make space for other courses. Subject specialism remains a concern since returning graduates are often seen as 'subject specialists' without having acquired the depth of knowledge and range of experiences to deliver in that role.

In response to the emerging needs of the graduates and issues identified in programme evaluation, the programme evolved to its current structure for the fifth cohort (see details of this for the Class of 2003 in the Appendix).

Profile of Course Participants

As indicated in Chapter 1, the participants are selected from AKU-IED's cooperating schools in accordance with IED's mandate of school improvement through developing institutional capacity. The participants are drawn from different educational systems including the government or public system. The composition of course participants has changed, to some extent, from year to year with a gradual increase in the number of candidates from the public sector, as can be seen in Table I. Presently, the course participants (CPs) come from a variety of contexts and geographical locations spread over eight countries in the developing world as can be seen in Table II. The balance of countries changes from one cohort to another. There is immense diversity in any one cohort of CPs that is apparent in terms of gender, age and teaching experience, their proficiency in the English language and the variety of regions and sectors that the CPs represent. For example, out of a total of 34 CPs in one cohort (Class of 2003), 46% are females and 54% males; age levels range from 22-52 years and teaching experience from 1-31 years. The CPs' proficiency in reading and writing academic English ranges from the level of beginners to intermediate and relatively advanced levels of attainment.

The diversity is also evident in the CPs' backgrounds and experiences at entry level such as the number of years of formal study and learning opportunities before joining the M.Ed. programme. For example, the minimum qualification required for entry in the M.Ed. programme is a bachelor's degree. However, some CPs also have either professional degrees and/or have attended training programmes such as the Language Enhancement and Achievement Programme and the Field Based Teacher Training Programme run by the Aga Khan Education Services (AKES) in the Northern Areas of Pakistan. Similarly, while most of the CPs have been classroom teachers, some have also worked as head teachers or teacher educators.

Tables I and II provide details of the CPs' distribution by sector and regions for the Classes of 1998 and 2003.

Sector	1998 No. of CPs	1998 %	2003 No. of CPs	2003 %
Public sector	12	34.28	15	44.12
Private Sector (including NGOs)	4	11.42	9	26.47
AKDN (including AKES)[4]	19	54.28	10	29.41
Total	35	100	34	100

Table I. Sectors represented in sample cohorts of CPs.

The success of the Master's programme can be seen in the enhanced confidence and knowledge growth of the CPs who went on to work as PDTs (see Ali et al, 1995; Khamis, 2000), as well as in the almost 100% success rate of the CPs in the final assessment. Preliminary findings of a longitudinal research study, *Narratives of Professional Development*, currently in progress at AKU-IED are similar to these earlier studies.[5] The external reviewers in their report (AKU-IED, 1998) described this programme as 'an exemplary model for graduate programmes in Education' (p. iv). They were impressed with a number of features which, according to them, set it apart as a 'distinctive and valuable programme'. For example, the 'grounding of all aspects of the programme in reflective practice' was identified as a major strength of the programme. This was further confirmed in the recent external reviewer's report (AKU-IED, 2002). However, certain issues and challenges arose when the theoretical principles underlying the programme were put into practice. The next section outlines the major issues and challenges faced in programme implementation. It also highlights attempts to deal with difficulties in maintaining the quality of teaching and learning in the programme as well as in enhancing the impact of the work of the M.Ed. graduates for school improvement.

CPs' Country and/or Region	Class of 1998		Class of 2003	
	No. of CPs	%	No. of CPs	%
Pakistan	28	80	24	70.58
Province of Sindh	16	45.71	16	47.05
Chitral/North West Frontier Province (NWFP)	2	5.71	4	11.76
Northern Areas	6	17.14	4	11.76
Balochistan	4	11.42	0	0
East Africa	3	8.55	4	11.76
Kenya	1	2.85	0	0
Tanzania (including Zanzibar)	1	2.85	3	8.82
Uganda	1	2.85	1	2.94
Central Asia	4	11.4	6	17.64
Tajikistan	2	5.71	4	11.76
Kyrgyzstan	1	2.85	2	5.88
Bangladesh	1	2.85	0	0

Table II. Countries and/or regions represented in sample cohorts of CPs.

Issues and Challenges

The issues and challenges that emerged were mainly of two types: first, those that were faced by the CPs and tutors in the course of the Master's programme, including issues of long contact hours and learner responsibility, the CPs' difficulties in taking a reflective stance towards their practice, their inadequate skills in the English language, varied expertise in subject knowledge and classroom experiences, and the diversity of the cohort in terms of prior learning experiences (see Chapter 4 for a discussion of issues pertaining to teaching and learning in different subject areas); second, those faced by returning graduates as PDTs, including the tensions that emerged as theoretical ideas were put into practice and in terms of time-sharing between the sponsoring schools and/or school systems and the AKU-IED.

Contact Hours and Responsibility for Learning

The intensive nature of the M.Ed. programme – 84 weeks of full-time study – has perhaps no parallel in graduate programmes elsewhere. However, there is general agreement amongst the faculty and the leadership in schools and school systems that the length of the programme is perhaps warranted due to the insufficient preparation of the CPs for graduate study in their educational contexts.[6] We also recognise that the M.Ed. programme is often the first experience for the majority of participants in alternative ways of thinking and learning which are vastly different from the transmission mode they have been exposed to traditionally as learners: for example, looking at learners as active participants in knowledge construction as opposed to passive recipients of external knowledge.

The M.Ed. programme began with very long contact hours (five and a half hours per day, four days a week, or 22 hours a week). Programme evaluations showed that CPs had insufficient time to 'mull over' new ideas and theories and relate them to their own contexts. It was also observed that the CPs had little time and energy after a long day in the classroom to extend their understanding of basic concepts through further independent reading and reflection. Furthermore, the long contact hours seemed to be giving the CPs a message that they could learn only from or in the presence of their tutors. This dependency culture was evident both in assessed and non-assessed tasks, for example, limited reading outside the specific topics focused on in the class. Some CPs also complained that they were being treated as children by being made to sit in the classroom for such long hours every day. The faculty, on the other hand, felt that the majority of the CPs might not be able to take responsibility for their own learning because of their weak educational backgrounds. To address these issues, a concept of 'Student Independent Learning Time' was introduced and contact hours were reduced from 22 to 16 hours per week for the Class of 2002 (for one example of programme structure and content, see the Appendix). This provided some time for independent study with various support structures. For example, tutors were available for consultation during self-study periods; the CPs were encouraged to read recommended texts in reading groups and to write reading responses and critical summaries wherever appropriate; and ongoing support in the English language was provided through weekly classes at three levels following placement tests. A focus on reflection was emphasised throughout.

Taking a Reflective Stance

Teacher-reflection through strategies such as maintaining reflective journals and participating in action research has been acknowledged as a robust form of teacher development leading to action based on critical thought (Schon, 1983; Carr & Kemmis, 1986; Johnson, 2001). However, issues emerged when the CPs in the M.Ed. programme were encouraged to engage in systematic reflection. For example, to begin with, the CPs' writings in their journals were mainly descriptive, and readily and uncritically 'accepting' of the new ideas to which they were being introduced. To enable and encourage the CPs to take a critical stance towards their practice and the experiences in the Master's programme, the course tutors began to set questions about which the CPs could think in the course of their reflections. For example, to help the CPs reflect on a lesson they taught in the curriculum areas, they were given a set of questions to recall the lesson, reflect on different aspects of the lesson, draw conclusions from this and consequently think about ways of improving their lesson. These focused questions helped the CPs to become more analytical about their classroom practice as was evident in their subsequent reflective accounts.

Asking the CPs to share their reflective journal with their tutors raised the issue of CPs' writing being constrained by the consideration of the tutors as audience. To address this issue the CPs were provided with an option to offer the course tutors only those parts of the journals that they felt comfortable in sharing. It was observed that as trust and confidence began to grow between the tutors and the CPs, the CPs were more willing not only to share their journal writings but also to discuss sensitive issues openly with their tutors.

Diversity

As is apparent from the profile of a cohort of the CPs there is immense diversity in the range and scope of experience that the participants in the Master's programme bring with them. On the one hand, this diversity is a strength of the programme because it enables the CPs to learn from each other and with each other. For example, one CP from a comparatively privileged private school in Karachi noted in her journal that

> I really appreciated this opportunity I got to work with the government school teachers. I had heard that they work in very impoverished conditions but never knew how impoverished until I saw the school that Nargis had been teaching in. A class of more than a hundred students!!! Really what can a teacher do under these circumstances? (Quote from a CP's journal)[7]

The diversity of the cohort was enabling this CP to widen her understanding of the issues and constraints prevalent in different educational settings. On the other hand the diversity in the group sometimes led to tension between the individual needs of the CPs and the institutional need of applying the same standards for all CPs. For example, one CP's struggle to deal with her relatively lower proficiency in the English language led to an uncomfortable and demoralizing situation:

> In one task of the module I took the initiative to be the group presenter and describing the task I wrote 'Roll model' instead of role model. The facilitator of the group laughed at my English and I was so hurt that immediately I lost all my confidence. Read my reflection of the day: 'today is the worst day of my life. I am very stupid. Why did I have a desire of learning? High qualification is only for the people who have the power of English language'.
> (CP's journal quoted in Jaworski, 1999, p. 198)

The differential language ability of the CPs and consequently their ability to read academic texts with understanding and to critique them posed immense challenges both for the CPs and the tutors as well as for the quality assurance of the programme.

A number of measures were taken early in the course to ensure that the learning opportunities created could be personally meaningful and relevant to all CPs, for example, support with the English language both through an eight-week intensive English language input before the main programme began, and in other ways described above. In addition, ongoing emotional and moral support, through structures such as personal tutors and a buddy system [8], is provided to all CPs, particularly to those who are away from home.

Issues in Relating Theory and Practice: the PDT programme

The principle of maintaining a close relationship between theory and practice is seen in a number of ways in the M.Ed. programme: for example, all the modules are school focused and the CPs are required to spend an equivalent of one day per week in a school throughout their programme. In order to prepare the CPs to undertake their role as professional development teachers after graduation, concepts such as mentoring and collaborative learning are introduced and the CPs gain some experience of their use during the M.Ed. programme. Theoretically speaking, mentoring is widely acknowledged as a strategy for school-based professional development of teachers (Gray & Gray, 1985; Feiman-Nemser & Parker, 1990; McIntyre, Hagger & Wilkin, 1994; Koeppen & McKay, 2000; Semenuik & Worral, 2000) and cooperative or collaborative learning approaches enable learning both for pupils in classrooms and in the professional development of teachers (Joyce et al, 1987; Slavin, 1987; Bennet et al, 1991). On their return to their schools, the

CPs, now PDTs, are expected to put their learned theory into practice, working as mentors with the teachers and using cooperative learning approaches to working with pupils and with teachers.

However, the concept of a field/school-based teacher education programme is fairly new for most senior managers in education and in schools in developing countries. The PDTs went back to school systems, or institutions, that had not changed with them. This became evident in issues such as ambiguity surrounding the role of the PDTs in the school; lack of infrastructure in schools to support teacher development; and the PDTs' isolation and need to sustain their own professional growth. For example, notions of mentoring and collaborative learning were quite strange for most teachers and for school leaders who were not familiar with the processes involved. Hence, they saw the PDTs as problem solvers, subject specialists, supervisors, and administrative assistants – roles with which they were familiar – rather than as mentors and collaborative workers. Such perceptions were at odds with those of the PDTs based on their M.Ed. learning as teacher educators and mentors. For example, PDTs had to negotiate with their school authorities, with varying degrees of success, to provide time for a group of teachers to meet and work together. Khamis (2000) confirmed that a lack of infrastructure and other forms of support became a major hindrance for the PDTs in playing their role as teacher educators effectively. Based on her own work as a PDT, Halai (1998, 2001a) judged that the ambiguity surrounding a PDT's role as a mentor was due mainly to a lack of understanding of PDTs' newly acquired skills and experiences during the M.Ed. programme by the schools and systems. Hence, PDTs' re-entry and efforts to put into practice theoretical concepts such as mentoring and teacher-collaboration were constrained by the contextual realities of existing school systems and practices.

The PDTs expressed the need for follow-up support from the IED to sustain their enthusiasm and strengthen their efforts, often in difficult circumstances, for school improvement. Elnazar (1999), in his study of the transition of 35 graduates of the second cohort of M.Ed. (Class of 1998) concludes:

> there is a need for community and the sharing of concerns and
> ideas with people who understand, support and encourage.
> Otherwise it would not be surprising if the PDTs' credibility were
> to evaporate and they would return to those beliefs and practices
> which they held and utilised prior to their experience at IED.
> (p. 52)

One kind of sustenance has come through the formation of professional associations for teachers by PDTs in various curriculum areas. The IED has provided support in principle and in small-scale funding (see Chapter 1). The PDTs have worked actively to form teacher networks and a platform for provision of continuing support to teachers from the cooperating schools and elsewhere. Presently eight professional associations are engaged in providing opportunities to teachers and PDTs for sharing experiences and continuing professional development through Saturday seminars, short courses and annual conferences on a small scale.

An important original feature of the PDT programme is the concept of time-sharing of graduates between their schools and the IED for the three years of their bond period following completion of the M.Ed. programme. This was motivated by the clinical model of apprenticeship and aimed to provide the graduates with opportunity to practice and develop further their skills as teacher educators in the relatively 'safe' and supportive environment of the AKU-IED. During this time the graduates have spent approximately six months at the IED and six months in their school. At the IED, the PDTs have worked in small teams to plan and conduct Visiting Teachers (VT) programmes (see Chapter 5) with guidance from faculty. While acknowledging the merits of this system of time-sharing for the development of the PDTs, the co-operating schools are now increasingly reluctant to release their PDTs for working at the IED. According to them, it disrupts their own plans and activities for school improvement. They point out that one of the objectives of the M.Ed. programme was to develop exemplary teachers; however, spending half the year in the university made it very difficult to develop this expertise. Also, the time out limited what the PDTs could do with other teachers in their school, since before any initiative was established the PDTs had to leave again. Thus, the six-monthly school/university division of time has come under scrutiny and is being reconsidered alongside modifications to the VT programme and developments in school management systems, (see Chapters 5 and 9).

Impact

There is immense complexity in the notion of impact of teacher education programmes on student learning outcomes. The complexity lies in the number of intervening variables and the distance of the programme inputs from the ultimate beneficiary, the student (Anderson, 2001). This is because the M.Ed. programme is part of a strategy for School Improvement through teacher education, described by Khamis (2000) as the IED model. A knowledge base on the impact of AKU-IED is emerging in the form of M.Ed. dissertations by the CPs (for example, Ahmed, 2000; Haque, 2002), doctoral theses (Khamis, 2000; Halai, 2001b; Fakir Mohammad, 2002) and the early findings emerging from the longitudinal study currently in process at AKU-IED. Furthermore, a pilot study of the impact of the M.Ed. programme through the lens of PDTs' roles and responsibilities is currently at the stage of analysis (Shamim, 2002).

Based on these studies we discuss the impact of the Master's programme through a consideration of the roles and responsibilities of PDTs in different educational contexts, of the CPs/PDTs as individuals, of learning in classrooms and of development in schools and systems.

Impact Seen through the Roles and Responsibilities of PDTs

Khamis (2000), studied the impact of the M.Ed. programme on PDTs in the variety of roles envisaged for them by AKU-IED, namely, exemplary teachers, teacher educators and teacher researchers.[9] He argued that, as the development of knowledge, skills and dispositions requisite for these roles underpins the design and ongoing development of the programme, determining the effectiveness of roles played by the PDTs is necessary before making any claims about the impact of the 'IED model'. The roles being played currently by PDTs, in vastly differing educational contexts, vary in terms of the nature and scope of their activities at the classroom, school and school systems or regional level. Also, there is increasing evidence of significant role shifts for the CPs, post graduation. For example, there is a major role shift from the CPs' original roles as teachers to PDT roles of teacher educator and/or educational leader and manager (Shamim, 2002; Siddiqui & Mcleod, 2004).

The various roles of PDTs at present can be summarized as those of teacher, teacher educator and senior or middle-level educational manager. In the IED model the three roles for graduates outlined in student handbooks as objectives of the programme, namely, exemplary teacher, teacher educator and teacher researcher, seem to be interlinked. However, there is no mention of preparing educational managers/leaders separately in this framework. This is possibly due to the focus of other IED programmes on developing heads and educational managers (see Chapter 9).

Most noticeable in the studies quoted above is the role of PDTs as teacher educators at different levels such as coordinating/leading teacher education activities across an entire school system. This role is particularly evident in the following excerpts from written reports of various PDTs (Shamim, 2002):

> After graduation from IED, my position has changed, now I'm working as Deputy Directress of Building Foundations School's School Improvement Centre, to grow teachers professionally. (M.Ed. graduate of 1998, current position: Deputy Director, School Improvement Centre)

> The main responsibility [of this PDT] is to structure, integrate and implement the academic staff's professional development in all AKES schools in country X. This is done in the form of in service workshops for teachers in respective schools and selecting staff members in conjunction with head teachers to attend professional development programmes. (M.Ed. graduate Class of 2000, current position: Professional Development Trainer)

We were a group of graduates from IED in the form of PDTs to work at PDCN.[10] It was helpful because we had the same professional language, same exposure similar understanding to work together, debate and reflect and learn from each other's experiences to deal with programmes and different circumstances at school level. We worked as a team and as colleagues ... In this way the continuation of our professional growth remained sustained. Working within the contextual realities of the school through WSIP programme [11] has provided us an opportunity to impact school improvement, student learning outcomes and influence system's policy. (M.Ed. graduate Class of 1998, current position: PDT at PDCN, Pakistan)

[I am] in charge of professional development in the junior section, KG [Kinder Garten]; I work with a group of 6-7 new teachers-individual meetings and a weekly one-hour session. Running a teacher leadership programme for 10 teachers in the school. Take [conduct] workshops held monthly. (M.Ed. graduate Class of 1996, current position: teacher educator)

Several PDTs have assumed senior leadership positions such as vice principal and principal in the management of a school. Their current range of responsibilities can be seen from the job description communicated by one PDT, currently working as vice-principal in her school (Shamim, 2002):

Administrative affairs: It mainly deals with the school management, i.e. writing and sending memos, framing time tables, giving allotments, interviewing teachers, taking demos, filling appraisals, taking care of school property, looking after maintenance, arranging curricular and co-curricular activities, checking fee defaulters, addressing/negotiating with the parents regarding behavioural problems, counselling students and parents, arranging orientation meetings for the parents and students, Parent teacher meetings etc. Also signing the bills and report cards etc. Sending report to the principal regarding Branch affairs.

Academic affairs: Informal classroom observation and feedback, attending co-ordination meetings, coaching VTs, monitoring the in-house training cycle (VT-non VT) [12], conducting workshops (needs based), writing papers for teachers, reviewing the assessment system, format and nature of papers; review textbooks; check student copies and guide the teachers regarding presentation and correction of students' copies, providing on-going professional support to the teachers etc. (M.Ed. graduate

Class of 1998, current position: vice-principal of a private
secondary school)

It seems that where there is incidence of role enhancement or adding other
roles to the returning graduate's already established role of classroom
teacher, the management role – always the more senior position in the
hierarchy – takes precedence over all other roles. For example, one M.Ed.
graduate, Tahira, moved very quickly from the role of teacher educator to the
vice-principal of a section in her school and then to the Principal of the
school comprising four sections located at three different campuses.
Currently, despite her very active interest in teacher education she indicates
that she cannot find time to engage in teacher education activities herself. In
her present role, she might be able to influence more lives, those of both
teachers and children. However, further research is needed to study the
nature and scope of the impact of PDTs moving into senior management
positions in their schools and systems.

One of the emerging findings of the pilot study is that few PDTs are
teaching classes alongside their other roles of teacher educator, head and
educational manager at different levels. In fact the PDTs who are 'merely
teaching classes' view themselves as unsuccessful and feel frustrated about
the lack of acknowledgement of their enhanced skills and abilities gained
from the M.Ed. programme, as is illustrated below (Shamim, 2002):

> Position is as usual normal teacher. No changes yet (like PDT) ...
> The concept/term PDT is not clear to the authority yet ... I'm
> assigned as usual like other teachers to teach at class. (M.Ed.
> graduate Class of 1998)

> Basically I am a subject teacher and have to spend most of the
> time in teaching higher classes which have to face Board exam. I
> need time to work with teachers but due to lack of job description
> I can't do it. (M.Ed. graduate Class of 2000)

Thus a review of PDTs' roles indicates role shifts mainly from teacher to
teacher educator and teacher educator to middle and senior management
position rather than role enhancement where PDTs take on the role of
teacher educators and/or educational managers/leaders *in addition* to the role
of a teacher in the classroom. Almost no PDTs seem to be engaged in
educational research at classroom level. The few PDTs who have remained
in their classroom feel frustrated at being unable to utilise their skills and
abilities for professional development of their colleagues. In contrast, the
PDTs who are responsible for the professional development of colleagues
have been taken out of the class to perform this role. Thus the 'teaching
expertise' of these PDTs remains largely theoretical and 'expert' without
developing further to meet the needs of the school (Khamis, 2000, p. 276).
Such PDTs could become isolated from the reality of the classroom leading

to their lack of empathy for teachers in introducing innovative ideas and techniques as well as stifling their professional growth as teacher educators.

To sum up, there needs to be further research to investigate whether the level of impact changes in relation to the changing roles and responsibilities of PDTs. At the same time it is important to explore the nature of the impact as PDTs move away from being practitioners to educational managers.

Impact on PDTs as Individuals

At the individual level, PDTs report a sense of major transformation both in terms of personal and professional growth – for example, more confidence, enhanced language and computer skills, enhanced content and pedagogical knowledge, and so forth. This is evident in the following excerpts from graduates who went on to work in different contexts after graduation:

> I believe that the MEd. programme equipped me with skills, knowledge, attitudes that enable me to execute my duties[as PDT]. For example, I do possess interpersonal skills that help me work with other teachers and colleagues at my place of work; the knowledge of ideas and concepts that are consistent with school systems demands and teacher training needs, and that are also relevant to the child-centred approaches upheld by AKES,U.; the attitude towards accomplishment of assigned duties and self directed activities. (M.Ed. graduate from East Africa, Class of 2000)

> Before going to IED I had no idea how professional development plan was designed and what was the role of teacher in it. As a teacher I was just following instructions of administration regarding professional development. Now I am looking at PD [professional development] in a different angle, I realised the importance of it for school improvement. I have started research on 'teachers' professional development needs' It will help me to match teachers' needs with available opportunities and to address them in our professional development plan. I also learned some skills that are useful in my job, such as for example, communicative skills. They are essential for me as I work with teachers, with adult people. Planning, writing and research skills are also of great help for me as a professional development advisor. (M.Ed. graduate from Central Asia, Class of 2000)

> I have become more analytical in my approach to my work and look critically at myself, teachers, school systems and the curriculum. I am more confident to carry out what I believe in. I am more able to deal with problems with individual

children/teachers and have a problem solving approach. (M.Ed. graduate from Karachi, Pakistan, Class of 1996)

MEd. programme changed me mentally, physically. My curiosity about education extended. I believe I am [more] professional than before. (M.Ed. graduate from Bangladesh, Class of 1998)

The emerging findings of the narrative study at AKU-IED also indicate that the major impact of the M.Ed. programme is at the level of individual CPs' or PDTs' knowledge, skills and attitudes (Andersen, 2001).

Impact on Classroom Practice and Student Learning Outcomes

As discussed earlier, PDTs in most cases have moved away from the classroom and become responsible for facilitating development of other teachers. This adds to the 'distance' between inputs in the M.Ed. programme and its impact on students' learning. Thus, in order for the impact of the M.Ed. programme to be visible in terms of students' learning outcomes, there is a need to investigate learning outcomes in classes of teachers working with PDTs for their professional development at the school or system level.

One such example can be seen in the doctoral research of Halai (2001b) which focused on students' learning in classrooms of AKU-IED graduates who had also worked closely with PDTs. Her study of mathematics learning in these classrooms revealed that the classroom organization and the teaching/learning environment were different from the traditional transmission mode of teaching: students were engaged in mathematical tasks that were open ended and challenging as compared to the closed and ritualized tasks prescribed in the textbook; group discussions related to these tasks showed elements of cooperative learning in action. There was strong evidence to show that these teachers were using their learning from the AKU-IED programmes. However, many students remained unclear about the mathematics on which they had been asked to work, and others seemed to have developed mathematically incomplete or incorrect conceptions. Thus, this study revealed teachers engaging with strategies introduced in the M.Ed. programme without the mathematical outcomes for students that such strategies were designed to achieve. It was clear that these teachers needed support at classroom level so that the issues emerging from implementing their learning from AKU-IED could be addressed. Here we see a study of students' learning revealing issues in teaching and teaching development that challenge the M.Ed.programme itself.

Impact Assessment in Relation to Schools and Systems

Different degrees of impact are visible in school improvement depending on the sector (public or private non-profit), degree of support available to the returning graduates and the size of the institution and/or system. For example, in the private sector, there is strong evidence of PDTs playing a central role in teacher development and school improvement provided the school management understands their role – for example, in planning and teaching systems-based VT programmes, [13] – and is supportive (see, for example, Huma, 2002). For example, the structural changes and other kinds of support increasingly being provided to PDTs are reflected in the recent establishment of a Professional Development Centre by one of the private school systems in Karachi. In addition, several systems have either created or are considering creating a cadre of PDTs or teacher educators. As such, the PDTs are given an explicit responsibility for planning and implementing school-based professional development programmes for teachers in their school system. Moreover, they are given a salary increase in recognition of their enhanced status and responsibilities.

In contrast, very little impact can be seen in the public sector as PDTs seem to get lost in the 'big' system. The PDTs from the public sector in Pakistan report that there is a general reluctance on the part of their management in using their skills even at the school level as they are often more 'knowledgeable' than their head teachers.[14] Also many of them are young junior teachers and are seen as a threat by the senior, more experienced teachers and educational mangers in the school and school system.

The stakeholders seem to have high expectations of the impact of the IED model of school improvement on the improvement of quality education in general (systemic level, national level) and the M.Ed. programme in particular. Such perceptions are supported by the following excerpts from the report of external reviewers (AKU-IED, 1998) of the M.Ed. programme:

> The Aga Khan University's Institute for Educational
> Development (IED) has provided an educational programme for
> the Master of Education students that will certainly contribute to
> educational reform and improvement in the efficiency and
> effectiveness of schools and other educational institutions in
> Pakistan, East Africa and Central Asia, as well as other countries
> and regions. (p. vi)

Impact at the regional levels can be seen from the variety of activities in which the PDTs are engaged, often as a result of special requests or commissions from educational agencies at a variety of levels. These activities include: (a) the PDTs' work in the Professional Development Centers (PDCs) in Gilgit, East Africa and at AKU-IED (see chapters 12, 7 and 10 respectively); (b) the PDTs' initiative in setting up professional associations; and (c) the PDTs' work with the Government in Pakistan to build capacity of teacher educators. For example, currently some PDTs are working with the faculty of the Provincial Institute for Teacher Education (PITE) in the province of Sindh, Pakistan, on a strategic plan for the development of PITE into an apex institute of teacher education in the province. Similarly, recently, the PDTs had an opportunity, through their respective professional associations, to undertake, with IED faculty, textbook revision for the Sindh Textbook Board from Classes I-V in four curriculum areas.

It is important to note that the work of the PDTs, and consequently, the sphere of their potential impact rests, on the one hand, on the opportunities made available by the school and system in which they work, and on the other hand, on opportunities created by them through professional associations and with colleagues, often in very difficult circumstances as seen above in the subsection 'issues relating theory and practice'.

Summary and Conclusion

The M.Ed. programme of the Aga Khan University in Karachi, Pakistan is aimed at developing Professional Development Teachers (PDTs) as part of its strategy for improving the quality of teaching and learning in Pakistan and other developing countries. The programme has been acknowledged as a very successful programme both by external reviewers and the AKU-IED's collaborating schools and systems.

While, initially, there was some ambiguity about PDTs' roles, now, there is increasing evidence that the schools and systems (principally those in the private sector) are beginning to utilize the human resources developed at AKU-IED through the M.Ed. programme for the professional development of their teachers. However, limited evidence is available about the impact on classrooms or students who are the final beneficiaries of the programme, as most of the PDTs are not practising teachers any more. Moreover, the teacher educator role of the PDTs seems to take precedence over the other two roles envisaged for them in the programme, that is, exemplary teacher and teacher researcher. This has the danger of isolating PDTs from classrooms and may have adverse effects on their future impact as teacher educators.

The impact of the M.Ed. programme is most visible at the individual level. However, most of the PDTs have also undergone significant role shifts and/or role enhancement on completion of the programme. Indeed, some of them have been assigned major leadership roles in their institutions.

The M.Ed. programme is a dynamic programme, constantly evolving in response to the emerging and/or changing needs of the course participants and other stakeholders. Amongst other things the growing trust and confidence of different systems in PDTs' abilities for educational leadership indicates a success of the programme.

Notes

[1] The second cohort was admitted after evaluating the entire programme. Similarly the fifth cohort was admitted after completing an extensive restructuring exercise in 2000. There is now an intake every year.

[2] The IED activities were funded mainly by international donors initially for the first six years. This is referred to as Phase I. At the end of this period, another proposal for activities during the next six years, referred to as Phase II, was prepared. This phase has also been funded by donors, primarily the European Union.

[3] By 'new' we mean curriculum areas that are traditionally not a part of the school curriculum in Pakistan and other developing countries.

[4] See list of acronyms.

[5] For example, Khatri et al (2001).

[6] For example, in Pakistan, only two years of study are required for a bachelor's degree after higher secondary school.

[7] Pseudonyms have been used throughout to maintain confidentiality of the participants.

[8] The personal tutor is an AKU-IED member of academic staff who is responsible for the development and welfare of M.Ed. Course Participants (CPs) during the two years of their stay at the university. The buddy system is where a CP from an incoming Master's cohort is paired with a CP from an ongoing Master's programme. The purpose is that the 'old CPs' would provide support to the newcomers in settling down and becoming members of the AKU-IED family.

[9] The experience of the first two cohorts of returning graduates indicated clearly that the focus of the M.Ed. programme should be on enabling the course participants to bring about change at all levels through developing their knowledge, skills and attitudes as teachers, teacher educators and researchers.

[10] PDCN is the second Professional Development Centre (PDC) of the AKU-IED established in Gilgit, Pakistan in 2000 to serve the teacher education needs of the Northern Areas of Pakistan (see Chapter 12). Two other PDCs are in the process of being established in Chitral, Pakistan and Tanzania, East Africa.

[11] The WSIP programme is the Whole School Improvement programme currently under way with the support of PDTs based at PDCN, in Gilgit and adjoining areas in Northern Pakistan.

[12] The VT-non VT cycle refers to a system of ongoing teacher development in the school initiated by the PDTs whereby teachers who have completed their Visiting Teachers (VT) programme at AKU-IED work with novice and inexperienced teachers providing them support in planning lessons, and through demonstration and feedback on observed lessons.

[13] VT programmes which are planned and delivered for teachers in just one system of schools, rather than the general model of the VT programme held at the IED – see Chapter 5.

[14] Personal communication with a PDT from the public sector.

References

Aga Khan University – Institute for Educational Development (AKU-IED) (1991) *A Proposal to the AKU Board of Trustees.* Karachi: AKU-IED.

Aga Khan University – Institute for Educational Development (AKU-IED) (1998) *Report of External Reviewers on MEd (Teacher Education) Programme.* Karachi: AKU-IED.

Aga Khan University – Institute for Educational Development (AKU-IED) (2000) *The Phase 2 Proposal (2000-2006).* Karachi: AKU-IED.

Aga Khan University – Institute for Educational Development (AKU-IED) (2002) *Report of External Reviewers on MEd (Teacher Education) Programme.* Karachi: AKU-IED.

Ahmed, S. (2000) Influence of the Secondary Science Professional Development Programme on Teachers' Beliefs. Unpublished M.Ed. dissertation, AKU-IED, Karachi.

Ali, M., Murphy, K. & Khan, G. (1995*) Documentation and Evaluation of Programmes. Report No. 1 Prepared for International Development Research Centre (IDRC), Canada.* Karachi: AKU-IED.

Andersen, S.E. (2001) *Impact Evaluation at IED: Consultant Report.* Unpublished report. Karachi: AKU-IED.

Bennet, B., Rolheiser, C. & Stevahn, L. (1991) *Cooperative Learning: where heart meets mind.* Ontario: Educational Connections.

Carr, W. & Kemmis, S. (1986) *Becoming Critical: education, knowledge and action research.* London: Falmer Press.

Cornbleth, C. & Ellsworth, J. (1994) Teachers in Teacher Education: Clinical Faculty roles and relationships, *American Educational Research Journal*, 31(1), pp. 49-70.

Elnazar, H. (1999) Exploring the Transition from MEd Graduates to Professional Development Teacher. Unpublished M.Ed. dissertation, AKU-IED, Karachi, Pakistan.

Fakir Mohammad, R. (2002) From Theory to Practice: an understanding of the implementation of in-service teachers' learning from university into the classrooms in Pakistan. Unpublished doctoral thesis, Department of Educational Studies, University of Oxford, Oxford.

Feiman-Nemser, S. & Parker, M.B. (1990) Making Subject Matter Part of the Conversation in Learning to Teach, *Journal of Teacher Education*, 41, pp. 32-43.

Gray, W. & Gray, M. (1985) Synthesis of Research on Mentoring Beginning Teachers, *Educational Leadership*, 43, pp. 37-42.

Halai, A. (1998) Mentor, Mentee, Mathematics: a story of professional development, *Journal of Mathematics Teacher Education*, 1(3), pp. 295-315.

Halai, A. (2001a) On Becoming a Professional Development Teacher: a case from Pakistan, *Mathematics Education Review*, 14, pp. 32-45.

Halai, A. (2001b) Role of Social Interactions in Students' Learning of Mathematics (in Classrooms in Pakistan). Unpublished doctoral thesis, Department of Educational Studies, University of Oxford, Oxford.

Haque, K. (2002) A Study of the Mentor's Role as a School Leader. Unpublished M.Ed. dissertation, AKU-IED, Karachi, Pakistan.

Huma, F. (2002) System Based Visiting Teachers Programme: major processes and their outcomes. Unpublished M.Ed. dissertation, AKU-IED, Karachi, Pakistan.

Jaworski, B. (1996) The Implications of Theory for a New Master's Programme for Teacher Educators in Pakistan, in C. Brock (Ed.) *Global Perspectives on Teacher Education*, pp. 65-76. Wallingford: Triangle.

Jaworski, B. (1999) The Plurality of Knowledge Growth in Mathematics Teaching, in B. Jaworski, T. Wood & S. Dawson (Eds) *Mathematics Teacher Education, Critical International Perspectives*, pp. 180-210. London: Falmer Press.

Johnson, G.C. (2001) Accounting for Pre-service Teachers' Use of Visual Metaphors in Narratives, *Teacher Development*, 5(1), pp. 119-139.

Joyce, B., Showers, B. & Rolheiser-Bennet, C. (1987) Staff Development and Staff Learning: a synthesis of research on models of teaching, *Educational Leadership*, 45(1), pp. 11-23.

Kanu, Y. (1996) Educating Teachers for the Improvement of Quality of Basic Education in Developing Countries, *International Journal of Educational Development*, 16(2), pp. 73-184.

Khamis, A. (1997) *The International Documentation and Research Study Report No. 3, Prepared for International Development Research Centre, Canada*. Karachi: AKU-IED.

Khamis, A. (2000) The Various Impacts of the Institute for Educational Development in Its Co-operating Schools in Pakistan. Unpublished doctoral dissertation, University of London, London.

Khatri, A. Siddiqui, N., Datoo, A., Mond, S. & Mcleod, G. (2001). *Narratives of Professional Development: A longitudinal study of M.Ed. graduates of AKU-IED*. Unpublished paper, AKU-IED.

Koeppen, K.E. & McKay, J.W. (2000) Who is Telemachus? Long-term Mentoring in Education, *Teacher Development*, 4(3), pp. 425-436.

McIntyre, D., Hagger, H. & Wilkin, M. (1994) *Mentoring: perspectives on school based teacher education*. London: Kogan Page.

Mithani, S. (1996) *The International Documentation and Research Study. Report No. 2. Prepared for International Development Research Centre*. Karachi: AKU-IED.

Schon, D. (1983) *The Reflective Practitioner*. New York: Basic Books.

Semeniuk, A. & Worral, A. (2000) Re-reading the Dominant Narrative of Mentoring. *Curriculum Inquiry*, 30(4), pp. 405-428.

Shamim, F. (2002) Role Shifts and Role Enhancement: the impact of an innovative Masters in Education programme. Unpublished report, available from the authors.

Siddiqui, N. & Macleod, G. (2004) Tracking Graduates of AKU-IED's M.Ed. Programme: the classes of 1999, 2000 and 2002, in A. Halai & J. Rarieya (Eds) *Impact: making a difference*. Proceedings of an International Conference. AKU-IED, 28-30 August 2003.

Slavin, R. (1987) Cooperative Learning: can students help students learn? *Instructor*, March, pp. 74-78.

APPENDIX
Academic Calendar

M.Ed. Class of 2003

Pre-Session Language Course: (8 weeks) 30 July 2001-23 September 2001.

Year One: 30 July 2001-11 August 2002		
Orientation	(2 weeks)	24 September-6 October 2001
Break	(1 week)	8-14 October 2001
Reconceptualization	(6 weeks)	15 October-24 November 2001
Primary 1	(3 weeks)	26 November-15 December 2001
Eid-ul-Fitr Break (2001)	(1 week)	16-23 December 2001
Primary 2	(6 weeks)	24 December 2001-2 February 2002
Primary 3	(3 weeks)	4-23 February 2002
Eid-ul-Azha Break (2002)	(1 week)	24 February-3 March 2002
Primary 3 (contd)	(3 weeks)	4-23 March 2002
Primary 1 (contd)	(3 weeks)	25 March-13 April 2002
Lower Secondary Subject Areas* (Maths & English)	(6 weeks)	15 April-25 May 2002
Break	(1 week)	27 May-2 June 2002
Lower Secondary Subject Areas* (Science & Social Studies)	(6 weeks)	3 June-13 July 2002
Teacher Learning	(4 weeks)	15 July-10 August 2002
Break	(5 weeks)	11 August-15 September 2002
Educational inquiry^		19 October 2001-2 August 2002

* CPs can select one of the two curriculum areas offered for study in these modules.
^ These are non-credit 'courses' and held on every alternate Friday for two hours in year one of the M.Ed. programme.

Year Two: 16 September 2002-1 August 2003		
Research Methods	(4 weeks)	16 September-11 October 2002
Teacher Learning	(2 weeks)	14-25 October 2002
Elective	(6 weeks)	28 October 28-6 December 2002
Eid-ul-Fitr Break	(1 week)	9-15 December 2002
School Improvement Programme	(6 weeks)	16 December 2002-25 January 2003
Developing Research Proposal	(2 weeks)	27 January 2003-8 February 2003
Eid-ul-Azha Break	(1 week)	10-16 February 2003
Alternate Exposure Module	(5 weeks)	17 February-21 March 2003
Break	(1 week)	24-30 March 2003.
Dissertation Process	(15 weeks)	31 March-11 July 2003
Proposal Presentation	(1 week)	31 March-4 April 2003
Field Work	(7 weeks)	7 April-23 May 2003
Write-up	(7 weeks)	26 June-11 July 2003
Break	(1 week)	14-20 July 2003
Re-Entry	(2 weeks)	21 July-1 August 2003
Dissertation Revision	(2 weeks)	4-15 August 2003

CHAPTER 4

Subject Studies in Teacher Education

BARBARA JAWORSKI, BERNADETTE L. DEAN & RANA HUSSAIN

Introduction to Subject Studies at the Institute for Educational Development at theAga Khan University (AKU-IED)

What is it Important to Learn and How Can Learning Be Organised?

If we answer the question, 'What is it important for children to learn', it is likely that we would include a variety of concepts relating to the world around us including aspects of language, mathematics and science; environmental, social, cultural and religious issues and concerns; music and the arts; physical education, and so on. As we consider how such concepts might be addressed, the ethics and values of addressing them, and the outcomes for children's growth and participation in society, a curriculum starts to form. Civilized societies that institutionalize learning into schools have developed curricula that relate to their particular contexts, values and political ideologies. In many countries, the resulting curriculum designated for schools has similarities, one of which, particularly in secondary education, has been its division into *subjects*. Although some schools in some parts of the world have resisted such division, it is a prevalent way of organising the curriculum. This is no less true in Pakistan and in other countries from which the AKU-IED draws its students, who are practising teachers.

Education at primary level tends to be more variable, with some places preferring a thematic division to the curriculum rather than a subject-based one. Thus, whereas subjects might include English, History, Geography, Mathematics, Science, and so on, themes would be broader and more socioculturally related: for example, buildings, fire, food, sport or trade. Study within a theme would draw on a wide range of subjects and encourage both subject-specific learning and development of values and skills for life. Thematic learning at secondary school level is seen to be more difficult to organize than at primary level since it is not obvious how certain concepts can be developed through a thematic approach except perhaps in a very contrived way. This, of course, varies according to subject discipline.

Teachers' Knowledge

What Forms of Knowledge Do We Recognise?

Learners need opportunities to address concepts in their experiential world, and the mantle of responsibility rests on teachers to interpret the given curriculum in ways that foster learning. Thus, teachers need knowledge appropriate to their interpretation of the curriculum. This includes the specialized knowledge to address concepts and issues that are subject related, the pedagogical knowledge to create learning environments and the social knowledge to address values and relationships. Scholars have written extensively about the knowledge teachers need, and the forms it might take. For example, Shulman's classification includes content knowledge and pedagogical content knowledge, both relating to subjects and approaches to teaching those subjects (for example, Shulman, 1987); while Eraut (1994) classifies knowledge into procedural knowledge, propositional knowledge; practical knowledge; tacit knowledge; and skills and know-how (p. 16). The latter may be seen collectively with respect to any one subject, or may be considered across subjects. However, it seems to make sense that in order to teach, for example, Science, whether directly as a subject or inter-thematically, teachers have to have knowledge of Science, and this has to be applicable to ways in which Science contributes to the experiential world of a student.

Content and Pedagogical Content Knowledge

Content knowledge involves the specialized knowledge that is the mainstay of each disciplinary field like Science or Social Studies. It also, to some extent that is negotiable, includes epistemological knowledge in the field. For Mathematics, for example, this might be seen as including the nature of abstraction, and how abstraction arises from particular cases, through generalization and proof. For example, the recognition that $3 + 7 = 10$ and that $5 + 11 = 16$ leads to a conjecture, expressed in general terms, that the sum of two odd numbers always gives an even number. We can prove this algebraically by starting with a general odd number $2n + 1$, where n is any whole number, and adding to it another odd number $2m + 1$. The sum of these is $2n + 2m + 2$ which we can write as $2(m + n + 1)$. This result has a factor of 2 which means that it is an even number. Thus we have proved a result that the sum of two odd numbers always makes an even number. Such reasoning, using algebraic symbolization and processes of generalization and proof is typical of mathematical formalism, and therefore indicative of aspects of mathematical epistemology. Although we may seem to focus on aspects of Mathematics that are regarded as hard and uncompromising, we must remember the conjecturing process, spotting patterns from trying out special cases, that leads to such results. The use of such recognition to encourage students to try out special cases, spot their own patterns and conjecture their own rules might be seen as a part of mathematical pedagogy. We shall show an example of this later in the chapter. The knowledge that teachers need in order to use such approaches to Mathematics and devise classroom activities that are conducive to students' learning is known as pedagogical content knowledge (Shulman, 1987).

In the case of Social Studies, content knowledge is sometimes viewed as knowing an enormous number of facts. For example, names of countries and capitals in Geography and dates and personalities associated with important events in History. Learners need to move beyond facts to appreciate concepts, concepts clusters and generalizations. In Geography we have concepts such as region, country, continent, longitude, latitude; concept clusters such as the climate, natural resources, population; and generalizations such as each region of a country interacts with other regions and makes economic contributions or human activities and natural forces cause changes on the earth's surface. Key concepts in History, particularly the concepts of time, continuity and change, causation, and the understanding of events and issues from the perspective of people in the past are important to enable learners to develop a sense of order of events in History and a coherent pattern of the stages that people have gone through to get to where we are today. The application of these concepts or 'tools of thought' helps to turn historical facts into historical knowledge (Sansom, 1987). Thus even when students are unable to recall specific details they still understand the significance of key events (which is an important educational outcome).

How Can Teachers Be Prepared for What They have to Teach?

In deciding how to approach the knowledge needed by teachers to provide effectively for students' learning, the IED had to consider both what is needed by teachers in their own national contexts as well as the ideals of preparing teachers for the comprehensive education of their students. The IED curriculum for teacher education in the M.Ed. programme has recognised teachers' needs for subject development, and for a more general growth of knowledge. This can be seen in relating subjects to each other and to wider aspects of students' life-worlds, and in developing understandings of educational process and development beyond specific subjects.

Within the subject studies part of the M.Ed. course, four subjects have been recognised as core areas: English, Mathematics, Science and Social Studies. These are areas in which many of the teachers recruited to the M.Ed. have a speciality, particularly those who have taught students at lower or higher secondary levels. They need to have a good understanding of their speciality subject in order to teach it effectively themselves and to help develop teachers more widely. However, for teachers who have taught mainly at primary or lower primary levels, there may be no specific speciality but a need for knowledge that is related to a wide range of subjects. Such specialisms and needs raise questions about the most appropriate structure in the M.Ed. programme for addressing those needs.

As Chapter 3 has indicated, the M.Ed. programme is a programme in Teacher Education. Its graduates will become teacher educators in schools or in institutions of higher education. Thus, it is not only their own subject specialism on which they need to focus, but also they require knowledge of areas of need for teachers with whom they will work. This complicates issues considerably.

The AKU-IED's Structure for Subject Teaching

As part of a two-year programme, there have been four modules, each of six weeks, each attending to one of the core areas of English, Mathematics, Science and Social Studies. In the early programmes, participants engaged in all four modules. In more recent programmes, each participant has selected two modules from four: one from English or Mathematics and one from Science or Social Studies. This recognises that some teachers feel very underprepared to engage with certain subjects and thus allows them to avoid those subjects; it also provides more space for other areas of the M.Ed. curriculum. However, it limits the extent of subject knowledge of teachers emerging from the programme and their possibilities for working with teachers in a range of subject areas. In early programmes, in addition to the four subject modules, each course participant (CP) participated also in one subject specialist module of their choosing. The module in subject specialism was called the EPCK (Enhancing Pedagogical Content Knowledge) module: these modules enabled CPs to study one subject to a greater depth.

In recognition of the special needs of those who will teach primary school children and those who mentor teachers at this level – namely, work with teachers to enable their reflective development of teaching – a cross-subject primary module has been taught. As the subject modules have been reduced, the primary module has grown accordingly. Thus all CPs address subject concepts in all four areas, relating specifically to primary education, and this study addresses subject content coverage to some extent. Also, particularly in English, approaches to developing understandings for learners at primary level are very different from those of older children at secondary and higher levels. Therefore a separate module to address such approaches is important. However, for some subjects, many issues in teaching transcend the primary-secondary phase boundary, so that a primary-secondary separation is less important.

There are many issues relating to structures of subject teaching within the M.Ed. programme. We address some of these below: firstly, through consideration of two cases (Mathematics and Social Studies) as examples, and, secondly, by extracting key issues across the four subject areas.

Areas of Mathematics and Social Studies: theory, practice and issues

Mathematics. Studies in Mathematics, from the start, have involved a partnership between the AKU-IED and the University of Oxford. This has emphasized a need for cultural rationalization between international theoretical perspectives and more local and idiosyncratic approaches to education. Those who planned and taught the module were aware of the IED's mission to develop teacher educators who are reflective practitioners and to encourage a broad conceptual understanding in learning. Such aims see the M.Ed. as fitting with a view of Mathematics as socially constructed, fallible knowledge rather than as an absolute body of knowledge outside the domain of the learner (for example, Ernest, 1991). Such a perspective has strong implications for how Mathematics is learned and taught. The learner of Mathematics is no longer seen as acquiring knowledge from outside herself, but rather as constructing knowledge within social settings. Piagetian and Vygotskian theories of human learning and development help formulate a social constructivist view of mathematical learning from which teaching approaches can be formulated (for example, Piaget, 1950; Vygotsky, 1978). Teaching becomes a process of creating environments in which learners can meet and engage with mathematical ideas and make sense of Mathematics jointly and personally (for example, Jaworski, 1994). The IED's commitment to cooperative learning and interactive teaching fits well with these perspectives of Mathematics, learning and teaching.

A major issue for some teachers in encountering such perspectives was that Mathematics has been seen, traditionally, as a subject of right or wrong answers, of procedures and rules, as hard and fixed. Changing such perspectives towards fallibility and social construction has not been easy or straightforward, and has presented a challenge for tutors.

To address this challenge, successive cohorts of M.Ed. teachers (CPs) have been invited to experience Mathematics themselves from a socially constructive perspective. They engaged in problem-solving tasks where they devised their own methods and analysed their solutions along with tutors. A simple question like, how many different numbers can you make using 4 fours, and operations +, -, x, / proved stimulating and rewarding. For example,

$$1 = \frac{(4+4)}{(4+4)} \qquad 2 = \frac{(4\times4)}{(4+4)} \qquad 3 = \frac{(4+4+4)}{4} \qquad 4 = (4-4)\times4+4 \; \ldots$$

and we can proceed for other numbers such as

73

$$1 = \frac{(4+4-4)}{4}$$

Some numbers can be represented in more than one way, for example,

$$63 = \frac{4^4 - 4}{4}.$$

Even those participants who were afraid of Mathematics, and believed they could not do it, could be successful with a problem such as this one. It challenged them; they enjoyed finding more numbers, and different ways of finding the same numbers, and in the process of working with numbers their knowledge of number relationships developed. Thus they learned Mathematics, and they also learned Mathematics pedagogy in how to challenge students and provide fruitful learning activities. When one CP who had said she was no good at Mathematics was successful in solving a problem, the tutor said, 'So you *can* do Mathematics'. The CP's response was, 'this isn't Mathematics, it's just common sense'. That Mathematics could derive from sense-making – making sense of something – was a completely new idea.[1]

So CPs were invited to engage in problems that opened up areas of Mathematics which they had found difficult previously. For example, tackling fractions, a notoriously difficult topic, from this new perspective was a complete revelation for many CPs: as a result they were now able to understand concepts in fractions. Geometry, algebra, statistics and trigonometry were all approached through investigative, problem-solving tasks involving activity and discussion. The idea was that the CPs together could construct mathematical knowledge, and that a tutor's role was to question and challenge. CPs learned to devise their own questions and set their own challenges. Solutions had to fit with the body of Mathematics socially constructed over millenia.[2] Tutors had to ensure that incomplete or incorrect solutions were challenged, discussed and corrected, with a main focus on student activity and sense-making through reflection and critique. The processes through which the CPs themselves learned were discussed and synthesized as a pedagogy for the classroom.

Simultaneously, CPs worked with students and teachers from local schools and put some of their own learning into practice. They also devised workshops for these teachers in which they offered and discussed what they themselves had learned. However, CPs recognised quickly that the approaches they were learning did not fit well with the systems used in many Pakistani schools. Although children responded extremely well to the activities they offered, teachers were less well disposed. Teachers had to follow textbooks, complete the curriculum in a limited time and prepare students for examinations. To achieve these requirements, students were expected to sit quietly, attend to the teacher, copy the teachers' methods, answer textbook questions exactly as they were presented, learn the material exactly as they had been given it and reproduce it for the examination. If students did all of this they were 'successful', and schools and teachers were measured by their success. Teachers felt enormous pressure from schools to keep to this pattern which was declared to be 'traditional', and which fits with a traditional view of Mathematics.

For the CPs, there was a clear dichotomy: in the IED environment, investigative Mathematics, questioning and sense-making were important; in schools the traditional methods were important. As teacher educators working in schools, how could they deal with this dichotomy? The dichotomy became even more real and potent when, as graduates of the M.Ed. programme, now Professional Development Teachers (PDTs), they had to work with other teachers in their schools and contribute to programmes for teachers (Visiting Teacher (VT) Programmes) at the IED. Their task became not just a case of working with teachers as they had worked at the IED, but of finding ways to reconcile fundamental differences between the two systems. They could not change textbooks or examinations, so they had to find ways of working with these traditional systems, but at the same time introducing the new approaches – a serious challenge and an uphill learning experience (see Chapter 13 and Mohammad, 2002).

This led to important learning also for their tutors. It was not sufficient just to work with the CPs in ways that encouraged mathematical concept building and conceptual understanding. They had to take into account the school systems and requirements on teachers. Thus, school textbooks became an important part of the Mathematics module. Investigative work had to be linked clearly to what was in the textbook. Tutors had to address the dichotomy from within the IED programme.

Another very important issue that became clear during the delivery of the first Mathematics module was that of the CPs' own subject knowledge, particularly those who were specialists in Mathematics and would be required to become future leaders in the subject. Traditional forms of teaching had resulted in understandings that were largely instrumental and lacked connections to other areas of Mathematics or to problem solving more broadly. It was clear that subject knowledge for these CPs needed to be enhanced. Through three subsequent programmes, CPs who chose Mathematics as their speciality attended the EPCK module in Mathematics. Here tutors taught Mathematics, modelling the pedagogic approaches and strategies that had been introduced and implemented in the Mathematics module. Thus CPs worked conceptually on number, functions and algebra, trigonometry, and calculus. The first such module (Class of 1998) was joined by PDTs from the first M.Ed. cohort (Class of 1996) who wanted extra mathematical experience. Learning in the module was researched during its practice through recorded observations of sessions and interviews with CPs (see Jaworski & Nardi, 1998). Deep learning of concepts and development of awareness of mathematical relationships were evident for all participants.

Tutors too acknowledged that the open and inclusive pedagogical approach had enhanced their own learning in important ways. It was a pity that the EPCK module had to be abandoned in later programmes to make room for other important aspects of a Master's programme in Teacher Education.

Social Studies. Social Studies in the M.Ed. curriculum was included as a response to a decline and neglect of the subject's status in schools. Teaching in the Social Studies module involved a radical shift from the 'traditional' implementation of Social Studies, in which knowledge is presented as facts to be learned, towards a participative curriculum in which learners are actively engaged in attaining key concepts. Activity included the use of concept attainment strategies such as identifying attributes through looking at examples and non-examples of the concept in the different disciplines that comprise Social Studies. This new curriculum encourages learners to apply their knowledge to understand present-day issues so as to become citizens capable of participating meaningfully in decision-making situations affecting their lives or engaging in social reform.

In its attempt to introduce a totally different way of dealing with content the Social Studies module faced a challenge. One or two course participants were Social Studies teachers and another one or two had taught History or Geography as separate subjects, but most had no experience of teaching Social Studies. Most CPs' knowledge was confined to the facts in the textbooks they used for teaching. Skills like map reading and chronology were negligible. In addition, most CPs' teaching practice comprised teacher talk. Alongside classroom lectures, the Socratic method of questioning is used. A typical lesson would include reading from the text followed by a lecture to explain the text and questions for in-class review. Repetition of material through reading assignments and answering textbook questions followed to prepare students to do well in examinations.

In introducing CPs to the idea that history is interpretive and perspectival, one CP commented, 'How can I interpret History from different perspectives? For me the history is given. Also by reinterpreting history I am going against patriotism'.[3] Since participants came to the module with such experiences of Social Studies, either as a subject teacher or as a learner, it was of crucial importance to help them reflect critically on their past experiences.

The module was planned to deal with limitations in CPs' prior knowledge. An approach was selected to help the CPs to reconceptualize the teaching and learning of Social Studies by critically examining the nature and role of Social Studies in school given the aim of developing members of society capable of taking responsible actions for improving their society. The course called for the CPs to put in considerable effort to enhance their own knowledge through research and enquiry. They were introduced to enquiry as a teaching/learning strategy. They chose a topic for enquiry and were then walked through identifying a question, collecting information, synthesis and presentation. Presentations facilitated the CPs' learning from each other. The use of enquiry and preparation of content for presentations to their colleagues, was seen as a valuable experience which helped them translate the term lifelong learning into 'I can improve in areas where and when I need it.'

The CPs also learned how to help students attain and develop concepts through the introduction to concept attainment and development strategies. Reflection, questioning and meta-cognition were important parts of the strategy. An important part of the Social Studies module was for the CPs to see themselves as 'Transformative Intellectuals' (Giroux, 1988), both in schools and in the communities in which they lived. They used enquiry to study social issues such as environmental degeneration, women's empowerment, and child labour, drawing on the various disciplines, applying skills learnt, developing attitudes and taking actions. For example, a small group studied why girls are not sent to school and possible ways to address the issue by interviewing parents and community leaders in addition to surveying the literature. They presented their findings to faculty and staff in the form of a role play following which they led a discussion on the topic. This approach to the development of subject knowledge with a focus on becoming a critical pedagogue remained a challenge for quite a few CPs as they moved from the position of 'doing as told' to 'acting after reflecting'.

Through the module the CPs began to question the content of Social Studies in the curriculum as well as the second-class status of Social Studies in most schools. This provided an opportune time to move to a key component of the Social Studies module which is CPs' work in schools. The M.Ed. programme required the CPs to translate into practice, in real classrooms, the knowledge and skills learned as theory in the seminar sessions. They engaged in unit planning, enriching the text with relevant content, instructional strategies and assessment practices. The CPs were not always able to teach as planned. For example, in their desire to include all students in the activity of the class, they kept calling on students to assess their prior knowledge, so that class time was used up before their plan was complete. The CPs found it difficult to deal with the noise during group work and to focus on one group while keeping an eye on all groups. Their self-reflections and feedback helped improve performance over time.

In order for the CPs to continue learning on their own and in collaboration with colleagues they were required to keep a reflective dialogue journal which was shared weekly with a colleague. In addition they collaborated with a partner to carry out an action research task in an area of their choice. This exercise enabled the CPs to see how, through systematic action and reflection, they could improve an area of practice.

Issues and Implications

Although there are clearly subject-specific ideas and issues in each of the cases reported, and the same is true for English and Science, there are nevertheless many subject-related issues that cross subject boundaries. The main issues, as we see them, can be listed as follows:

1. The shaking up of teachers' perceptions of subject as they meet new perspectives and formulations.
2. The traditional curriculum and traditional approaches to teaching it. The influence of textbooks and examinations.
3. Teachers' lack of subject knowledge and its implications for learning and teaching. How subject knowledge can be enhanced.
4. The theory–practice interface: interpreting theoretical perspectives such as a social constructivist view of learning and critical reflective practice in relation to the practice of subject teaching. Cultural dimensions at odds with recommended practices.
5. Pedagogic practice: the need for rationalization of methods across individual subject modules.

Teachers' Perceptions of Subject

The nature of Science, or of Mathematics, or of Social Studies, as seen by CPs, was challenged in the modules. Seeing Science as a tentative human construct rather than an abstract external truth; Mathematics as fallible and socially constructed rather than rule driven with right and wrong answers; Social Studies as being about controversial issues, rather than historical or geographical facts; was seriously challenging. Pedagogical approaches in these subject areas were premised on such alternative perspectives of subject, and only made sense if these epistemological foundations were in place. One of the problems that emerged from subsequent studies of the teaching of VTs (Visiting Teachers, taught by the PDTs: see Chapters 3 and 5) was the implementation of pedagogical approaches without the epistemological understandings that allow such approaches to make sense. The result was 'methods without meanings', and hence ineffective outcomes in terms of students' subject learning (Halai, 2001; Mohammad, 2002).

The 'Traditional' Curriculum

The way that curriculum is presented traditionally, in Pakistan and beyond, is to list topics that are to be taught and learned. Such topics are then presented by teachers to students through forms of direct instruction in which teachers tell and demonstrate what is to be learned and students internalize through repeated practice and memorization. Textbooks present the 'knowledge' to be learned in culturally acceptable forms; teachers follow textbooks closely; and examinations test what has been set out in the textbook. According to sociocultural theories, such practices are perpetuated by newcomers, new teachers and students, being enculturated into accepted ways of doing and being (for example, Lave & Wenger, 1991; Wenger, 1998). In order for such perpetuation to be modified, epistemological positions of teachers need to change, so that alternative practices can be introduced in meaningful ways. However, this alone is not sufficient without wider systemic change. A massive challenge for the AKU-IED is to influence educators and policy makers, across the countries it serves, to look at critically, and modify, syllabuses and examinations [4], to support change.

Teachers' Lack of Subject Knowledge

In all subjects, teachers' knowledge of their subject was limited, thus constraining potential to teach well according to new beliefs and practices, and to mentor other teachers (Khamis, 2000; Halai, 2001; Mohammad, 2002). Partly, this was due to instrumental learning deriving from their own schooling; partly it was due to the limited nature of the curriculum they had followed. All subject modules addressed 'content' knowledge as part of the overall delivery of the module as can be seen from the two cases above. However, the module time was insufficient to cover all necessary content adequately. The EPCK module provided an excellent opportunity to address further content and its teaching at a range of levels. We feel it would be valuable to reinstate such provision in future programmes.

The Theory–Practice Interface

The subject modules made heavy demands on CPs in terms of new theory, philosophy, pedagogy and content. In the (relatively) luxurious surroundings of the AKU-IED, with the expertise of their tutors always on hand and resources readily available, it was possible to espouse new ideas and translate them into tentative belief systems. It was too easy to forget the constraints that faced teachers in the realities of schools and classrooms. Mohammad (2002 and in Chapter 13) points out the very seriously disjointed nature of these systems. Teachers in general, and especially those in government schools, face curriculum and examination constraints; large classes; poor buildings; inadequate furniture or resources; heat; lack of water; lack of concern for their physical and mental well-being; family concerns; needs to earn extra money to support their families, and so on. Translating AKU-IED theory into classroom practice is a greater challenge than just that of translating theoretical ideas into classroom practice, although this alone is a serious challenge. Module leaders are tackling issues of how to address the theory-practice transformation, taking into account all the above factors. For example, in Science, the need for resources has been addressed through a focus on simple, readily available or home-made materials that can support scientific enquiry. However, dealing with practical concerns while maintaining a focus on epistemological groundings of subject teaching and the associated pedagogies is still a serious challenge.

Barbara Jaworski et al

Pedagogic Practice

Key factors of personal preparation to teach and strategies for classroom teaching include questioning, use of interactive activity, a range of resources and modes of cooperative learning, critical reflection and action research. Use of these modes, strategies and ways of thinking has manifested itself differently in different modules, but their overall theoretical basis has been common to all modules. In addition, theoretical positions related to learning, such as a social constructivist perspective, have underpinned approaches and strategies. There is thus a case for CPs to work generically on such ideas before or after seeing their individual interpretation in subject areas.

For example, all subject area modules have incorporated some form of activity related to the assessment of the module, in which CPs have conducted some small-scale action research and analysed their findings. Such activity has been highly revealing of issues related to learning, teaching, mentoring or classroom practice. Thus, depending on which module has come first, this has involved CPs' first introduction to action research. They have then revisited action research in successive modules, from different perspectives and often using a different, subject-related discourse. Such differences have impeded a generic perspective of action research and its contribution to development in teaching and learning. Module leaders have recognised a need for collaborative cross-subject addressing of such common areas of pedagogy, so that CPs are encouraged to build a coherent sense of theoretical notions and a critical sense of how they are interpreted in practice. A clear example of this necessity can be seen in the concept of *cooperative learning*. This term has been employed in Social Studies, but pedagogical discourse in Mathematics has included terms like 'group work' and 'pair and small group discussion', and their relation to knowledge construction, without ever referring to them as cooperative learning. Thus, cooperative learning has come to be seen, erroneously, as a strategy for Social Studies, but not necessarily for other subject areas. Theories of learning form a backdrop to thinking about classroom practice in all subjects, but it is in Mathematics and Science that *a social constructivist perspective* has been addressed most overtly, with a possible consequence that it is seen as particular to these subjects.

A different kind of issue has arisen with respect to the use of enquiry or 'questioning' which is fostered in all subject modules. In Pakistani schools children are not encouraged to question teachers, or teachers their superiors in the school. The educational practice of questioning goes against accepted norms in Pakistani society. This has raised ethical as well as social issues. How are the PDTs to deal with such issues as they work with teachers in Pakistani schools as part of their M.Ed. learning and beyond?

Concluding Remarks

It is clear to us as writers of this chapter, that each of the above sets of issues could form a chapter of a book about subject studies. Perhaps such a book might be prepared in the future. We feel that we have, here, just alerted readers to the issues we have found in addressing subject studies. Some of these are issues that will be found prevalent internationally; others are more particular to the developing world. Where our CPs are concerned, as they emerge from the M.Ed. programme to become PDTs and to mentor other teachers, they are potent issues that PDTs and their tutors are still addressing.

As PDTs ran courses for Visiting Teachers (VTs) at the AKU-IED, they were more able to recognize such issues for themselves. Although the AKU-IED's ethos and environment provided a supportive atmosphere for working with the new approaches, and the IED's walls an insulation from the realities outside, the problems were passed on to the VTs who had to contend with the dichotomy when they returned to their schools. Subsequent research has shown VTs confused by trying to reconcile their new learning and old practices in subject teaching (Halai, 2001; Mohammad, 2002). Many revert to the old practices as the only way to cope. In just a few schools, particularly where head teachers have followed the AKU-IED's head teacher programmes, schools have recognized the need for support and teachers have been encouraged to bring the new methods into general school practice (see Chapter 10).

The knowledge of issues that we see reflected briefly in the above sections forms the roots of a new epistemology of subject teaching to which the developing nature of AKU-IED practices is making a very significant contribution.

Notes

[1] There is a considerable literature related to mathematical development, learning and teaching from a social constructivist learning perspective which relates to the contexts addressed here: see for example, Jaworski (1994, 2001) and the literature reviews of Halai (2001) and Mohammad (2002).

[2] For helpful pedagogic analysis relating to mathematical topics, see Prestage & Perks (2001) and Ollerton & Watson (2001).

[3] This quotation derives from the experience of the authors.

[4] The Aga Khan University has now been chartered to set up an examination board which would contribute to changing the systemic condition.

References

Eraut, M. (1994) *Developing Professional Knowledge and Competence*. London: Falmer Press.

Ernest, P. (1991) *The Philosophy of Mathematics Education*. London: Falmer Press.

Giroux, H.A. (1988) *Teachers as Intellectuals: Towards a CP of learning*. Grandby, MA: Bergin & Gravey.

Halai, A. (2001). Role of Social Interactions in Students' Learning of Mathematics (in Classrooms in Pakistan). Unpublished D.Phil. thesis, University of Oxford, Oxford.

Jaworski, B. (1994) *Investigating Mathematics Teaching: A Constructivist Enquiry*. London: Falmer Press.

Jaworski, B. (2001) Social constructivism in Mathematics learning and teaching, in L. Haggarty (Ed.) *Teaching Mathematics in Secondary Schools*. London: Routledge.

Jaworski, B. & Nardi, E (1998) The Teaching-Research Dialectic in a Mathematics Course in Pakistan, in A. Olivier & K. Newstead (Eds) *Proceedings of the 22nd Conference of the International Group for the Psychology of Mathematics Education* Stellenbosch: Program Committee of the 22nd PME Conference.

Khamis, A. (2000). The Various Impacts of the Institute for Educational Development in Its Co-operating Schools in Pakistan. Unpublished doctoral thesis, University of London.

Lave, J. & Wenger, E. (1991) *Situated Learning: legitimate peripheral participation*. Cambridge: Cambridge University Press.

Mohammad, R.F. (2002) From Theory to Practice: an understanding of the implementation of in-service mathematics teachers' learning from university into the classroom in Pakistan. Unpublished Ph.D. thesis, University of Oxford, Oxford.

Ollerton, M. & Watson, A. (2001) *Inclusive Mathematics 11-18*. London: Continuum.

Piaget, J. (1950) *The Psychology of Intelligence*. London: Routledge & Kegan Paul.

Prestage, S. & Perks, P. (2001) *Adapting and Extending Secondary Mathematics Activities: new tasks for old*. London: David Fulton.

Sansom, C. (1987) Concepts, Skills and Content: a development approach to the history syllabus, in C. Portal (Ed.) *The History Curriculum for Teachers*. London: Falmer Press.

Shulman, L.S. (1987) Knowledge and Teaching: foundations of the new reform, *Harvard Educational Review*, 57(1), pp. 1-23.

Vygotsky, L.S. (1978) *Mind in Society: the development of the higher psychological processes*. Cambridge, MA: Harvard University Press.

Wenger, E. (1998) *Communities of Practice: learning, meaning and identity*. Cambridge: Cambridge University Press.

CHAPTER 5

Creating a Critical Mass: the Visiting Teacher Programme

BERNADETTE L. DEAN

Perhaps the paramount issue facing education planners in Pakistan today is how to recruit, train, deploy and improve the quality of teachers in primary and secondary education. (The World Bank, 1988, p. 22)

The momentum this VT Programme has generated (among the course participants) is overwhelming in spirit, ideas, energy, commitment and desire to seek new avenues for change and make change happen. (Mithani, 1996)

Introduction

The Institute for Educational Development (IED) began the first Visiting Teacher Programme (VTP) [1], in October 1995. The Visiting Teacher programmes are offered in the areas of social studies, English, mathematics, science and primary education to teachers from the IED's cooperating schools in Pakistan and other developing countries in the region. These schools send teachers for their professional development to the IED for eight weeks of rigorous and supervised work, after which they return to their schools. The programmes are designed to prepare classroom teachers who, in concert with Professional Development Teachers (PDTs) [2], would form a critical mass of teachers with a shared outlook and who would support each other in enhancing the quality of education in their schools.

This chapter provides a description of the VTP. It highlights the key objectives and features of the programme, the role of the PDTs, and the impact of the programme on PDTs and the visiting teachers (VTs) as evident in programme reports and impact studies.

Description of the Visiting Teacher Programme (VTP)

The VTP is based on the teaching hospital model (Cornbleth & Ellsworth, 1994). In this model teachers learn theory at the university followed by practice in school. Of the eight weeks approximately three weeks are spent in teaching practice in real classrooms.

Teachers selected for the VTPs must have a first degree [3], three years' teaching experience, indicate a willingness to endure the rigour of the programme and have the desire to develop professionally. The VTPs are designed, implemented and evaluated by a team of PDTs serving as part-time faculty. The PDTs are supported by an IED faculty member and, in the initial programmes, by a faculty member from a partner university (PU) as well.

The philosophy of education and approach to teacher education advocated by the IED is radically different from that advocated by other teacher education institutions in Pakistan. Unlike most of these institutions where transmission of knowledge through the lecture method predominates, the VTP is based on the constructivist philosophy of learning and adopts an active participatory methodology. Learners are active creators of knowledge who reconstruct their knowledge when faced with new experiences (Piaget, 1977). Interaction with others through communication, reflection and interpretation enhances their potential to learn (Vygotsky, 1981).

Aims and Objectives of the Programme

The programme has two aims: the in-service professional development of classroom teachers and the development of the PDTs as teacher educators. The PDTs, supported by the faculty, plan, conduct and review the programme. This experience is expected to prepare them as teacher educators. The programme also aims to contribute to the professional development of classroom teachers through the realization of the following objectives:

1. *Improving subject matter knowledge.* Research in developing countries suggests that teachers' subject matter knowledge is probably the most important factor influencing their students' academic performance (Warwick & Reimers, 1995). Therefore a key objective of the programme is to attempt to deepen knowledge and understanding of the nature and content of the subject they teach.
2. *Improving existing and introducing new instructional skills and strategies.* Teaching in most classrooms in Pakistan is based predominantly on the transmission of knowledge, attitudes and values through lectures, reading from textbooks and teacher directed questions (Aziz, 1992; Warwick & Reimers, 1995; Hoodbhoy, 1998). The VTP attempts to provide teachers with both general and subject-specific teaching skills and strategies.

3. *Broadening the conception of their role as teachers.* Teaching is generally viewed as helping students to perform well in tests and examinations. The VTP seeks to broaden teachers' view of education by encouraging them to see teaching not simply as an activity aimed not only at raising the academic performance of students, important though it is, but also at their holistic development and preparation to deal with persistent and emerging challenges of their societies.

4. *Increasing understanding of students and the learning process.* Teachers often focus their attention on the academically brighter students and those who show an interest in their classrooms. The VTP attempts to increase teachers' ability to recognize the individuality of their students and adjust the learning process to suit students' individual differences.

5. *Developing greater confidence in their own abilities as teachers and facilitating independent learning.* There is a belief that pre-service teacher training with occasional in-service training is sufficient for the professional development of teachers. The VTP takes a different approach. It attempts to enable teachers to become critical enquirers into their own practice and introduce them to the knowledge, skills and attitudes required to continue to learn independently.

6. *Preparing VTs to play a supportive role to the Professional Development Teacher.* Two to three PDTs would not be able to bring about sustainable change in their schools. Graduates of the VTP together with the PDTs would form a team to facilitate the in-service professional development of their colleagues and create a critical mass for school improvement (Bacchus, 1994).

The above objectives are met by making the following features an integral part of the total instructional programme.

1. *Maintaining a dialectical relationship between theory and practice.* Theoretical inputs on teaching and learning are followed by application in the real classroom and classroom practice is followed by reflection to review theory. The dialectical link between the two is made meaningful by promoting reflection.

2. *Developing the ability for critical reflection.* Reflective practice forms an integral part of the programme and is encouraged through such activities as journal writing, self-reflection and collaborative reflection on teaching, and problem-solving activities;

3. *Mentoring.* Mentoring is seen as a means of facilitating the professional development of both the PDTs and participants of a VTP. The role of the mentor is to challenge assumptions, encourage independent and critical thinking, encourage self-identification of strengths and limitations and find ways to address them.

The above features facilitate VTs' and PDTs' learning from the programme and are expected to be particularly helpful when they return to their school contexts and engage in the professional development of their colleagues. On return to school PDTs are expected to mentor VTs and facilitate contextually appropriate use of their learning from the course. Together they would conduct professional development activities at school such as workshops, lesson demonstrations and peer coaching for their colleagues.

The Role of the PDTs

The PDTs are seconded from their schools for 4-6 months to conduct the VTPs. While engaged in conducting the VTP they learn the importance of designing a contextually relevant programme, the need for a safe learning environment and of building on the VTs' prior knowledge and experience.

Planning the VTP

Planning a VTP usually begins a month or two prior to its commencement. The team meets regularly to select the VTs, identify their needs, frame specific objectives of the programme, decide how best to realize the objectives and how to assess the VTs and the programme.

The VTP depends on effective teamwork. The initial phase of coming together to plan helps to develop a collaborative working relationship among the facilitating team. The team members learn with and from each other as they reflect on their own experiences, and from the literature on teaching and learning. They learn how best to address the needs of the VTs and realize the objectives of the programme. Once the knowledge, pedagogy and teacher development aspects to be covered in the programme are identified, each PDT identifies his/her areas of strength and interest. Often PDTs sharing similar interests but different strengths are assigned responsibility to develop and teach a specific area. Given that this is a professional development opportunity for the PDTs, they are often encouraged to take up a new area perceived as difficult, and to acquire new knowledge and skills with the guidance and support of more knowledgeable colleagues or the faculty member. The sub-teams come together regularly to discuss plans for teaching and receive feedback in a supportive yet challenging environment.

During the planning phase, the faculty member acts as mentor, tempering the PDTs' desire to teach all they have learnt in their Masters Programme; raising questions that lead team members to question their assumptions and experiences; encouraging them to ground practice in their experiences and the literature; and providing personal and professional support as and when needed.

Implementing the Plan

The VTP usually begins with introductory activities for VTs to get to know each other. Introductions are followed by critical reflection on their past practice: their teaching methodology, the curriculum and textbooks, teacher-student relationship and assessment practices.

This is seen as an opportune time to introduce VTs to the concept of reflective practice. They are encouraged to continue critical reflection on their learning through daily writing of a reflective journal. PDTs collect journals each week, read them and provide critico-constructive feedback. Difficulty in reflective writing has led teams to find creative ways of promoting reflection such as having VTs answer guided questions, post-lesson conferences and small group and whole class reflection activities in the classroom.

The programme continues with an introduction to the processes of children's physical, intellectual and psychosocial development; and to how children learn through discussion of theory and reflection on observations of children in real classrooms. VTs also learn how to plan effective lessons. Usually two members of the team lead teaching sessions, which include some mix of sharing relevant knowledge and experiences, engaging VTs in activities which challenge and question their existing ideas and help them to construct new ideas and to reflect on their learning. Other team members act as observers recording data for feedback and occasionally contributing to the session. The responsibilities of teaching and observing are rotated so that all team members get the opportunity to grow in all aspects of the PDT role.

An important focus of the programme is to improve teachers' content knowledge. The PDTs have consistently found that the subject matter knowledge of many VTs is quite superficial despite the fact that most have an undergraduate degree in the area. Even those with considerable teaching experience at higher levels admitted that prior to the VTP they 'did not truly understand certain fundamental ideas' or 'had never thought about certain ideas' (Lakha, 1999). The question PDTs have to address is: to what degree can teachers' content knowledge be improved in eight weeks and what is the best way to do so? The PDTs have addressed this question by directly teaching content as well as teaching VTs how to develop their content knowledge on their own. In teaching the content, misconceptions and gaps in knowledge are addressed. VTs are helped to identify what they know, what they do not know and where and how to find out.

A number of instructional strategies (questioning, cooperative learning and enquiry/investigation) are used while teaching content and helping VTs learn how to learn. VTs are asked to reflect on the processes in which they engage and to identify key elements of the strategy. First-hand experience of the strategy as learners enables VTs to assess its strength and limitations for themselves. These instructional strategies are also explicitly taught and practised in preparation for use in real classrooms. In using instructional strategies which focus on process rather than product, VTs begin to see the need for alternative assessment practices. For example, when VTs conduct an inquiry in small groups and make classroom presentations, they begin to realize that learning has been demonstrated. What is required are ways to record and assess this learning. PDTs help VTs to improve current practices by teaching them how to design better essay and objective test items, and develop the skills to implement the alternate assessment practices introduced.

During the programme, a conscientious effort is made to ensure that the VTs spend at least a third of the programme in real classrooms. They spend time closely observing a student or a small group of students when studying theories of development and examining how children learn. Besides this, VTs teach individual lessons or a planned unit on topics of their choice. Lesson planning involves development of objectives, selection of content and instructional strategies, preparation of teaching and learning materials for teacher and students, and development of tools to assess learning outcomes. Lesson planning facilitates synthesis of their learning and helps VTs recognize that they do have some control over the curriculum. Implementation of the plan in the real classroom is observed by a peer and guided by a PDT. Teaching is followed by self-reflection and group reflection. Reflection on practice is crucial to identifying possibilities and challenges and finding ways to address them. One VT wrote about her experiences in a VTP:

> Each concept and idea that was conveyed and exposed was given
> time and opportunity to practice in real classroom situations. This
> repeated and reflected practice removed doubts, made the
> understanding very clear and gave us confidence in practicing the
> new concepts. (Dean & Niyozov, 1996a, p. 35)

Joyce et al (1987) notes that teachers must have at least 25 opportunities to practise a teaching strategy before it can become part of their repertoire. The lack of sufficient practice is one great limitation of the eight-week VTP and is one of the reasons for a shift to other forms of VTPs (see Chapters 6, 7 and 8).

As the VTP draws to a close, the participants focus their attention on discussion of the process of educational change and the preparation of a realistic action plan to bring about change in their own classrooms and schools. These plans are shared so that VTs can learn from each other.

Behind the Scenes

The PDTs critically reflect on their teaching at the end of each day, usually in the presence of the faculty member. The reflections seek to identify what went well, what did not, and why. The debriefing sessions eventually turn into planning sessions. Each sub-team shares plans and receives input from other team members. Each day's learning contributes to improving future sessions. The critical reflection sessions encourage the PDTs to strive constantly to improve their teaching and become more reflective practitioners.

At the end of the VTP, the PDTs evaluate the VTs and the programme. Evaluation of VTs is based on criteria shared at the beginning of the programme. VTs receive qualitative feedback on the degree to which they met the criteria and what they can do to improve. Evaluation of the programme is based on analysis of written feedback provided by the VTs on the end-of-the-programme evaluation form and the PDTs' own reflections. The evaluation results in the PDTs identifying successes, challenges and dilemmas faced, and lessons learnt during the programme. They suggest ways to build on the successes, address the challenges and raise issues that require thoughtful resolution. All these form part of a report from which PDTs can learn and to which IED can respond.

Impact of the VTP

The VTP had an impact on both the PDTs facilitating the programme and the VTs participating in it. The impact on the PDTs has come from their reports on the programme. A number of Masters and Ph.D. dissertations (Ghulam Muhammad, 1998; Vazir, 1998; Lakha, 1999; Mankeia, 1999; Ahmed, 2000; Rehmani, 2000; Fakir Mohammad, 2002) have been undertaken to gauge the impact of the VTP. Some are studies of the VTs during the VTP while others are studies of the VTs a few years after programme completion. These studies have used interviews, analysed documents and observed VTs teaching in classrooms to identify the influence the programme has had on VTs' knowledge, skills, beliefs and practice of teaching. The studies have consistently revealed a profound impact of the programme on the expressed beliefs of the VTs about the subject they teach and about teaching and learning processes. Less evident, however, is the translation of their learning from the programme into significantly different teaching practices in the classroom. The studies reveal that the difficulty in shifting from traditional to innovative practices are due to a combination of programme and context factors which include what was offered in the programme and how it was offered, the overly supportive environment at IED, and the environment and expectation of the school to which they return.

Lessons Learnt by the PDTs from the Programme

Reports of the VTPs indicate that participation in the conceptualization, implementation and evaluation of the programme is a transformational experience for most of the PDTs. Preparation of the VTP provides them the opportunity to evaluate critically the knowledge they acquired during the M.Ed. and find ways to adapt it to the needs and contextual realities of the VTs. While conducting the programme they realize the truth of the statement, 'one learns best when one teaches'. Reflection on the experience brings forth many valuable lessons, such as, the importance of creating a conducive environment for learning and the need to build on the VTs' prior knowledge and experiences. They recognize the importance of cooperation for effective teamwork and the need to provide practice and follow-up support for knowledge use. Following are the lessons learnt by the PDTs.

A safe and caring environment promotes learning. The PDTs learnt that creating a safe and caring environment is necessary for effective learning. Creating such an environment takes time and requires consistent modelling of caring behaviours such as listening attentively, respecting persons and ideas and giving individual attention. When VTs realize that their ideas are respected and valued, their self-esteem and confidence increases, facilitating their active participation in learning. (Halai et al, 1996; Shah, 1999; Alvi et al, 2000; Baber et al, 2000; Hayyar et al, 2000).

To build on prior knowledge and experiences. The PDTs learnt that a complete break from past practice can create doubt and confusion leading to a loss of confidence as described by a VT in her journal:

> Now I know that I have to revise all my previous conceptions and learn new approaches, but I am a little confused whether I would be able to find a better way of teaching or whether I'll take only this idea that 'I don't know how to teach'. Before coming here I had the feeling that I am a very good teacher. Now I have to get this feeling again. (Halai et al, 1996, p. 11)

Journal entries like the above made PDTs realize the need to begin from where the VTs are at a particular point in their career and build on their prior experiences rather than try to replace them. They are therefore, first introduced to simple generic cooperative structures, such as, think-pair-share or round table, which they can use during a lecture and then to more complex structures, such as, a jigsaw which can be used as a strategy itself.

To contextualize teaching. PDTs know that conceptual understanding is promoted by the use of teaching aids. They are acutely aware that most VTs come from resource deprived schools. They, therefore, teach VTs how to make low cost/no cost teaching aids, from recyclable materials, easily available in their contexts. Similarly, VTs have difficulty recognizing the utility of learning how to conduct knowledge inquiry because of a lack of books and other reading materials in their contexts. The PDTs help them identify organizations from which they can acquire free materials and to see the community as a resource.

Understanding what cooperation and collegiality involves. Although cooperation and collegiality are stressed during the M.Ed. programme, the competition for marks often results in contrived collegiality among the PDTs. However, working closely together for 3-4 months towards a common goal, they learn that showing respect for others, giving due weight to alternative viewpoints, being honest with and trusting of others, being willing to say 'I don't know' or 'please help me', putting team goals ahead of personal goals, participating in joint problem solving and decision-making results in authentic collaboration and collegiality. (Dean & Niyozov, 1996a, b; Halai, 1996; Muhammad Sheikh et al, 1996)

Practice and support are required for knowledge use. During the VTP, VTs have relatively few opportunities to use their new knowledge, skills and strategies in the real classroom. The PDTs realized that if VTs are not provided opportunities to practice, and, given constructive feedback, they would revert to old practices. Becoming aware of the limitations of an eight-week university-based programme, PDTs suggested that the course be divided into shorter periods alternating between university and school or a systematic programme for follow-up of the graduating VTs should be put in place.

Influencing Teachers' Beliefs and Practices through Teacher Education

There are different perspectives regarding the relationship between beliefs and practices. One perspective is based on the assumption that beliefs guide practice. When teachers become involved in new experiences, they question their held beliefs and alter their practice (Thompson, 1992) Another perspective is that beliefs and actions are not explicitly distinguishable so that one cannot identify which changed first, but acknowledges that change requires awareness either of one's own thought or experience (Fennema et al ,1996). Research on the impact of the VTP revealed that teachers expressed a change in their beliefs about the subject, about how students learn and about teaching but change in practice was hindered because they did not know how to convert these beliefs into effective practices and because of the imperatives of school (Ghulam Mohammad, 1998; Lakha, 1999; Ahmed, 2000; Rehmani, 2000; Fakir Mohammad, 2002).

Change in beliefs about the subject. Research studies (Ghulam Mohammad, 1998; Mankeia, 1999; Ahmed, 2000; Fakir Mohammad, 2002) have reported a change in VTs' beliefs about the nature of the subject. For example, before attending the programme, social studies VTs perceived social studies as the study of historical events and names of places in geography. From the programme they learnt that 'social studies creates social awareness among people, develops their thinking ability and creates [responsible] citizens' (Ghulam Mohammad, 1998, p. 34). Similarly, VTs' belief of scientific knowledge as factual and true and therefore more valid and authentic than other forms of knowledge was changed to recognizing the tentative, controversial and sceptical nature of science (Ahmed, 2000).

Change in beliefs about how students learn. Changing teachers' beliefs about how students learn is important because as Harlen (1993) states:

> A teacher's view of how learning takes place is very important,
> since it determines what experiences and materials s/he provides,
> what role s/he takes in the learning and what role the pupils are
> expected to take, what is assessed and how success is evaluated.
> (p. 37)

At the time of entry to the programme most VTs believe that learning is a passive reception of knowledge from an authority such as the teacher or the textbook. Many VTs categorize students as 'intelligent' or 'slow' believing the children have an innate ability that predisposes them to learn. They also believe that a student's motivation to learn determines the degree to which learning takes place. Motivation, however, is seen as emanating from the student. These beliefs are evident in the comment of a VT,

> Learning can only take place if students themselves are willing. It
> is the first pre-requisite. They should be enthusiastic and curious
> by nature. They should be willing to devote much of their time to
> reading. (Ahmed, 2000, p. 33)

After a few weeks of active engagement with new ideas and materials that facilitate their learning, VTs realize that while innate ability and motivation to learn are important, the learning experiences provided by the teacher in the classroom can develop students' abilities and enhance motivation to learn.

These emerging beliefs are further strengthened after practice teaching in which VTs involve students in the teaching and learning process. Lakha (1999) observes that during a post-practice teaching discussion a VT remarked, 'I was surprised to see students coming to the blackboard and explaining', and in his journal noted, 'it was [a]very interesting incident for me because I [did not] expect that the students [could] also explain their answer' (p. 40).

The knowledge that students are not empty vessels but can think is likely to influence teaching practice. Fennema et al (1996) notes that, 'there is increasing evidence that knowledge of children's thinking is a powerful influence on teachers as they consider instructional change' (p. 405).

Change in beliefs about teaching. Most VTs entering the VTP view teaching as largely teacher centred and didactic. After a few weeks in the programme, a radical change in thinking about teaching is expressed. Many VTs who perceived Mathematics as product-oriented, procedure-driven and learnt-through practice, initially could not see the purpose of practical activities in teaching Mathematics. However, as they found their understanding of mathematical concepts improving through activities, they realized that they could use activities to promote conceptual understanding in their own classrooms. This is what one VT said, 'I was [a] traditional teacher, encouraging rote learning, but now I have realized, Maths is not rote learning and we can do practical work' (Rehmani, 2000, p. 72). Another VT, who prior to the programme stated that the aim of teaching is to complete the textbook, remarked at the end 'Now I am thinking [whether] the concept of the lesson is clear in [the] student's mind and not about how much of the lesson [is] left' (Lakha, 1999, p. 41).

Some VTs were stressed because they saw the value of what they were learning but felt contextual pressures and constraints would hinder implementation. A VT lamented:

> I am feeling stressed at the end of the programme, [because] it will be difficult to apply what we learn here in our context as there are many problems ... lack of cooperation of teachers, the strength of students, the environment of the schools and the headmaster behavior. (Lakha, 1999, p. 38)

Other VTs were deliberately setting aside new information, as they perceived this information to be inappropriate for and inapplicable in their context. VTs, especially those teaching classes 9 and 10 in which students sit for the Matriculation Board examinations felt they could not use activities as they were time consuming. A VT stated, 'The time that we have is not adequate to cover the syllabus through activities, [as activities] require time' (Lakha, 1999, p. 32).

The observation (Fakir Mohammad, 2002) that teachers set aside new information when it is not relevant to their own teaching situation seems to be true here. For these VTs their perception of the challenges of teaching in their context proved to be a barrier the VTP had not helped them address.

Change in the practice of teaching in their own real classrooms. At the IED, VTs seeing the benefits that accrue to students during practice teaching, express a desire to bring about change in their own classroom practice when they return to their schools. Classroom observations indicate that VTs have changed their attitude towards their students, tried to engage students as active participants in the learning process, and have used some skills and strategies to improve their traditional classroom practices. They, however, leave out ideas and strategies that are new and relatively difficult to translate into effective classroom practice without further support.

Classroom observations (Mankeia, 1999; Rehmani, 2000; Fakir Mohammad, 2002) indicated a change in VTs' attitude towards their students. This was reflected in the way they dealt with students in the classroom. Instead of 'yelling and punishing students when they made mistakes', VTs now tried to 'understand' why their students were making mistakes. They dealt with the mistakes by providing oral and written feedback (Fakir Mohammad, 2002), and working with them individually often outside of their regular class (Mankeia, 1999).

Students were more active in VTs' classrooms. They came to the board to work out problems and explain the process used to their colleagues; they worked in small groups; and they made presentations based on group work and inquiry (Mankeia, 1999; Fakir Mohammad, 2002). However, in many cases this active involvement was more physical than intellectual. The VTs praised students when they worked out a problem correctly but did not explore their thinking when they made mistakes. Group work consisted largely of solving questions or explaining material in the textbook, and presentations consisted of sharing the group findings with the rest of the class.

Teachers usually use questioning as a way of finding out what students know prior to teaching and checking for understanding after teaching. Prior to the VTP, these questions usually required students to recall facts, and if students could not answer they were not encouraged to do so. Classroom observations following the VTP revealed that VTs have improved their questioning strategies. They ask questions to promote different levels of thinking, provide wait time, call on many students and encourage the students to answer their questions (Mankeia, 1999). Fakir Mohammad (2002), however, found that 'the major criterion of success in the lessons was emphasis on students' right answers to teachers' mainly closed questions' (p. 135).

Skills related to the subject, such as map skills in social studies, are used by the VTs in their teaching. Mankeia (1999) observed a VT teaching longitude and latitude and how to draw an outline map and noted that 'the teacher has a sound understanding of map skills' (p. 36). In the post-lesson interview the VT proudly stated, 'Before the VTP, I was facing difficulty in drawing (maps) and understanding the direction on maps but now my students are getting distinctions in the board exams in the map drawing section' (Mankeia 1999, p. 36).

The VTs seemed to have great difficulty in using the new instructional strategies introduced in the VTP and adapted a few of them to suit their needs. For example, VTs get their students to practise the social skills of listening actively and using quiet voices, introduced in the VTP as part of the strategy of cooperative learning, because it results in a quiet and orderly classroom and promotes the transmission of knowledge. This has been so effective that one school has made the use of these two social skills a school policy, encouraging students to use them even during break time! (Vazir, 1998).

Personal Change

Joyce et al (1987) state that professional development is, first of all, a matter of personal development. Most VTs noted a change in themselves. These changes include discovering strengths and building confidence; developing respect for others and valuing others' perspectives; asking questions and seeking information from others (Ghulam Mohammad, 1998). A VT claimed, 'I have become more flexible. I am trying to understand people. I cannot say I have changed a hundred per cent but it has started' (Lakha, 1999, p. 51). Another noted that 'Before the VT course I thought it was useless to seek information from others, but after working there I realized I can learn from others also (Ghulam Mohammad, 1998, p. 55). Yet another VT recalled 'Before coming to IED when workshops were conducted in school, I could not participate but here I try to take part and I have got confidence' (Lakha, 1999, p. 33). VTs credited gain in confidence to the presentations they had to make and to microteaching. More female VTs mentioned gaining enough confidence to present in front of male colleagues. They felt their confidence had prepared them to talk to their seniors and superiors who are often male.

Facilitating and Hindering Factors

What Facilitated These Changes?

In studies of the impact of the VTP two factors were mentioned by VTs as facilitating change in themselves and in the knowledge, beliefs and attitudes required for effective teaching and learning. These were the enabling environment provided by the PDTs and IED and the different approach to teacher education used in the programme.

Enabling environment. The constant support and encouragement from the PDTs and other faculty members and the facilitative intellectual and physical environment of IED helped the VTs build confidence. This is exemplified in a VT's comment:

> The most important aspect of the course was that one never felt stressed, although we had set goals and deadlines to meet. The course was conducted in a pleasant, friendly, success promoting and encouraging manner. It helped to develop my confidence. It taught me to critically question and examine every aspect of teaching and learning, to reflect on the current practices, syllabus and make decisions to bring about a change for the betterment of the society by developing critical citizens. (Dean & Niyozov, 1996a, p. 41)

> The lack of a similar facilitative intellectual and physical environment in schools, however, makes it difficult for VTs to use their new learning and results in their reverting to routine practices. (Fakir Mohammad, 2002)

Another VT expressed a similar view:

Nobody [in school] there had a similar perspective of teaching
such as I had developed at the IED. And after a few weeks I
locked my files in a cupboard and resorted to the routine way of
teaching. The IED environment is far away from the real situation
of school; IED's methods negate the applicability of its philosophy
in school. IED provides relaxation in timing and luxury in
resources and satisfies all basic needs, which [is] quite in contrast
to school[s] where teachers have difficulty in getting a chair or a
glass of water. IED's learning could be only sustained in the IED
environment. IED represents an artificial environment for
teachers. (Fakir Mohammad, 2002, p. 109)

The approach to teacher education. Most VTs come from contexts in which
teaching and learning follows what Freire (1970) calls 'the banking concept
of education' where teachers 'deposit' knowledge into students. Students are
expected to memorize and regurgitate this knowledge in examinations. Since
the education system is driven by examinations that assess students'
knowledge of textbook facts, teachers use methods, such as lecture and
recitation, to ensure students know the facts well enough to pass the
examinations.

The VTP, on the other hand, is based on the social constructivist
perspective which assumes that learners construct knowledge for themselves
through encounters with new ideas or situations. Interaction with others
facilitates knowledge construction. The role of the teacher is to provide new
ideas for learners to interact with and construct knowledge. The VTs soon
recognize that it is not the transmission of knowledge but the nature of the
activities provided and their engagement in meaning making that facilitates
their learning. They realize that the same process can be used with students
in their own classrooms as evident from this VT's comment:

I can use some activities in my large classroom teaching. I [can]
use [this] paper activity, this I can use. This will not be a problem.
Low cost/no cost resources will be easy [to] use and the
headmaster and colleagues cannot disturb or object because it is
in my classroom. (Lakha, 1999, p. 40)

Another VT credited the change in her teaching to the approach used in the
VTP:

My style of teaching is different, I don't consider myself as an
expert, both students and teachers play an equivalent role, I learnt
this on the VTP from the tutors' roles. I am more flexible in my
teaching; previously only content mattered; now the method is
also important. The best part is if one thing does not work I
modify it to my students' needs. (Vazir, 1998, pp. 57-58)

What Hindered the Change?

The factors that hindered the conversion of programme learning into effective classroom practices can be placed in three categories: programme factors, school factors and out of school factors.

Programme factors. Some programme factors hindered learning and subsequent change in practice. First, the instructional language of the programme, namely English, is a foreign language for many VTs and not the medium of instruction in their schools. Their limited prior exposure to English may have hindered conceptual understanding and use of the ideas presented during the programme. Second, an emphasis on covering the broad curriculum rather than spending the required time for in-depth understanding of a particular content area or strategy was also a problem. VTs recalled struggling with ideas and sometimes being left confused because of the need to move to the next topic (Ghulam Mohammad, 1998). Third, VTs were not always helped to make their tacit learning explicit during the programme. Lakha (1999) observed that many VTs recognized the changes that had occurred in their attitudes and personal behaviour; they, however, were not able to articulate changes in their thinking. Fourth, not enough time was spent on how the ideas and strategies being taught could be adapted in different contexts (Rehmani, 2000). This may be due to the fact that some PDTs teaching the programme had learnt but not themselves applied the new ideas and strategies in real classrooms as they went straight from being students in the Masters programme to becoming teacher educators without the opportunity to teach in real classrooms. Fifth, PDTs sometimes seemed to lack awareness of the contextual realities in which VTs worked and the constraints these realities may pose to change. Consequently, they did not pay adequate attention to VTs' fears of not being able to use 'group work' or 'activities' because these 'require time' which they did not have as they had to 'complete the syllabus and prepare for exams' (Dean & Niyozov, 1996a, b). PDTs often interpreted these concerns as arising from personal factors rather than from the acute awareness of the challenges VTs knew they would face in their schools.

School factors. Lack of support from administrators and colleagues is an important hindering factor. Fullan (1991) argues that if administrators are not actively involved and highly visible supporters of particular practice, the likelihood that efforts to use these practices will continue, is minimal. In many cases, the head teacher had restrained the returning VTs from changing their practice instead of supporting them. One VT recalled,

> Once my students were busy in discussion and there was noise in
> the class, [the head] entered the class and scolded the students
> about discipline and asked me to stop this game and start to teach
> as before. (Mankeia, 1999, p. 55)

Another VT stated regretfully,

> Now I am not using my VT learnings because when I came back I was very enthusiastic and I used them. But nobody observed my classes, checked my planner or asked me what I was doing. (Mankeia, 1999, p. 48)

Guskey (1995) observes that teachers need support for change. Support can take 'the form of coaching, providing practitioners with technical feedback, and guiding them in adapting new ideas and practices to their unique contextual realities' (p. 124).

All VTs pointed out that the pressure to complete the textbook and to revise it so that students would have sufficient practice to pass their examinations hindered the transition from teaching for rote learning to teaching for understanding. Teachers preferred to teach to complete the syllabus and obtain good results in the examination. This is evident from a VT's comment,

> I have to complete the syllabus before the final examination. We check their memory and skills of drawing [geometrical shapes] in the examination; conceptual clarification is not a basic requirement of the examination. If we 'check' [assess] their concepts, none of them will pass the examination. (Fakir Mohammad, 2002, p. 263)

Most of the VTs noted the lack of time to plan lessons, to complete lessons and to reflect on their lessons. A constructivist approach to teaching requires teachers to think of how they can build on students' previous knowledge. This entails designing activities and organizing them so as to facilitate learning. For VTs in resource- deprived schools it involves much more as is evident from this VTs' comment:

> Last evening I spent my time buying material and drawing triangles. I bought paper sheets and a geometry box to prepare these worksheets. It is not easy to plan a lesson the way I learned at IED. (Fakir Mohammad, 2002, p. 255)

Despite spending time on lesson planning, the limited time allocated for classroom teaching affects the learning outcomes that the teachers can actually achieve. In most schools a teaching period is of only 35-40 minutes' duration, which is insufficient for students to engage in activities aimed at facilitating conceptual understanding. Teachers have to negotiate with colleagues to take two consecutive periods or revert to transmission of knowledge towards the end of class time.

There is no notion of time for reflection in most schools even though there is a growing body of evidence (Schon, 1983, 1987; Pollard & Tann, 1993) that reflection is an important source of learning and of continuing professional development. The question that comes to mind is, where is the time going to come from? What changes will be required to make the time for learning for understanding in our schools?

Out of school factors. The prescribed national curriculum that comes to teachers in the form of a textbook they are bound to teach and board examinations which are based entirely on recall of textbook content seem to be the two greatest hindrances to change. Teachers are torn between facilitating acquisition of knowledge, skills and attitudes, which they feel are important for life and completing the syllabus so as to prepare students for their exams. Teachers often look for support to parents but find that they too have come to see teaching as covering the textbooks and learning as memorization of textbook content. A VT claimed, 'I tell my students to read the newspaper and watch National Geographical movies but their parents want them to memorize answers and go through exams' (Mankeia, 1999, p. 47). Pressure from all stakeholders for good results in the examination reinforces tradition (Fakir Mohammad, 2002).

Conclusion

The above discussion based mainly on the VTP during the first five years shows that some learning did accrue to the teachers who participated in the programmes. They left the programme with a better understanding of the concepts in particular subjects, with enhanced teaching and learning skills and with the desire to move from being the 'sage on the stage' to a 'guide on the side' in their classrooms. However, there was limited and often superficial change in classroom practice. It was clear that while the VTP had from the very beginning included opportunities to practice the newly learned strategies, these were not enough. Also, during the programme, the VTs did not practise in their own classrooms but in a new classroom acquired for the purpose and which was therefore new to them. Acknowledging these problems, the VTPs have become more school-based over the years. At present the course participants spend at least half (120 hours of the total 240 hours) of the course time in their own classrooms implementing the strategies learned in the face to face part of the course. During this period, they participate in weekly seminars to discuss problems of implementation and together try to find solutions. PDTs and IED faculty visit them in their classroom at least five times during the term to provide classroom support.

Despite this change, the institutional imperatives of curriculum and examinations, the resource constraints, and acceptance of the orders of their school authorities continue to be a challenge for implementation and continuation of classroom change. For the VTs choice, to change existing practice, is limited by their own capacity as well as by the structures of the school and society within which they have to choose (Corrigan, 1990). The VTs perceive school culture as static, authoritative, and impossible to change and hence they either do not initiate change or give up quickly. The programme facilitators and the graduates must both recognize that teaching is a site of conflict and struggle, which are individual and social, complex and evolving (Dean, 2000): a practice they must understand in order to influence the conditions in which they work.

IED now has a 'critical mass' of teachers in many of its cooperating schools. To the emphasis in the VTP on classroom change must be added ways for VTs to work in concert with PDTs and head teachers to bring about change in schools. For as Margaret Mead the famous sociologist reminds us, we should never doubt the power of a small group of thoughtful, committed teachers to change school, since it is the only thing that ever has.

Notes

[1] This programme was renamed as Certificate in Education in 2002.

[2] Professional Development Teachers are graduates of IED's M.Ed. programme. See Chapters 1 and 3 for a more detailed description.

[3] The first degree is in most cases a bachelor's degree. However, in the case of the programme for primary teachers, this requirement had to be flexible and teachers with a lesser qualification, namely higher secondary school certificate, were accepted. This flexibility was necessary because a large number of primary school teachers in Pakistan do not have a graduate degree.

References

Ahmed, S. (2000) Influence of the Secondary Science Professional Development Programmes on teachers' beliefs. Unpublished Master's dissertation, AKU-IED, Karachi.

Alvi, V., Shafi, I., Mustafa, S., Yousafi, S. & Bano, Y. (2000) *Secondary Science VT Program Report*. Karachi: AKU-IED.

Aziz, K.K. (1992) *The Murder of the History of Pakistan*. Lahore: Vanguard.

Baber, S.A., Ahmed Khan, S., Rodrigues, S., Kimani, N.A. & Najari-us-Scher, K. (2000) *Report on the Secondary Mathematics Visiting Teachers' Programme*. Karachi: AKU-IED.

Bacchus, M.K. (1994) Towards an Outline of the Programme for Visiting Teachers at IED (The VT Programme). Memo to faculty, AKU-IED, Karachi.

Britzman, D.P. (1991) *Practice Makes Practice: a critical study of learning to teach*. Albany, NY: State University of New York Press.

Cornbleth, C. & Ellsworth, J. (1994) Teachers in Teacher Education: clinical faculty roles and relationships, *American Educational Research Journal*, 31(1), pp. 49-70.

Corrigan, P. (1990) *Social Forms/Human Capacities*. London and New York: Routledge.

Dean, B.L. (2000) Islam, Democracy and Social Studies Education: a quest for possibilities. Unpublished doctoral dissertation, University of Alberta.

Dean, B.L. & Niyozov, S. (1996a) Inservice Teacher Education: going beyond the surface (reflections from Pakistan). Paper presented at the Conference on Innovative Approaches to Teacher Education, 2-4 April 1996. Karachi: AKU-IED.

Dean, B.L. & Niyozov, S. (1996b) Converting Theory into Practice: lessons learnt, dilemmas faced and insights gleaned from the first Visiting Teacher Programme conducted at AKU-IED, Karachi.

Fakir Mohammad, R. (2002) From Theory to Practice. D.Phil. thesis, University of Oxford.

Fennema E., Carpenter, T.P., Franke, L.M., Jacobs, V.R. & Empson, S.B. (1996) A Longitudinal Study of Learning to Use Children's Thinking in Mathematics Instruction, *Journal for Research in Mathematics Education*, 27(4), pp. 403-434.

Freire, P. (1970) *Pedagogy of the Oppressed*. New York: Seabury Press.

Fullan, M. with Steigelbauer, S. (1991) *The New Meaning of Educational Change*, 2nd edn. Toronto: OISE Press.

Ghulam Mohammad, N. (1998) What Have the Teachers Learned? The Impact of Social Studies VT Programme on Selected Government School Teachers. Unpublished Master's dissertation, AKU-IED, Karachi.

Guskey, T. (1995) Professional Development in Education: in search of the optimal mix, in T. Guskey & M. Huberman (Eds) *Professional Development in Education*, pp. 114-132. New York: Teachers College Press.

Halai, A., Ali, F., Zahid, M., Fakir Muhammad, R. & Mehta, Y. (1996) *Report of Mathematics Visiting Teachers Programme*. Karachi: AKU-IED.

Harlen, W. (1993) Children's Learning in Science, in Rosemary Sherrington (Ed.) *Science Teachers' Handbook*, pp. 37-54. Hatfield: Association for Science Education.

Hoodbhoy, P. (1998) *Education and the State: Fifty Years of Pakistan*. Karachi: Oxford University Press.

Joyce, B., Showers, B. & Rolheiser-Bennet, C. (1987) Staff Development and Staff Learning: a synthesis of research on models of teaching, *Educational Leadership*, 45(1), pp. 11-23.

Lakha, S. (1999) Exploring Changes in Teachers' Thinking during a Mathematics VT Programme. Unpublished Master's dissertation, AKU-IED, Karachi.

Mankeia, P. (1999) The Impact of Social Studies Visiting Teacher Programme on Teachers' Perception and Classroom Practices. Unpublished Master's dissertation, AKU-IED, Karachi.

Mithani, S. (1996) *Programme Evaluation, Summary and Implications*. Karachi: AKU-IED.

Muhammad Sheikh, N. et al (1996). *Report on the English VT Programme*. Karachi: AKU-IED.

Nayyar, I., Lone, A.H., Khan, B.A., Shah, J.I. & Rodrigues, S. (2000) *Report of Visiting Teacher Programme in Primary Education*. Karachi: AKU-IED.

Piaget, J. (1977) *The Principles of Genetic Epistemology*. London: Routledge.

Pollard, A. & Tann, S. (1993) *Reflective Teaching in the Primary School: a handbook of the classroom*. London: Cassell.

Rehmani, N. (2000) Teachers Linking Professional Development to School Improvement: A Case study of VTP of the AKU-IED. Unpublished Master's dissertation, Institute of Education, University of London.

Schon, D. (1983) *The Reflective Practitioner*. New York: Basic Books.

Schon, D. (1987) *Educating the Reflective Practitioner*. San Francisco: Jossey-Bass.

Shah, J. (1999) The Impact of the Institute for Educational Development Visiting Teacher Programme on Teachers of English. Unpublished Master's dissertation, AKU-IED, Karachi.

Thompson, G. (1992) 'Teacher' Beliefs and Conceptions in Synthesis of Research, in D.A. Grouws (Ed.) *Handbook of Research on Mathematics Education*. New York: Macmillan.

Vazir, N. (1998) The Impact of IED's Visiting Teacher Programme Case Study of a Co-operating School in Transition. Unpublished Master's dissertation, AKU-IED, Karachi.

Vygotsky, L.S. (1981) *The Genesis of Higher Mental Functions. The Concept of Activity in Soviet Psychology*. New York: M.E. Sharpe.

Warwick, D.P. & Reimers, F. (1995) *Hope or Despair? Learning in Pakistan's Primary Schools*. Westport: Praeger.

World Bank (1998) *Pakistan: education sector review*. Washington, DC: World Bank.

CHAPTER 6

Mentoring as an Alternative Approach to In-service Teacher Education in Balochistan: some successes and challenges

MUHAMMAD MEMON, FIRDOUSALI LALWANI & RAKHSHINDA MEHER

The Context

Balochistan is the largest but least populated province of Pakistan with 4.6% of the total population of Pakistan. The majority of this population lives in small rural settlements. Educational attainment in the province is lower than in the rest of the country with an overall literacy rate of 10.3%. This indicates that the education system in Balochistan has not performed well. The reasons attributed to poor performance include ineffective educational plans and policies; inadequate number of schools; lack of qualified teachers; gender inequity; non-conducive learning environment; overemphasis on cascade approach to teachers' development; lack of innovative programmes; ineffective school governance and management; lack of follow-up mechanism for providing professional support on-the-job for teachers; and unrealistic objectives and outdated content of in-service teacher education programmes. Warwick and Reimers (1995) mention that:

> Teacher-certification programmes in Balochistan faced the
> greatest obstacles of any in Pakistan. Because of its severe shortage
> of teachers Balochistan appointed candidates to teaching posts
> with no preservice training. Most of them obtained their positions
> through recommendations from provincial and national
> politicians. The province assigned them to teach for five or more
> years before they received any training. By that time they had
> formed teaching habits that would be hard to dislodge even with
> the most effective training courses. They saw their training not as

a way to improve their teaching but to get the certificate that they
needed to be called trained and to be promoted. (p. 48)

The above situation has significant implications for the quality of education
in general and teacher education in particular. The Government of Pakistan
(1998) has also acknowledged that the existing programmes are not
adequately responding to the increased demands for quality education and
advised that in-service teacher education programmes must incorporate
modern teaching methodologies.

In the late 1980s, learning coordinators were recruited in Balochistan
with the assigned task to provide on-the-job professional support to primary
school teachers. However, a majority of the learning coordinators acted like
'inspectors' and 'evaluators', involving themselves in 'stock-taking' exercises
rather than serving as 'mentors' or 'facilitators'. Before the emergence of the
Provincial Institute of Teacher Education (PITE) in Balochistan, the Bureau
of Curriculum and Extension Education Centre developed and conducted
short courses in different subjects included in the curriculum. The
programmes focused on enhancing content knowledge and pedagogical skills
but the balance between these two was hardly established. These short
courses were conducted mainly by a group of master trainers from secondary
school education and college education. Most of them had never taught in
school or had never gone back to the classroom after becoming master
trainers. Master trainers usually focused on imparting a battery of mechanical
skills to teachers rather than using an integrated approach to enhance
teachers' pedagogical content knowledge, pedagogical approaches,
communication, interpersonal and reflective thinking skills. Graybill (1999)
pointed out that

Prior to 1996, the only in-service training primary teachers in
Balochistan received ... formal two-week in-service courses at
centralized training venues delivered by so-called 'master trainers'
who had no experience at the primary level ... . After participating
in the two courses, most teachers reverted back to their former
didactic and teacher-centred approaches to teaching, and the
learning process in schools has continued to be relatively
uninspiring for most primary students. (p. 1)

Warwick & Reimers (1995) argue that teachers who attend in-service courses
consider it as one source of earning a modest extra income through travel
and daily allowances and spend a lot of time resolving related issues. If the
allowances are not as per their expectations, they would participate in the
programmes only half-heartedly.

In the early 1990s, the Government of Balochistan introduced a
number of new initiatives to transform teacher education. These included the
condensed primary teaching certificate, bridged courses, female mobile
teacher courses and crash programmes. These were conducted through a
'cascade model'. Although a substantial number of teachers were trained in

these programmes, they failed to introduce any change in teachers' beliefs and attitudes and instructional approaches. Teachers remained afraid of taking risks. One of the problems associated with the cascade model was that cascading of information always resulted into 'watering down' and 'misinterpretation' of concepts by master trainers who lacked confidence, knowledge, and understanding to deliver the goods (Pardhan et al, 2004).

The cascade model has been widely criticized as being an ineffective approach to teacher education due to various reasons. These include short duration of teaching practice; superficial approach to teaching practice; inadequate guidance provided to trainees; lack of conducive environment for professional learning; single shot training approach; lack of relevance of curriculum and instructional materials; lack of trained teacher educators; and theory-driven delivery (Anzar, 1999; Qaisrani et al, 1999).

Anzar (1999) argued that the quality of education in Balochistan would not improve until curricula and instructional methodologies are changed. Therefore, an alternate approach to in-service teacher education programmes was necessary to provide continual professional support for teachers at the classroom level to overcome their fear and anxiety while implementing innovations in curricula and methodology. The Institute for Educational Development at the Aga Khan University (AKU-IED) initiated a cluster-based mentoring programme in four selected districts of Sindh and Balochistan provinces. Mentors were developed through intensive in-service teacher education programmes with a focus on mentoring, problem solving, reflective practice and teaching skills. These mentors worked with their mentees by conducting interactive workshops in their respective school clusters and providing follow-up support in the schools. AKU-IED has since used this model with NGO-supported community schools in Sindh with considerable success (Memon & Mithani, 2003). This approach seems to suit the local needs and conditions since it allows 'hands-on' activities, experiential learning and enquiry for building individual and institutional capacity. In the rest of this chapter, we describe and discuss the planning, implementation and outcomes of the cluster-based mentoring programme in Balochistan.

Initiating the Cluster-based Pilot Mentoring Programme in Balochistan

In the 1990s, the Government of Balochistan, in collaboration with the international loan-giving agencies, launched a major initiative entitled Primary Education Development Project (PEDP) for improving the quality of primary school teachers. Under this initiative, the Government established the Primary Education Directorate (PED) and delegated it some fiscal and administrative autonomy. The PED was made responsible for the planning, development, and management of primary schools as well as for the in-service training of primary teachers. Earlier, in-service training was the responsibility of the Bureau of Curriculum and Extension. In order to accomplish the demanding task of training a large number of primary teachers, the PED established a Teacher Training Support Unit (TTSU) within the organization, headed by the Deputy Director, to develop plans for initiating a needs-based innovative in-service teacher education programme. TTSU was provided with a small number of professionals and a small support staff as the Teacher Learning Resource Team (TLRT). The team was responsible for managing, monitoring, and documenting in-service teacher education programmes in the province. TLRT conceived and developed the cluster-based pilot mentoring programme in three selected districts of Balochistan. This was considered as an innovative initiative based on a decentralized model of teacher education (Anzar, 1999; Graybill, 1999; Qaisrani et al, 1999). The quality of the cluster-based pilot mentoring programme was assured by the technical advisor for teacher education hired by the loan-giving agencies. The overall purpose of the cluster-based pilot mentoring programme was to try out an alternate approach to in-service teacher education which could provide an outreach facility for the continuing professional development of teachers at the grass-roots level. Qaisrani et al (1999) described the following objectives of the pilot mentoring programme:

1. to assist the teachers to upgrade their content knowledge in primary curriculum and school subjects;
2. to enable the teachers to use teacher guides;
3. to develop reflective practices and problem-solving skills; and
4. to facilitate a process of collegiality among teachers and bring about positive changes in their beliefs and teaching practices.

Anzar (1999) found that the cluster-based pilot mentoring programme was able to achieve its objectives with minimum human, financial and material resources. An element of ownership and accountability was also found among the mentors and district education officers. Anzar (1999) quoted a district education officer, 'once I started the cluster training programme in my district, teachers became confident in their dealing with children and got a sense of progress by going to school every day. This helped us to loosen the control of teachers' unions which were basically there to protect the incompetent teachers. I tried to cover every teacher' (p. 36). The teacher community also found this programme useful as it allowed them to learn, apply, reflect and evaluate their new experiences. Loan-giving agencies and district education management also seemed satisfied with the outcomes of the pilot programme. Overall, the experiment with the new model was found to be successful, although the role of teachers as mentors who played a role in the 'actualization of professional reformation' was not formally recognized (Smith, 2001).

The Notion of Mentoring and Models

Mentoring is perceived as an effective developmental process for new teachers but it can be equally effective for experienced teachers who need to further improve their content knowledge, pedagogical and classroom management skills (Ganser, 1996). Mentoring is generally defined as a process of establishing personal and professional contacts between mentors and mentees for their professional development. Koki (1997) considers mentoring as a complex and multidimensional process of guiding, teaching, influencing and supporting teachers in their workplaces through mutual trust and beliefs. Anderson & Shannon (1995) suggest that mentoring is a nurturing process in which more experienced teachers assist the less experienced teachers for their personal and professional development through reflective, collaborative, shared inquiry and caring environment.

Sometimes the terms mentoring and coaching are used interchangeably; however, mentoring is a process which may include coaching as an instructional strategy. To be effective, a mentor must be able to demonstrate a range of coaching competencies such as posing thought-provoking questions, probing, and gathering and analysing response for improving teaching and learning processes (Gray & Gray, 1985). Koki (1997) suggests that an effective mentor must have qualities such as a range of interpersonal skills, good working knowledge of teaching methods, ability to use a coaching process for fostering increased self-direction and self-responsibility among teachers, effective communication skills and understanding teacher development needs.

The significance of mentoring has gained wide recognition in the developed world (Anderson & Shannon, 1995; Maynard & Furlong, 1995; Tomlinson, 1995; McIntyre, 1996). However, in many parts of the developing world, including Pakistan, mentoring has not yet been fully recognized as an alternate approach for in-service teacher education. Mentoring is becoming increasingly complex because of its various forms and models. These include the apprenticeship model, the reflective coach model, the co-inquirer model, and the staged model. The apprenticeship model entails mentoring as a form of apprenticeship training where novice teachers observe a skilled teacher and then attempt to emulate the mentor. Within a reflective coach model, a mentor acts like a critical friend (Schön, 1983) and the process of learning is determined by experiences. In the co-inquirer model, the mentor acts as a co-inquirer with the mentee who sets targets, analyses and evaluates student performance. The mentor encourages the mentee to engage in and share critical reflections. In the staged model, the mentor's role varies from stage to stage as summarized in Figure 1.

Balochistan's mentoring model was a blend of three models – reflective coach, co-inquirer and staged mentoring within the broader framework of a cluster-based mentoring approach.

Stages	Mentor's role
Beginning teaching	Model
Supervised teaching	Coach
Focus on learning	Critical friend
Independent teaching	Co-inquirer

Figure 1. Mentor's role at various levels.

The Role of the Aga Khan University, Institute for Educational Development in Developing Mentors

As a result of the keen interest of senior government officials, practitioners, policy makers, teachers and other stakeholders in the pilot programmes in selected districts, the Government of Balochistan decided to replicate the cluster-based mentoring programme in all districts of the province. However, it was felt that the programme should be conducted by an educational institution that had practical experience and institutional capacity to develop primary school teachers as mentors. Consequently, the Government of Balochistan signed a Memorandum of Understanding (MoU) with the Aga Khan University, Institute of Educational Development (AKU-IED), Karachi in 1996 to help prepare primary school teachers as mentors.

AKU-IED agreed to build the institutional capacity of PED. Two of its faculty members held a series of meetings with the provincial and district education officers, policy-makers/implementers, teacher educators and teachers to understand the context and identify the needs of teachers and mentors. They also met with the instructional team which had led the mentoring programme in the piloted districts and the mentors who had implemented the cluster-based programme for teachers.

In these meetings, the needs of primary teachers and of potential mentors were identified. They included the need to learn strategies for effective delivery of primary school curriculum in the context of multigrade teaching, to develop low cost material, to enhance pedagogical content knowledge and to understand the dual role as classroom practitioners and mentors. With these needs in mind, AKU-IED designed a programme for mentors using the framework of its regular Visiting Teacher (VT) Programme (see Chapter 5). A three-week orientation programme was also organized for district education officers to familiarize them with the purpose, strategies, processes and practices of mentoring programmes.

Gray & Gray (1985) remind us that the mentors must be carefully selected. Primary teachers from each district were selected, through a rigorous process, jointly by AKU-IED and TLRT. Similarity in the linguistic, ethnic, and socio-economic background of the potential mentor and the teachers they would be working with was considered in the selection. Other attributes such as willingness, commitment, enthusiasm and leadership potentials were also considered. Ten mentors (seven males and three females) were identified from each district. The programme was conducted in six phases. In each phase, three or four districts were included in the mentoring programme. Altogether 166 teachers (121 male and 45 female) from 20 districts were prepared to become mentors through six programmes. Out of these, four programmes were conducted by AKU-IED's M.Ed. graduates, called Professional Development Teachers (PDTs), at AKU-IED in Karachi. The fifth programme was conducted in two stages. Stage one, consisting of six weeks, was conducted at AKU-IED in Karachi and stage two, consisting of two weeks, was conducted at the Primary Education Department in Quetta, the capital of the Balochistan province. The TLRT staff included a few graduates from the AKU-IED's M.Ed. programme who assisted the planning and delivery of the first five programmes and took on the major responsibility for conducting the sixth programme delivered entirely in Quetta. By end of the programmes, 20 out of 23 districts had implemented the mentoring programmes. Three districts could not be reached because donor funding which had supported the programme ended.

Mentoring was a cross-cutting theme of the programme. Sessions on mentoring were organized every day with 'hands-on' activities where participants were engaged in role-plays and simulations of mentor and mentee roles. They were also given hands-on experience of conducting interactive workshops. Demonstration interactive workshops were organized by faculty members after which course participants, in groups, planned and conducted similar workshops on various topics such as students' meaningful learning, formative and summative assessment, students' learning difficulties and so on, for their fellow participants. This experience helped the course participants to improve their skills of planning, conducting and evaluating workshops. They felt that hands-on experiences boosted their confidence and sharpened their mentoring skills. Several practicums were carried out to develop communication, interpersonal, negotiation, mediation, counselling, active listening, problem-solving and conflict resolution skills.

Implementing the Cluster-based
Mentor Programme in Balochistan

After completion of each programme, mentors initiated cluster-based mentoring programmes in their respective districts. At level one (the Level of School Cluster), mentors met with 30-40 mentees in their cluster for two days each month to conduct interactive workshops. During these workshops, mentors and mentees focused on academic and professional aspects such as teachers' content knowledge; pedagogical approaches; classroom environment; school management; student assessment; effective use of low cost material; use of teacher guides; effective use of textbooks; community participation; professionalization of mentor's role; parents' participation; students and teachers' absenteeism; students' drop out rate and teachers' retention and transfer. Principles of learning such as mutual trust and respect; relationships; self-esteem and image; self-responsibility and accountability for learning were employed during the cluster sessions. A common structure of a day's mentoring session was as follows:

- Share and discuss a day plan of activities.
- Share reflections on new experiences.
- Identify a problem and build session around it.
- Discuss and seek solution to problems.
- Develop action plans for implementing new learning.
- Review/analyse new experiences in relation to students' learning.

Sometimes, mentees would share academic, professional, management and logistic problems with their fellow mentees and discuss possible solutions. If the group could not find solutions in the cluster, the problems were forwarded to the concerned district education officers or TLRT for solutions. District education officers or TLRT were expected to come up with a solution and share it with the concerned mentors.

At level two (District Level), TLRT members, in collaboration with the respective District Education Officers who were ultimately responsible for the implementation of the programme in their respective districts, conducted a one-day meeting with ten mentors within the district every month. This was a regular activity throughout the programme. The purpose of these meetings was to provide an opportunity for both mentors and TLRT to discuss academic, professional, and administrative matters at length and identify alternate strategies to deal with them. Mentors were also encouraged to approach TLRT members through the telephone, personal visits to PED, or through letters if they needed academic or management support.

At level three (Provincial Level), matters related to policy and finance were referred to TLRT but due to the bureaucratic process mentors could not get timely feedback and support. The process at all three levels is summarized in Figure 2.

One might argue about the similarity between the cluster-based mentoring programme and the cascade model of teacher education as far as the levels were concerned. However, the cluster-based mentoring programme was completely different from the cascade model in terms of its rationale, framework, strategies, processes and practices. The cluster-based mentoring model allowed teachers to create a sense of 'togetherness' for promoting professionalism among teachers. Mentors and mentees developed a sustainable professional relationship which helped create the 'critical mass' needed for managing change effectively.

Currently, a one-on-one situation of mentoring is more common in teacher education programmes but the Government of Balochistan adopted a cluster-based mentoring approach which seemed more economically viable to achieve the maximum benefits within minimum resources.

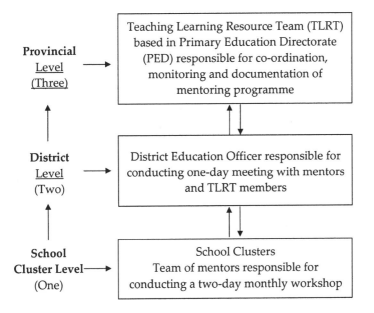

Figure 2. Levels of mentoring programme.

Some Strengths of the Cluster-based Mentoring Programme

A few studies (Anzar, 1999; Graybill, 1999; Lalwani, 1999; Qaisrani et al, 1999) were conducted to study the process of mentoring in the cluster schools and to identify the successes and challenges of the cluster-based mentoring programme in Balochistan. All these studies indicate that on the whole the programme achieved its objectives to a great extent within the short span of time. Some strengths of the programme are discussed below.

1. The mentoring programme was perceived as an innovative in-service teacher education programme which enabled mentees to learn from their mentors who came from the primary school background (Lalwani, 1999; Qaisrani et al, 1999). The cluster became a hub of professional development where teachers discussed their academic, professional and contextual issues and searched for relevant solutions. As one of the visitors to the programme said: 'every mentor we met was committed to the strategy of supporting colleagues in local schools. Primary Teachers Mentoring Programme (PTMP) is a sound idea, which nicely balances professional support with the realities of distance, culture and resources ... We sensed a spirit of collegiality and mutual respect emerging which augurs well for the growth of all teachers in the cluster. Whereas some mentors had influenced colleagues to make both the school environment more attractive and functional' (extracts from the correspondence of the UNICEF Regional Office for the South dated 6 November 1997).

2. The programme also provided access to teachers for enhancing their content knowledge and pedagogy. Generally, primary school teachers in Pakistan have poor content knowledge (see chapter 4). The monthly interactive cluster workshops provided an opportunity for teachers to share problems related to content knowledge with their fellow mentees and seek support from them and from the mentors. They spent considerable time clarifying concepts in Science, Mathematics and Social Studies. One of the male mentees described that, 'We brought textbooks related problems and jointly discussed and tried to solve them. If we were not successful in solving these problems, then we would send them to the Directorate. In the past, we did not have a practice of sharing our weaknesses with others. Now, we do not have any hesitation to get help from each other' (interview with a male teacher). The mentor maintained a balance between content and pedagogy and the mentees enhanced their content knowledge while learning how to teach a particular subject matter.

3. By appointing primary teachers as mentors, the programme gave recognition to the fact that primary teaching requires special knowledge and skills. Traditionally, secondary school teachers are considered higher in status and stronger in knowledge, and become master trainers in programmes for primary teachers. The mentoring programme also broke teachers' isolation and loneliness by creating opportunity for mentees to learn from each other. Qaisrani et al (1999) noted that by attending the cluster-based workshops, teachers came out of chronic isolation and created opportunities to learn from each other. A mentee described how the programme had affected them. 'We made our teaching learning process better. In our meeting we were forty teachers, therefore, forty minds. We jointly worked and solved problems. Before joining this programme, we were under the impression that only senior teachers could guide junior teachers, but in this programme junior teachers could also guide senior teachers. Some of us, who were newly appointed teachers, were also able to develop confidence to teach effectively' (Lalwani, 1999, p. 63).

4. One of the major purposes of this programme was to improve students' learning. Some positive effects on students' learning were noted by the programme evaluators. Comparing students of teachers who had participated in the mentoring programme with those who had not participated, Qaisrani et al (1999) reported that 'Performance of the students taught by the mentees was to some extent better than the students taught by non-mentees' (p. i). District education officers and TRLT members also confirmed that mentees introduced activity-based teaching which contributed towards enhancing and sustaining students' interest in learning. It helped in reducing students' absenteeism and drop-out particularly among girls. Students also reported that their teachers had become more caring and supportive and their teaching style had also changed.

5. Mentors were able to create all possible conditions to conduct an effective mentoring programme. They were committed, motivated, friendly,

open-minded, flexible and empathetic towards mentees' professional development (Graybill, 1999). One of the mentees shared her view of the mentors. 'We found our mentors different from the instructors of Bureau of Curriculum and Extension Wing and Colleges of Elementary Teachers. Mentors encouraged us questioning their view points and styles, engaging us in the learning process, providing individual feedback, and respecting our opinion ... Of course, the mentors belonged to the community of primary school teachers whereas the instructors don't ... We feel proud of our fellow primary school teachers who assisted us in our professional learning' (interview with female mentee).

6. Mentors performed several roles such as facilitators, moderators, counsellors and critical friends in their cluster workshops. They developed personal and professional relationships with their mentees based on mutual respect, understanding, need and trust. According to one mentee, 'I liked the mentor's attitude....He worked with us as a friend; therefore, I discussed personal matters as well. While discussing a problem, we became critical, but he never reacted. He personally arranged classroom settings, material display etc for us' (interview with male mentee).

7. The programme provided ample opportunities for mentees' professional growth at the grass-roots level. Through this programme mentees learnt from their own and others' experiences and took charge of their own professional development. This programme allowed mentees to reflect on the implementation of new ideas and assess implications for the teaching/learning process. Mentees felt empowered while dealing with the critical issues of teaching and learning. Some mentees brought their instructional material to cluster workshops and shared them with their fellow mentees. This encouraged others to further improve their lesson plans and develop instructional material to improve teaching. Sometimes mentees would invite each other to observe their classes. In each cluster, mentors and mentees worked together on developing low and no cost material. They were encouraged to try new ideas and share their successes and challenges. Qaisrani et al (1999) report that

> Teachers found cluster meetings useful for their professional development. They also learned new techniques of teaching. They considered themselves as professionals and talked about professional problems and difficulties. They were open-minded, confident, courageous and curious. They would sometimes challenge their mentors' viewpoint, which helped them to develop more confidence.

8. Mentors were able to develop and promote positive relationships with mentees. As one female mentor said: 'As a mentor, my prime responsibility is to create a friendly environment in the workshop so that everybody contributes to it which helped mentees in improving their professional learning' (extract from a female mentor's correspondence). Literature also

considers a positive relationship as one of the prerequisites of an effective mentoring programme. This programme helped develop and promote collegiality and collaboration among mentors and mentees (Graybill, 1999). The professional relationships provided a reciprocal process contributing to the personal and professional development of both mentor and mentees; strengthening their self-image and professional positions. For successful mentoring, positive personal and professional relationships are necessary. The relationships in this programme were based on the principles of mutual respect, trust, confidentiality, academic honesty, shared understanding and expectations, common goals and good will.

9. Mentors served as link persons between teachers and District Education Officers to discuss issues related to teaching and learning. This was a significant achievement of the programme since prior to this programme, teachers were not allowed to talk directly to their senior officials. The programme helped to minimize the communication gap and break the hierarchy by regularly bringing together primary teachers (both mentors and mentees) together with the district officers to discuss issues and find solutions. The close and continuing interaction regarding primary teaching at and between the cluster, the district, and the provincial education department was a new and potentially effective approach for improving the quality of primary schools. The level of communication among teachers, district education officers and TLRT members had substantially increased. Senior and junior teachers worked together on a regular basis and the education officers worked more closely with teachers to provide logistic support. Thus the programme contributed towards creating a culture of harmony and togetherness among teachers and education officers. In the programme, some mentors were less experienced teachers and they encountered difficulties while working with more experienced mentees. However, they were able to gain respect and influence the traditional thinking that one learns only from the number of years spent teaching.

10. District education officers were found to be supportive and committed to mentees' professional development for enhancing the quality of education in Balochistan. TLRT and the concerned district education officers also attended district based mentoring meetings and provided adequate feedback for mentors to continuously upgrade and improve their knowledge and skills. This helped mentors to keep their morale high. It was observed that those officers who supported mentors in a variety of ways in their clusters became more successful than others. Some clusters are still functioning without any further monetary, professional and logistic support.

Some Challenges of the Cluster-based Mentoring Programme

A number of successes of the programme have been highlighted above; however, there were also several challenges which affected the effectiveness and sustainability of the programme.

1. Loan-giving agencies' sudden withdrawal from their financial commitment badly affected the institutionalization of the programme.
2. The majority of mentors were 'generalists' rather than 'specialists' in their teaching subject areas, hence, they lacked adequate content knowledge in Science and Mathematics. They also lacked understanding and skills of multigrade teaching and students' assessment (Qaisrani et al, 1999).
3. Even though the programme was effective in many respects, as discussed above, a majority of stakeholders, especially higher provincial education authorities and district education officers, developed very high and unrealistic expectations from mentors and were looking for quick results in terms of improvement in teaching and learning.
4. Those mentors who performed well started leaving their jobs and joining the private sector which normally pays more salary and fringe benefits.
5. The TLRT was responsible for providing academic support but instead remained more preoccupied with management chores. Moreover, the team at the TLRT was not large enough to support all mentors. A TLRT member confirmed this limitation when he said, 'We had a small team of four members. It was impossible for us to look after all districts and in each district there were ten clusters. We tried our best to visit one or two clusters (interview). Some mentors did not find meetings with TLRT useful. According to one mentor, 'Monthly meetings with TLRT were a waste of time and resources because they could not help us in improving our understanding about content knowledge' (extract from male mentor's letter). As soon as the project was over the level of enthusiasm of many officers went down, hence, they could not continue providing support for the mentors. According to a male mentor, 'In the beginning the PED took keen interest in solving problems, but later they lost their interest' (extract from correspondence).
6. High turnover of education officers at the directorate and district levels also affected the sustainability of a cluster-based mentoring programme.
7. The majority of district education officers were replaced with new officers who were not able to provide continued support to mentors.
8. Many mentors were not able to provide professional on-the-job support for their mentees because of the distance, the harsh climate in winter and summer seasons, the teaching workload, the immobility of mentors and the lack of intrinsic and extrinsic incentives.

Conclusion

The cluster-based mentoring model of teacher development implemented in Balochistan offered a decentralized, economically viable and contextually-driven approach to in-service teacher education (Graybill, 1999). It also introduced a 'paradigm shift' in in-service teacher education from 'competency-based training' (Pring, 1995) to 'inquiry-based teacher education' The programme developed confidence, commitment and competencies among those it prepared as mentors. The programme focused on the building and maintaining of relationships, exchanging information, exploring ideas and opinions, discussing difficult issues, sharing experiences and working towards the future. The mentoring programme became well known for its effectiveness both in the national and international community and received a technical achievement award from the Academy for Educational Development, USA, in 1998. Through this programme, an innovative approach to in-service teacher education was introduced as an alternative to the centralized and hierarchical approaches to teacher education which were predominant in the context.

References

Anderson, E. & Shannon, A. (1995) Towards a conceptualization of mentoring, in T. Kerry & A.S. Mayes (Eds) *Issues in Mentoring*. London: Routledge.

Anzar, U. (1999) *Education reforms in Balochistan 1990-98: a case study in improving management and gender equity in primary education*. Washington, DC: The World Bank.

Ganser, T. (1996) Preparing mentors of beginning teachers: an overview of staff developers, *Journal of Staff Development*, 17(4), pp. 8-11.

Government of Pakistan (1998) *National Education Policy (1998-2010)*. Islamabad: Ministry of Education.

Gray, W. & Gray, M. (1985) Synthesis of Research on Mentoring Beginning Teachers, *Educational Leadership*, 43(3), pp. 37-42.

Graybill, D. (1999) *Change and Continuity in Primary Education in Balochistan: an evaluation report of three innovations introduced by the BPEP programme*. Report submitted to Directorate of Primary Education, Quetta.

Koki, S. (1997) *The Role of Teacher Mentoring in Educational Reform*. PREL briefing paper, Pacific Resources for Educational and Learning, pp. 1-6.

Lalwani, F. (1999) A Study of the Impact of the Mentoring Process on Primary Teachers' Professional Development in District Lasbella, Balochistan. Unpublished M.Ed. dissertation, Aga Khan University, Institute for Educational Development, Karachi.

Maynard, T. & Furlong, J. (1995) *Mentoring Student Teachers*. London: Routledge.

McIntyre, D. (1996) *Mentors in Schools: developing the profession of teaching*. London: Foulton Press.

Memon, M. & Mithani, S. (2003) Enhancing Institutional Capacity Building of Non-governmental Organizations and Community Based Organizations: impact of an innovative initiative, in A. Halai & J. Rarieya (Eds) *Proceedings of an International Conference on Impact: making a difference*, Aga Khan University, Institute for Educational Development, Karachi, 28-30 August.

Pardhan, H., Memon, M., Qureshi, F., Baber, M., Solangi, S., Hussain, M., MacLeod, M., with Zafar, F., Rashid, A., Niaz, I., & Mashallah, M. (2004) *Effectiveness of In-service Teacher Education Programmes Offered by the University of Education, Lahore: A report of an evaluation study carried out by the Aga Khan*

University, Institute for Educational Development, Karachi and the Society for the Advancement of Education, Lahore submitted to DFID and Punjab Government, Department of Education and the University of Education, Lahore.

Pring, R. (1995) Standards and Quality in Education, in T. Kerry & A.S. Mayes (Eds) *Issues in Monitoring*. London: Routledge.

Qaisrani, M., Rassani, R., Mujahid, A., Huq, S. & Bano, A. (1999) *Evaluation of Primary Teacher Mentor Programme*. Quetta: UNICEF.

Schön, D. (1983) *The Reflective Practitioner*. New York: Basic Books.

Smith, P. (2001) Mentors as Gate-keepers: an explanation of professional formation, *Educational Review*, 53(3), pp. 313-324.

Tomlinson, P. (1995) *Understanding Mentoring: reflective strategies for school based teacher preparation*. Buckingham: Open University Press.

Warwick, D. & Reimers, F. (1995) *Hope or Despair? Learning in Pakistan's Primary Schools*. London: Praeger.

CHAPTER 7

Continuing Professional Development and the Relevance of the IED Model in East Africa

JANE RARIEYA & FRED TUKAHIRWA

Introduction

This chapter addresses the introduction, implementation and impact of the AKU-IED (Institute for Educational Development at the Aga Khan University) teacher education programmes in East Africa.

East Africa consists of three countries: Kenya, Tanzania and Uganda. In their first decade of independence, the governments of the three countries had to identify new goals and objectives to guide the growth and development of education. Educational developers saw a competent, well-trained and dedicated teaching force as a critical factor in establishing an education system for the development of a high quality and skilled workforce for all the three countries.

Despite varying political systems in the three countries, the commitment to improving the quality of education is reflected in the following objectives of teacher education in Kenya, which are similar to those of Tanzania and Uganda:

> Develop the basic theoretical and practical knowledge about the teaching profession, so that the teachers' attitudes and abilities can be turned towards professional commitment and competence; enable teachers to recognize the pupils as the centre of education; create a national consciousness for educational excellence in every teacher; develop in the teacher the ability to adapt to new situations; and, develop in the teacher an awareness and appreciation of innovation in the field of education and to utilize them. (Njoka, 1995, p. 104)

Concern about the quality of teaching in schools in East Africa has seen the creation of various commissions appointed to review and evaluate the education systems at all levels and recommend measures and strategies for their improvement. For example, the Uganda Government White Paper (1992) recommended a review of the condition of education, beginning with primary education reform and calling for restructuring in teacher education. Reform aimed at improving the quality of teachers (including their pedagogical skill development); improving learning materials, supervision and assessment; improving the financing of primary education and management of resources; building the management and implementation capacity of educational institutions; and promoting universal access to education and equity.

All three countries have adopted Universal Primary Education (UPE) – the provision of free education for all eligible primary school children. Whilst UPE in the three countries has led to an increase in the enrolment of children in school at the primary level, this has not been accompanied by similar expansion of teacher personnel, support and services. This discrepancy has been compounded by lack of regular in-service programmes for capacity building and enhancement of teachers' knowledge which are necessary for teachers to cope with educational reforms. For example, in Tanzania, many teachers are ill-prepared and poorly motivated to teach. A large number of teachers who were hired under the UPE programme continue to teach with little more than a primary school education as their training. 'According to the Ministry of Education and Culture, in 1997 only 44% of all primary school teachers had a diploma or Grade "A" qualifications, and not even one of the total 110,000 primary school teachers held a university degree' (Kuleana Centre for Children's Rights, 1999). Subsequently, the competence and morale of the teaching force have dwindled. This has been exacerbated by socio-economic, political and environmental changes, which have placed additional responsibilities on teachers. For example, as teaching becomes more learner-centred, teachers are expected to play a more active classroom role. Head teachers are expected to take on further responsibilities in the management of their schools. As a result of such expectations, teachers and head teachers wish to see improvements in their careers, such as access to training and upgrading.

Response of Both Government and Private Agencies

According to Sitima (1995, p. 105), continuing education for teachers in East Africa serves three main purposes, namely:

1. provision of further personal and professional education;
2. enabling teachers to review and modify teaching methods and curricula in the light of present-day changes be they technological, economic, cultural, social or political; and
3. meeting in-service needs of a stable teaching force due to the fall in demand for new teachers in some areas such as music, art, agriculture and home economics.

At the Third Education Conference in Nairobi in 1995, which brought together all the important stakeholders in education in Kenya, the following recommendations were made with regard to continuing education for teachers:

> There should be regular in-servicing of teachers and teacher trainers.

> All teachers should have opportunities for academic and professional advancement which should form a basis for their promotion by their employers. (Lodiaga, 1995, p. 102)

All three governments recognize that teacher effectiveness is largely influenced by the nature of support teachers receive; thus they have attempted to put in place programmes that would help provide continuing professional development to both teachers and head teachers. This responsibility has been mandated to a number of institutions, departments and organizations, which work either as part of directorates of education or in partnership with the respective Ministry of Education, sponsored by donors, in the three countries. Institutes have been established with specific objectives to strengthen the management and planning capacity of various cadres of education as well as provide support to practising teachers.

However, in implementation of such initiatives for improving teacher education major constraints have been identified. For example,

- For donor-dependent programmes, the withdrawal of donors has often led to the collapse of the programmes due to lack of sustainability. Even in instances when the withdrawal has not been total, lack of efficient provision of services has always been the case.
- Financial constraints limit some programmes. Funding for courses, like any other public service activity, is done by the Treasury which is guided by what is considered as priorities. Unfortunately, 'in-service training ... tends to be placed rather low in the priority list for public spending' (Lodiaga, 1987, p. 50).
- Recognition of a need to provide continuing education support to teachers has not been matched by the development of a strong cadre of teacher educators. More systematic development of teacher educators and strategies to retain those competent in a particular field are needed.
- Frequent deployment of staff affects teacher services: often teachers and head teachers are deployed elsewhere before they can implement what they have learned in an in-service course.
- Although current trends globally are for teachers to take more responsibility in identifying their own development needs, the trend in East Africa is still for teachers to expect centralized training programmes.

Existing In-Service Programmes in East Africa

In order to determine the relevance of the AKU-IED model in East Africa, it is imperative that some comparisons be made between this model and the existing ones.

In East Africa, in-service programmes for teachers are usually conducted to help teachers understand better the demands of newly introduced curricular reforms with the aim of enabling curriculum implementation. In other words, the thrust of most of these programmes is to familiarize teachers with the new reform. There is no established way in which teachers of a particular subject area can be helped to improve their teaching skills. In-service programmes tend to take a theoretical stance during training. Those who conduct the programmes *tell* trainees what should be done rather than demonstrating the relevant practices. Teachers who attend upgrading courses find themselves being offered new, often academic, content areas while little effort is made to seek out and build on their classroom experiences. Although, some of these programmes claim to be field-based, this does not seem to be so at the practical level. Most of the local in-service programmes are of short duration ranging from a day to a week and conducted at a central venue with participants sometimes numbering as many as 70. Participants are given materials to read for the sake of preparing for examinations pertaining to the course. When these teachers have been 'trained' there is little or no follow-up when they return to their respective classrooms. Thus, the graduates of such programmes end up not improving their teaching practices; instead they use the qualification acquired to enhance their career opportunities in terms of promotion and salary increment.

The demands placed upon teachers today in East Africa and the almost non-existent support structures for teachers to meet these demands has led to the demoralization of the teaching force which tends to view teaching as a routine task with little challenge or attraction.

Most in-service courses in East Africa are either conducted by donor agencies and their personnel (who may not necessarily be locals) or personnel from the respective Ministries of Education or their institutes. In the case of the former, such programmes are not contextualized to fit the demands of the local contexts, thereby being out of touch with the very participants they are expected to serve. In the case of the latter, often the methodology employed by these trainers is little different from that which the teachers practise in their classrooms, thereby resulting in teachers feeling that they have learnt nothing new at such courses.

Such factors have led to current East African in-service or professional development programmes for teachers being deemed as inadequate to meet educational aims and teaching needs. For example, Uganda's Ministry of Education's Teacher Development and Management Plan (TDMP, 2000) identifies issues concerning current continuous professional development programmes as follows:

- Continuous professional development for practising teachers – taken to mean refresher courses and upgrading – is inadequate. Teachers do not adequately apply knowledge and skills acquired from refresher courses. Current upgrading for primary teachers does not necessarily lead to better classroom performance.
- No incentives are offered to teachers to encourage continuous professional development initiatives.
- The organization of continuous professional development for teachers at secondary school level is non-existent.
- Schools do not prepare staff development plans, neither are there school and district initiatives.

AKU-IED/Professional Development Centre (PDC) courses in contrast are designed to try to meet current educational aspirations and associated needs in East Africa.

The Advent of AKU-IED

The entry of the Aga Khan University's Institute for Educational Development (AKU-IED) into the arena of provision of continuing education for both teachers and head teachers in East Africa is partly a response to the shortcomings and recommendations identified above which was revealed by a survey conducted by a specially appointed task force by His Highness, The Aga Khan. This looked into the need to establish a PDC similar to that at the AKU-IED in Karachi. Following this survey, the PDC Lead-in Project was established in 2000 to conduct a two/three year preparatory phase for the establishment of PDCs in East Africa.

The first programme offered by the AKU-IED in East Africa was the Visiting Teachers Programme (VTP), currently referred to as Certificate in Education Programme (CEP), in August 1998 in Nairobi. It drew participants from Kenya and Tanzania. This particular programme, adapted by a facilitating team of Professional Development Teachers (graduates of the Masters in Education at AKU) from the model developed at the AKU-IED (see Chapter 5), is now referred to as the East African Model. In this model, courses run for five-six months with both central and school-based elements. They target primary school teachers and dwell on a specialist focus (English, Mathematics, Science, Social Studies and Primary Education). They are tailored to the needs of the teachers and attempt to enhance teachers' pedagogical skills, particularly exposing teachers to non-traditional teaching methodologies, and developing their understanding of students' learning processes, curriculum development and enrichment, and subject content knowledge.

Following implementation of the certificate programmes, a certificate course in Educational Leadership and Management (CE:ELM), based on the same model as the CEPs, is now in place for head teachers and school inspectors. The thrust of this course is a shift from the traditional administrative approach to educational leadership to the development of pedagogical leaders who can effectively contribute to school improvement initiatives. Similar courses are being planned for education officers, centre co-ordinating tutors (Uganda) and teacher advisory centre tutors (Kenya).

Both the CEP and CE:ELM courses are conducted by Professional Development Teachers (PDTs), CEP and CE:ELM graduates and carefully selected personnel from local educational institutions and government departments under the supervision of a faculty member of the AKU. The use of the above range of facilitators is partly to build a large group of teacher educators across the region which is likely to enhance the sustainability of the change initiatives. Participants find these courses enriching since they dwell on improving teaching and school leadership and are based on their identified needs. Unlike most professional development courses, these ones do not solely focus on curricular innovations or reform of the time as directed by ministry officials.

The East African Certificate in Education Programme

AKU-IED/PDC programmes in East Africa are geared towards enhancing teachers' pedagogical skills and pedagogical content knowledge. First, a survey is carried out on a sample of teachers who would be eligible for the programme and their perceptions of need form an important component of the programme content. Second, teachers' perspectives and classroom experiences are taken into consideration during the delivery of the programme. Thus the relevance of programmes to the teachers' classrooms is ensured in the duration of the programme. Furthermore, the facilitation of the AKU-IED/PDC Lead-in Project programmes is such that the participants actually experience the teaching strategies proposed in the programme, thereby providing them with the opportunity to see the feasibility of the suggested ideas. It is against this context, that they are able to better appreciate the workings of the teaching strategies proposed. For example, one graduate of a CEP course commented,

> This programme [VTP] is very intensive and very enriching. I
> have learnt so much more in the past five months than I ever did
> during my two-year teacher training programme. (Course
> Participant, Reflective Journal Entry, December 2001)

Programmes run for five to six months depending on the country where the programme is being conducted and cater for 27 participants in any course. A programme is divided into three modules. For modules 1 and 3, participating teachers converge at a central venue (a school) for a period of three weeks, usually during a school vacation. This has helped to resolve problems of releasing teachers during the school term. Participants meet face to face with each other and with the course facilitators. They are introduced to the content of the course, to ways of working and thinking as part of the course, and to approaches to reflecting on and evaluating their own teaching. In the second module, participants return to their schools for one school term. During this period, they are provided with support by the course facilitators as they try to implement in their classrooms whatever they had learnt in the first module. Saturday seminars are held during this time to bring participants together to discuss their challenges and successes during this module, as well as to provide an opportunity to the facilitators to address issues emanating from their observations of classroom practice and discussions about it with the participants.

IED/PDC programmes are highly practical in nature, with participants often having to demonstrate their understanding of the issues discussed through micro-teaching and presentations. Experiences registered from the participants clearly indicate that they find these easily applicable in the real classroom/school situation as reflected in the comment made by one participant:

> We have learnt that it is initiative and innovation that makes Mathematics more practical and makes a learner more of an active participant and not just a mere passive listener. (Course Participant, Reflective Journal Entry, May 2001)

Thus it can be seen that the practical nature of the programme is one of the factors that make the participants more willing to adopt the principles of teaching and learning shared at these courses. This prevents the course from being a one-stop workshop that may not result in improved teaching skills on the part of the teacher. Indeed, one of the aspects of the programme that is greatly appreciated by the participants is the fact that the participants leave the programme looking at things anew. As one such participant stated:

> You see these things are not really new, but now we are looking at them differently. When I was in college, I came across some of these things that we are discussing here, but they were rather theoretical and the purpose then was to pass exams. I never really understood what they all meant. Now, I have the chance to fully do so and see how they relate to the way I teach or am expected to teach. (Course Participant, Reflective Journal Entry, August 2002)

IED programmes aim at getting teachers to reconceptualize their roles as teachers and at creating an attitudinal shift among teachers. One important aspect of the programme is that it seeks to develop teachers into reflective practitioners. Thus, it is as a result of continually engaging in reflection that teachers are able to evaluate and re-evaluate their teaching practices, and this often results in a shift in attitude as regards teaching. For example, one participant in the Certificate in Educational Management course (which uses similar approaches to VT courses) commented,

I did not know how to reflect. Reflection has been a big thing for me. This has enabled me to understand who I am, how I can come down and work with others. (Course Participant, Reflective Journal Entry, September 2001)

Reflection is a skill most participants have identified as the most beneficial as it enables them to make professionally informed decisions.

Significant Features of AKU-IED Programmes

One of the strengths of the AKU-IED programmes in East Africa is that they are planned, organized and conducted by teacher educators who are graduates of the Masters in Teacher Education Programme at the AKU-IED and have specially been trained to run such programmes. These graduates are teachers in their respective countries. Upon graduation from AKU-IED, they start to work as teacher educators in their schools. These facilitators understand the philosophy of AKU-IED programmes and are in a position to translate it to the participants through the way they design and conduct the programmes. Many participants have commented on the way course facilitators work with participants, and the following statement by one such participant aptly sums it up:

One of the things that impresses me about this VT[P]is the way the facilitators work as a team. The way they relate to one another as well as to us [participants] has made me realise how important it is for me to be positive about my work as well as the way I deal with my students. I'm beginning to realise that teaching is not so much about me but about my students. (Course Participant, Reflective Journal Entry, August 2001)

However, the PDC Lead-in Project, under whose aegis IED programmes are run in East Africa, still does not have a sufficient number of IED graduates to facilitate programmes entirely. Thus, facilitators of the courses in East Africa are drawn from the pool of AKU-IED graduates in the region and former participants of Certificate in Education Programmes run by AKU-IED as well as staff from other institutions in the region that have the personnel able to contribute. This has led to close collaboration between the AKU-IED/PDC Lead-in Project and the respective government agencies in the field of education. It has also ensured that the programmes in place address contextual needs. Thus programmes in East Africa have developed a flexibility that has contributed to establishing their relevance for the East African participants.

The content of the courses is also another flexible aspect of the course. When the courses first began, they aimed at improving the pedagogical knowledge of the teachers. However, it soon became apparent to the course facilitators that a large number of the participants faced huge challenges in implementing new ideas learned in the programmes because they were weak in the content knowledge of the subjects they taught. For example, the courses advocate that children should be at the centre of the teaching-learning experience; this requires teachers to take children's prior experiences into account and calls for the teachers to allow students to ask questions freely in class and discuss issues. Many teachers often felt vulnerable as they realised that they did not have strong enough content knowledge of their teaching subjects to work in such ways. As a result, they often reverted to their old traditional teacher-centred methods that provided a safety net for them. Now, the programmes have been modified to teach both content and pedagogy to the participants. Participants are consulted to determine what subject content should be handled during the course. The content taught is also determined during Module II of the programme when classroom observations of the participants reveal particular needs.

Another important distinction, yet likely to be considered minor by some, is that modules 1 and 3 of the IED programmes provide participants with the materials they require for the course, including meals. Although this raises the cost of running the programme, it contributes to making the participants comfortable and gives them a sense of being well cared for. Participants are, therefore, in a position to relax and concentrate on the course. Indeed, this is one area of the programme that is often rated highly during the programme evaluation in overt contrast to other in-service programmes which expect participants to provide their own stationery and meals. This actually deters many teachers from participating in these programmes as they find attending the courses costly. Such provision is, of course, an issue to be considered when funding for programmes is limited.

Finally, as mentioned earlier, IED programmes in East Africa provide in-service courses to all cadres of education that are necessary for whole school improvement. The purpose of this is to ensure that all involved (teachers, head teachers, school inspectors and education officers) work together in trying to improve the quality of teaching and learning offered in schools by having a shared understanding of the processes involved. This is because the AKU-IED/PDC Lead-in Project has realized that if the participant teachers are to be the change agents that the programmes ask of them, then they are more likely to play this role effectively if they have people of like mind within their environment. In contrast, other in-service programmes in the region target specific cadres who are then trained in isolation. The link between all these sectors is not really established and thus participants leave the courses with their own agenda that may not involve collaboration with others.

Challenges Presented by Use of the AKU-IED Model as a Tool for Continuing Education for Teachers in East Africa

The success of the IED model as an in-service approach can be seen in the increased participation of schools in the programmes. In Nairobi (the latest course site), there are five government participating schools instead of the usual three. There have been numerous appeals from both ministries of education agencies and non-participating schools for inclusion in the programmes.

Furthermore, the cooperation extended to the PDC Lead-in Project by the Ministries of Education in putting up the programmes is an indication of the success and high regard the governments have for these programmes. For example, in Zanzibar, the provision of programmes was initially at the request of the Minister of Education. In Uganda, the first course for School Inspectors was at the request of the Ministry of Education. The linkages that have been established between AKU-IED/PDC Lead-in Project and local universities and Teacher Training Colleges, leading to their participation in AKU-IED programmes is yet another indication of the positive regard with which these programmes are viewed.

However, the above successes notwithstanding, there are several challenges that are presented in using the IED model of in-service teacher education in East Africa. They include the following:

1. The first challenge comes in the form of certification of the courses attended. In East Africa, a lot of value is placed on the certificate one receives at the end of a course as it is used as a basis for promotion. In as much as most participants view the IED programmes as powerful in terms of their personal and professional growth, this does not count much for promotion for teachers in Kenya and Tanzania. The accreditation of Aga Khan University certificates by all the East African governments would go a long way in ensuring that participants and their employers take the programmes much more seriously.

2. The second challenge comes in the form of facilitation of the programmes. Like AKU-IED, Karachi, the leading facilitators in the programmes are graduates of the institution. Currently East Africa has a total of 25 such graduates spread throughout the region. These graduates also work as teachers in their respective schools. As a result of the demands placed upon them by their respective schools, they find themselves constrained in developing and conducting the programmes as required. This, if unchecked, is likely to affect the quality of programmes offered to participants.

3. At the moment, the training approach used by the PDC Lead-in Project is to provide training opportunities to selected schools, which are referred to as collaborating schools. The collaborating schools are expected to send three teachers to any given programme. This means that few teachers get to take part in these programmes in a given year. Therefore, the bulk of teachers from a given school do not get the opportunity to participate in the programmes and are therefore unlikely to provide the cooperation the course participants might require when they return to their schools. This also means that based on this approach, it would take several years for all, or a majority of the teachers in a school to undergo such a programme.

Given that high teacher turnover is quite a common phenomenon in schools in East Africa, the programme could have little effect on the teaching and learning in some of the collaborating schools.

4. The follow-up of the participants who have undergone AKU-IED/PDC Lead-in Project programmes is at the moment inadequate. Once participants are through with the course, they move on to their schools and a new group of teachers are taken through a similar programme. It is assumed that once the participants have completed the programme, their approach to teaching will have changed; yet all indications are that with lack of systematic follow-up, which could be in the form of classroom visits, seminars, reflective dialogue groups, formation of professional associations, among others, teachers would revert to their old practices.

Recommendations

As stated earlier, IED programmes in East Africa are perceived to be a success, with the demand for such programmes growing within the region. It is in the light of this that the following recommendations for AKU-IED/PDC are made:

- AKU-IED/PDC needs to seek government accreditation (consideration of the certificates awarded in terms of promotion and monetary attachments) for its courses within the East African countries. Otherwise, most course participants might shun them due to lack of financial attachments at the end of the course. This is in contrast to courses that are usually run by government institutions and whose participants often receive some form of promotion or salary increments upon completion of the course.

- There is need to develop follow-up mechanisms for those who have completed the courses to ensure that the courses do not assume the one-stop workshop/programme approach that usually shrouds most in-service programmes. This would also minimize the possibility of course graduates reverting to their former teaching practices.

- It would be valuable to extend the fieldwork component of the programmes as this would allow the course facilitators to consolidate the change initiatives into the school systems, and thereby provide support where necessary.

- In all the programmes so far piloted: CEP and CE: ELM, there has always been a request from the participants that more time be allotted to the concepts covered. It is recommended that the programmes be extended to a whole year so that ample follow- up of the participants is done before certification.

- Finally, for the real worth of programmes to be felt in East Africa, there is a need to expand the programmes so that teachers, especially those in rural and disadvantaged areas, and who need these programmes most, can benefit from them. This can be done in collaboration with teacher advisory centres and teacher coordinating centres.

Conclusion

This chapter has attempted to review the relevance of the AKU-IED model of continuing education for teachers against a backdrop of past and prevailing teacher professional development courses in East Africa. From the foregoing, the AKU-IED model can be said to be relevant and this, no doubt, stems from the fact, that prior to its entry into the East African educational arena, AKU-IED was engaged in a series of studies and discussions with the relevant stakeholders in the education sector in East Africa. This has resulted in programmes that are quite responsive to the local needs. However, the challenge that now faces AKU-IED is largely one of how to meet a rapidly growing demand for its programmes, especially now when the effects of UPE are acutely being felt in East Africa.

References

Government of Uganda (1992) *Education for National Integration*. Report of the Education Policy Review Commission. Kampala: Government of Uganda.

Kuleana Centre for Children's Rights (1999) *The State of Education in Tanzania: crisis and opportunity*. Mwanza: Kuleana Centre for Children's Rights.

Lodiaga, J. (1987) *Staff Training and Development*. Report of the Education Administration Conference held at Jomo Kenyatta College of Agriculture, 21-25 April, pp. 48-51. Nairobi: Jomo Kenyatta Foundation.

Lodiaga, J. (1995) *Continuing Education for Teacher Supporters and Facilitators*. 3rd Report of the Teacher Education Conference, 5-9 December, pp. 116-127. Nairobi: Jomo Kenyatta Foundation.

Njoka, E.N. (1995) *Teacher Management and Professional Support Services*. 3rd Report of the Teacher Education Conference, 5-9 December, pp. 104-108. Nairobi: Jomo Kenyatta Foundation.

Sitima, T.M. (1995) *Maintenance of Standards in Teacher Education. 3rd Report of the Teacher Education Conference, 5-9 December*, pp. 109-115. Nairobi: Jomo Kenyatta Foundation.

Teacher Development and Management Plan (TDMP) (Primary Education) (2000) *Formal Draft of the Department of Teacher Education*. Ministry of Education and Sports, Kampala.

CHAPTER 8

Professional Development and School Improvement in Central Asia

GULGUNCHAMO NAIMOVA

This chapter is based on my experience as a resident of Tajikistan; a teacher for over 20 years, first in Dushanbe, the capital of Tajikistan, and later for over 20 years in Badakshan province; and a professional development teacher (PDT) in Badakshan for over five years. I lived through the period of transition from the Soviet Union (USSR) to independence, civil war and after, and saw the influence of these upheavals on schools, teachers and students. In writing the chapter I have also conducted discussions with other teachers and teacher educators including PDTs from Tajikistan and Kyrgyzstan. Because of lack of resources on educational issues of the country my readings were limited to some dissertations, Education Ministry documents and other information available about the region on the Internet.

While the chapter is about central Asia, a focus of this study is on the province of Badakshan in Tajiskstan and the city of Osh in Kyrgyzstan because that is where my own experience and that of my fellow PDTs is derived from.

This chapter will discuss briefly the educational system of the two Central Asian countries Tajikistan and Kyrgyzstan, particularly the experiences of teachers' Professional Development and School Improvement during the Soviet era and at the present time. The chapter will also describe the relationship of the educational institutions in these two countries with the other institutions and especially with AKU-IED and their impact on the Educational Development and School Improvement in these countries.

Education System in Central Asia: Soviet and post-Soviet period

According to Abdushukurova (2002), Soviet social policy created a modern education system in Tajikistan, Kyrgyzstan and the other 13 republics that were part of the Soviet Union. These countries had a public education system. The system was financed from Moscow and education was provided free of charge to all the citizens. Male and female citizens had equal educational opportunities from the kindergartens upwards. As elsewhere in the Soviet Union, the system was co-educational and was divided into schools for primary (grade 1-4), middle secondary (grade 5-9), higher secondary (grade 10-11), and higher education (at the special technical or professional schools, universities and institutes).

The achievements of the Soviet Union were a high literacy rate and a good quality of education in terms of students' strong knowledge base, especially in science, mathematics and literature. The teachers were well respected, degrees and diplomas sought after and students were employable upon graduation. All the teachers working at schools even in the remote areas were qualified. They had either University, Pedagogic Institute or Special Vocational Pedagogic qualifications. There were many other structured programmes for the students, including subject clubs, sports, camping, and so forth.

The centralized education system did not prepare the republics for independence in 1991. Everything was uniform and ready-made – curriculum, resources and even the lesson plans were prepared by the central education offices in Moscow. Very little attention was paid to the questions of relevance, sustainability, culture and context. The teachers were not flexible to modify curricular or other resources according to culture or context, or according to the needs of the students. There were 'Teachers' Guides' – books with all the lesson plans, from which the teachers were expected to deliver the lessons step by step following the books.

Education in pre-independence Tajikistan and Kyrgyzstan was considered as the responsibility of the USSR with the Republic's Ministry of Education subordinate to the Ministry of Education of the USSR. There were lower departments of education in the regions, districts and cities of the republics. These departments were implementing state policy. By the time the republics became independent, the quality and availability of education was lower than the Soviet Union-wide average. The newly independent countries were left with the Soviet infrastructure and curriculum, but without resources to maintain the buildings, pay salary, carry out extracurricular activities and programmes and keep up with the information revolution. Additionally, in Tajikistan, civil war had destroyed the economy and damaged the social fabric. The education sector along with other social sectors sharply declined.

Tajikistan

The republic of Tajikistan is a small country comprising 143.1 thousand square kilometres. It borders on Kyrgyzstan, Uzbekistan, Afghanistan and China. The population of the country exceeds 6 million of which 73% live in the rural districts. Tajikistan is an agrarian country. Agriculture is mainly based on cotton growing, although other agricultural crops like rice, grain, tobacco, corn, potatoes and vegetables are grown. Vineyards and gardens are also cultivated. Livestock production comes after cotton growing. Mining, chemicals, metallurgy, oil processing, energy, construction, food processing industries, mechanical engineering and handicraft industries are all developed in Tajikistan (Encyclopedia: Tajikistan).

Figure 3. Map of Tajikistan.

Within Tajikistan, the autonomous Province (MBAR) lies in the high Pamir mountain range and its capital is Khorog. The population of MBAR consists of 206,000 people. There are 318 schools, about 5000 teachers working for 55,000 students from grade 1 to 11. A student-teacher ratio of 11:1 is as required by law in all areas of Tajikistan (Country Guide, The Times of Central Asia).

Data from the Ministry of Education shows that Tajikistan is short of 72,200 teachers. The political non-stability and deterioration of the inter-ethnic relations resulted in the migration of a huge number of teachers to Russia and other countries. The prestige of the profession fell, together with the value of education. Having low economic conditions and working in hard conditions for a miserable salary, the teachers lost their desire to work at school. They left their workplaces at school to engage in trade. Children also dropped out of schools because they had to help their families with earning. They left their desks at schools for a place in the bazaar. The Department of

Statistics reported that only about 79.8% of school age children attend classes (Bruker, 2002).

We can observe very similar problems in the education system of Kyrgyzstan, the neighbouring country to Tajikistan.

Kyrgyzstan

The Republic of Kyrgyzstan has an area of 198,500 square kilometres. It borders on China, Kazakhstan, Uzbekistan and Tajikistan. Its population is 4.832 million. The majority of the population is Kyrgyz.

Osh is the second biggest city in Kyrgyzstan. There are 50 public schools, two private (Iilim and AKS) and two Turkish Lyceums funded by the Turkish government plus several professional lyceums (Kyrgyzstan Development Gateway).

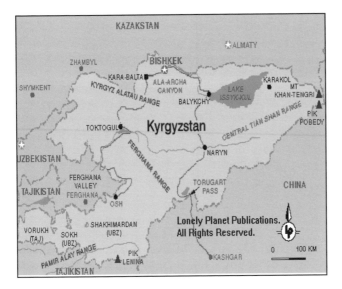

Figure 4. Map of Kyrgyzstan.

According to Karim (2003), 'The secondary education in Kyrgyzstan is facing a number of problems, most of which are due to lack of resources. Among these, shortage of qualified teachers and lack of the textbooks are the most serious problems.' According to the information provided by the Ministry of Education and Culture of the Kyrgyz Republic, there is a shortage of 2,863 teachers and about 2,500 schoolchildren have dropped out of schools (Karim, 2003).

It is clear from the above descriptions that education systems in Tajikistan and Kyrgyzstan are beset with similar problems. Considerable effort is needed to reform the system and improve the quality of teaching and learning in schools.

Professional Development and School Improvement

Tajikistan

The goal of the Ministry of Education is to develop an education system and an education policy which will meet international standards, provide quality and equal access to education and encourage teachers to use modern methods of teaching (Rashidov, 2000).

Education has always been considered important in Central Asia. Here education is not only identified with schools as it covers a wider range of issues rather than just training and professional development. Education is a process that influences all life. It is a process which is oriented towards the formation of the individual; it is a process of development of human resources. Education concerns the quality of life for all members of society. Its purpose is to satisfy the requirements of the person in all-round development for the realization of all abilities, survival, existence, and improved quality of life and work, thereby improving the economic, cultural and spiritual legacy for maintaining the social and economic development of the republic (Rashidov, 2000).

The constitution (Article 41) and (Article 12), says that all the children must complete nine years (Class 1-9) of compulsory education. After this, education is not compulsory but every child is guaranteed a place in the state-run higher secondary school (years 10 and 11), in the schools for professional education and in the university. All state schools are free of cost. (Rashidov, 2000).

According to Rashidov (2000), on 4 June 1997 the Tajik government accepted Resolution No. 266 on the State Standard of General Secondary Education of the Republic. This resolution identified disciplines and skills to be taught at each level of education and emphasized the holistic development of a child. The document also talks about the creation of conditions for supporting the child and realizing the rights of children for high-level physical, intellectual, spiritual, moral and social development. It recommended material support to large families, and the development of public health services and educational services for children. To develop a normative document is admirable, but to apply it is challenging if not impossible in the existing situation as described above. Teachers are the key to students' achievements, and every student deserves an experienced, well-prepared teacher. Especially needed are teachers for the primary and secondary schools in almost all subjects. However, as I said earlier, few well-qualified teachers are available.

During the Soviet era, professional development for teachers consisted of self-study and organized training designed to improve the content knowledge, methodology and pedagogy of the teachers. Teachers were expected to do research on their own and present it at the teachers' seminars and conferences. Professional development or training courses were designed and conducted by Institutes for Professional Development. Teachers would attend these courses once in five years. Once every few years some teachers could get the opportunity to attend professional development courses offered at the national level by the Central Institute for Professional Development in Dushanbe, the capital of Tajikistan. Also, every year the teachers had to attend a one to two day conference on different areas such as methodology, pedagogy, innovations in education, and so forth. In addition, there were monthly subject-wise 'methodology sessions' at schools' subject departments. The Professional Development courses for the heads of the schools and other administrative staff were organized the same way by the Central Education Departments for all the areas.

The overall control of the implementation of the Professional Development courses and teachers' professional growth was led by the Ministry of Education. We can say that Professional Development courses for the teachers were intentional – the teachers were expected to attend them in an ongoing and systematic process. They consisted of a short (the longest being one month) retraining of the teachers and educators. In Tajikistan they were usually conducted by the educationalists from the universities and institutes. Most of these educationalists were not aware of the school contexts and their history, of classroom situations, teaching learning processes and accessibility of facilities/resources. Also as the ideas for the professional development came from the centre, from Dushanbe, they were not very applicable for all the areas in the republic. These courses did not meet the needs of the teachers from the different areas.

As a teacher, I have attended several training courses. The approach to them was always top down, never bottom up. There was no needs assessment conducted in the beginning to know what the teachers really need from these courses and what are their objectives for attending these courses. Almost all the Professional Development courses involved theory-based lectures on content and methodology. Instead of practical approach, there were lectures on child-centred learning, on group and pair work techniques and on classroom discussions. The Professional Development courses had nothing practical, neither practical demonstrations, presentations, nor model teaching and no classroom observations at schools or follow- up activities in the field.

As a result, classroom teaching was mainly teacher centred; with teacher-talk, teacher at the front and activities directed to the whole class. No element of a child-centred approach could be observed. There was very little group work, pair work, or debate and discussions. Teachers had very little or no understanding of these approaches to teaching so that they just put the students in groups or pairs and gave them a task to do. They gave no instructions about how to work in the group nor distributed roles and responsibilities (such as idea generator, writer, timekeeper and presenter) among group members. Thus the strong students who had better knowledge of the subject would do the task without sharing with others and without asking for and considering others' ideas. The other group members would engage in off-task talk. As a result there was always an unhealthy noise in the classroom. After giving the group task, teachers themselves would mark the students' exercise books, fill in the register or do other things instead of observing the students and facilitating and monitoring their work.

From my own experience as a teacher, I know that the teachers were bound by the curriculum and the textbooks. Even if they had good ideas about teaching approaches they were not confident to apply these approaches. They had a fear that they would not be able to finish the textbook, or cover the syllabus and they would not be able to meet the curriculum requirements. Also there was a fear of inspection starting from the administration (head, deputy heads) of the school up to the educational officers of the departments. Inspections from the school administration – head and deputy heads and subject department leaders – were quite regular. There was the so-called 'Frontalnaya proverka' – the whole school inspection by the team from the Regional Education Departments (RED) once in three or four years. This team spent about a month in one school observing all the teachers teaching, and checking all the documents starting from the students' notebooks and diaries up to all the curriculum and syllabus, matching them with the topics in the registers. The consequences were very bad if the teachers were not teaching according to the curriculum.

There was very little or no room for the development of the students' thinking skills or creativity in lessons. Mainly the teachers' understanding was that the students have no outlook and very limited knowledge; therefore they have to gain knowledge from the teachers, who know everything. The teachers' questions to the class were usually open but time was limited, so that the students did not get chance to think and respond to them fully. So the teacher would do it instead of them. The students were taught to be good listeners and to respect their teachers. Therefore there were no questions from them during the lessons, no enquiries, as if they knew everything from what their teachers taught them.

To develop the students' thinking skills and creativity there were extracurricular and very good outdoor activities, called subject clubs. A student could choose the area of his/her interest and attend these clubs. These clubs were very interesting with hands- on activities, where the students could develop their creativity, thinking and other skills. And the most interesting thing was that the same subject teachers could conduct activities at these clubs. These activities were very interesting and applicable for the classroom sessions, but as the teachers were bound to the time and the textbooks, they could not bring them to the classroom. Unfortunately, because of family commitments or other interests, not all students attended these clubs.

All of the above refers to pre-independence in Tajikistan as a whole. I am now going to refer to my own experiences in the MBAR, post-independence; since this is where the IED has been involved.

Mountainous Badakhshan Autonomous Region (MBAR)

After the Soviet era, during the early years of independence, as in other parts of the country, many qualified teachers left their places in the schools because of the poor economic situations of their families. The new graduates of the pedagogical institutes and universities did not choose to work in school and opted to work with international development agencies working in the region who could give them higher salaries. This raised serious problems for the education system. According to Ismailova (2000), the schools in the Mountainous Badakhshan Autonomous Region are short of almost 800 teachers, both in the primary and secondary schools. She says that only 12 out of 264 graduates of the higher educational institutions sent to the MBAR applied for a job in the educational departments of the region. The other graduates sought work with a private organization.

Nowadays, many teachers are not certified. These teachers have a higher secondary school certificate but no professional training and were employed during the war or in postings in remote areas where no teachers were available. These teachers have either limited or no understanding about methodology and subject content knowledge and no knowledge of curriculum. They usually face lots of problems such as classroom management, resource development, giving instructions and, of course, teaching methods. This problem is evident in the following quotation from a history teacher from Niyozov (2001).

> The current programs for all the subjects are being developed in
> Dushanbe ... Many important themes are not in the program.
> There are debates around the meaning of (the history behind)
> Badakhshan and Pamir and we teachers even do not have enough
> knowledge about them. I would include the view of the
> mountains, the traditions of the people of Badakhshan, the needs
> of Badakhshan and the problems we face today. (pp. 222-223)

The Ministry of Education is now concerned not only with the retention of teachers and school administrators but also with the development of their professional skills (Rashidov 2000). A policy requiring formal certification of teachers and retraining of all teaching staff was developed and authorized by a Government Resolution (4 June 4 1995, no. 264). The government expects that certification will lead to improvement in teachers' professional skills, increase in their salaries and overall improvement in schools.

Regional Education Departments

After independence, the Regional Education Departments took charge of the financial and pedagogical needs of the schools. The local authority (Hukumat/Government of the areas, towns and regions) implements the state policy in education, develops and realizes regional programmes for the development of education within the national context and takes into account the socio-economic, cultural, demographic and other peculiarities of individual districts. Having a small budget, the Regional Education Departments cannot afford to change the curriculum and purchase or develop all the needed resources for the schools in a short period of time. They are not able to develop and conduct courses for all the teachers of the area. Even when training courses are offered, they do not always lead to improvement in teaching practice. It is hoped that strategies to increase incentives for teachers to help them improve the economic situation of their families, may also provide opportunities for more exposure outside the school activities and may also lead to development of teachers and improvement in the quality of teaching and the school as a whole.

According to Rashidov (2000), the new policy paper on the National Schools (3 January 1995) is the most important document in the education sector which defines the purposes of education. The Ministry of Education issued the order for the implementation of the policy. Various measures were developed for addressing various aspects of school organization including maintenance of the school norms, rules and regulations, preparing teachers and improving their qualifications, solving of the urgent problems, defining the contents of school education and studying the existing educational programmes, textbooks and educational methodological literature for comprehensive schools. All this has to be done by the authorities from the central education office in Dushanbe, through the regional educational offices in the regions.

The influence of independence was different in the MBAR in Tajikistan from the rest of the country and from other Central Asian countries. Badakhshan has a lot of problems in schooling but fortunately the educational departments as well as the teachers and the students are very open and supportive of making changes and improving the system. The greatest motivation for the teachers of Badakhshan to work in school and to improve the students' knowledge comes from the Aga Khan, the spiritual leader of the Ismaili community, a sect of Muslims, which forms almost 100% of the population of MBAR. The Aga Khan development has supported the community through many initiatives, particularly in the education sector in MBAR, since 1991. The speech the Aga Khan IV made at the opening ceremony of the Aga Khan Lycée in Khorog in 1998 was particularly inspirational for the teachers. He expressed high praise for the teachers, who in a very difficult time of poverty (because of the civil war) did everything to keep the education alive. He said: 'I should pay My compliments, My respect and My gratitude to the teachers who have kept education alive in Badakshan' (Aga Khan IV, 1998).

Teachers are considered the most honest, most educated and most important people in Badakshan. Those teachers who had continued to work as teachers had kept education alive without getting any salary or promotions. From 1992 to 1994 teachers did not get any salary and starting from 1994 they could get only half of their salary. I myself was a teacher and remember the faces of foreigners who were surprised when they learnt that I received only US$4 per month as salary and still continued to work as a teacher. My response was similar to a teacher quoted in Niyozov (2001):

> Mavlo sends us everything, food clothes, his love and care. He
> said that we were always in his thoughts and heart ... The only
> thing that Mavlo wants from us is to work hard, seek knowledge
> and teach the children. (p. 201)

All the teachers and students thought that this was the best way to pay back to Hazir Imam; therefore they were all trying their best to improve educational standards

There is another example of teachers and students being highly motivated in the teaching and learning process. Case (2002), a professor at the University of Toronto who worked as an education consultant in Badakhshan, described his visits to classrooms of Khorog (capital city in Badakhshan) in the south-eastern part of Tajikistan:

> Classrooms have no heat, and children sit in their winter coats,
> the wind whistling through cracks in the walls and the windows ...
> The situation is excruciating, classrooms are inhabited by cold and
> often hungry children and teachers who attempt to learn and
> teach using methods abandoned decades ago in other parts of the
> world. Teachers continue to teach and students continue to learn
> ... nowhere else in the world have I ever seen teachers as highly
> motivated and giving of themselves. (p. B19)

The teachers in the MBAR are very lucky in the sense that the Educational Departments are very supportive of their professional growth, although they still lack funds and opportunities. Regional, local and district governments in this area are paying much attention to the improvement of the education system. There are still economic difficulties in the area but in 1996 the National Assembly of the region set up a programme called 'The programme of future education development' to conduct ongoing training programmes and to introduce new reforms such as the introduction of English medium sections in existing schools. Teacher training motivated teachers to return to school, leading to improvement in the quality of schools as well as in the economic conditions of the teachers themselves. Due to this programme in 1996-2002, education achieved some successful results in improving the schools' performance in examinations judging from the number of students securing admission in universities.

The Ministry of Education and the local educational department bodies work strongly in collaboration with the non-governmental organizations working in the education field and assist in their charitable activity. There are several institutions – the Aga Khan Foundation Education Department [1], the Aga Khan Education Service and the Aga Khan University, Institute for Educational Development – that have great impact on the development of the education system and school improvement in Badakhshan. The greatest and most valuable contribution to the development of education in Badakhshan was made by His Highness the Aga Khan and His Development Network (AKDN).[2]

Kyrgyzstan

I cannot speak personally about Kyrgyzstan. However, writing about the secondary education in Kyrgyzstan, Karim (2003) says that there are acute problems in the rural areas. She says: 'Schools in remote villages desperately lack teachers of English and Russian. There are cases when people without proper qualification have been teaching some subjects. As a result the quality of secondary education is suffering greatly.' She also says that the secondary education system in Kyrgyzstan has the same problems as the other former Soviet Union republics particularly the lack of and high price of the textbooks. As a result, the situation of the schools in the rural areas is very bad. 'Most of the people do not have access to books and even if they do, not all of them can afford to buy them.'

Educational reform in Kyrgyzstan aims to change the economic organization in education. It talks about the establishment of a variety of education facilities at all levels, democratization of the education system, and introducing new technologies. According to Jusenbaev and Ryskulueva (2002), since 1991 the republic of Kyrgyzstan has started drastic, social, political and economic reforms. In 1992 the law of the republic of Kyrgyzstan called 'On Education' was adopted. This document determines the state education policy and the main principles of managing and functioning of the system of education to be implemented in the republic. It is associated with a set of comprehensive measures aiming to change radically its economic organization, institutional structure and content. According to different sources, there has been constant growth in the number of schools and the number of children enrolled and teachers in Kyrgyzstan have more opportunities for professional development and school improvement now than they had in the Soviet era. There are many Professional Development Institutions in Osh such as the Institute for Professional Development, Osh State University, foreign organizations and non-governmental organizations (NGOs) which support teacher education. Despite these institutions the area still lacks qualified teachers.

Impact of AKU-IED on the Education System of Central Asia

This section will highlight the impact of the Aga Khan University Institute for Educational Development (AKU-IED) on the professional development of teachers and the overall improvement of schools in Tajikistan and Kyrgyzstan. AKU-IED's impact in Tajikistan started from 1994 and in Kyrgyzstan from 1996. These are the years when the first students joined

AKU-IED to do their Masters in Education (M.Ed.). Since then a number of teachers have had the opportunity to do their M.Ed. and get the qualification of Professional Development Teacher (PDT) from the AKU-IED. Also, a large number of the teachers from these countries attended two-month courses of the Visiting Teacher Programme (VTP). Table III shows the number of M.Ed. and VTP graduates from Tajikistan and Kyrgyzstan participating in the courses run by the AKU-IED.

Year	Tajikistan		Kyrgyzstan		Total per year
	M.Ed. graduates	VTP graduates	M.Ed. graduates	VTP graduates	
1995	1				1
1998	2	5	1	4	12
1999	2	9	2	3	16
2000	2	11	1	6	20
2002	2	7	3	5	17
2003	3		2		5
2004	3		1		4
2005	2		1		3
Total	17	32	11	18	78

Table III. M.Ed. and VTP graduates from Tajikistan and Kyrgyzstan participating in the courses run by the AKU-IED.

Five PDTs from Tajikistan and three from Kyrgyzstan have left the areas to which they had returned after graduation to take up jobs with another institution within the country or another outside the country. All the other PDTs are working in their respective areas. This study will talk about their achievements and problems later.

AKU-IED prepares all the graduates academically and with the work skills required to return to their areas. PDTs are very good in administration, in the practicalities of designing and delivering workshops on teaching methodology and improvement of content knowledge. Out of the 21 graduates of the M.Ed., 13 have remained within the education system of the two countries; 7 in Tajikistan and 6 in Kyrgyzstan. By 2006, 7 more PDTs from the two countries will return after graduation. These PDTs along with the VTP graduates (all of whom have returned to their schools) have returned confident and better equipped to take leadership roles in their respective areas. They are very confident; they have good knowledge in pedagogy and methodology and have the potential to bring changes in the educational system of the area. The PDTs aim to support the education systems providing models of teaching, education and development by conducting workshops and seminars for the teachers and other school staff. They are considered as exemplars of practice, builders of knowledge and sources for communicating professional understanding amongst the teacher educators, and experienced and non-experienced teachers.

PDTs in Khorog and Osh

The Aga Khan Education Service (AKES) Tajikistan [3] opened the first private Aga Khan Lycée (AKL) in Khorog in 1998. The first two PDTs upon their graduation from IED joined AKES and started working at the Aga Khan Lycée, presently considered as the best school in Tajikistan, as classroom teachers and school-based teacher educators. They worked closely with teachers conducting content, methodology and English learning proficiency courses. Later one of the PDTs worked as a manager of the newly developed Learning Resource Centre of the school. This PDT developed and organized training courses on methodology and English proficiency for the primary and secondary schoolteachers; prepared teachers for the Visiting Teacher (VT) courses at AKU-IED and for English proficiency courses at the American University in Bishkek, Kyrgyzstan. The other PDT rejoined his position at the Kharog State University and developed and conducted methodology and English proficiency courses for the teachers and university students (years 4-5).

Today there are three PDTs at AKL and two at the Institute for Professional Development (IPD) in Khorog. The three PDTs at AKL have been asked by the AKES and the Ministry to lead the development and modification of curriculum for all subjects to be taught at the Lycée, especially for the newly opened English medium classes in the primary and secondary sections of the school and for the lower secondary school classes. They involved teachers in material development for the new curriculum thus creating ownership of the new curriculum among them. The PDTs also develop and offer ongoing school-based professional opportunities for the AKES teachers. Sessions of two to three hours are conducted after classes four times a week, with a focus on primary methodology twice a week and on science and English once a week. Also, throughout the year, PDTs continue to do classroom observations, demonstration lessons and presentations. Similar inputs are made in the secondary schools for all subject areas. Attendance in these professional development activities is part of the teachers' contract and PDTs and head teachers are involved in performance appraisal. However, there are many difficulties also since it makes too much work for teachers after they are already tired after taking all their classes.

PTDs are involved in other initiatives as well. AKES, in partnership with AKF and government, has started a new educational development project called the Allied School Project. Some selected government schools are targeted for provision of resources, teacher training and repairs. The teachers come to AKL from the districts, observe the classes, attend workshops and short courses and return to their schools to apply their learning in the classrooms. The PDTs facilitate teachers through observations, workshops and courses, and teaching them to prepare low cost or no cost materials.

The PDTs also work at the Institute for Professional Development (IPD) which is a government institution. According to the deputy director (DD) of the IPD, the PDTs, along with the VTP graduates from the Primary section of AKL, developed and conducted some training sessions in teaching primary English and mathematics. They also conduct training in content knowledge and pedagogy for primary and secondary teachers of different subjects from the government school. IPD has a Mobile Training Resource Centre (MTRC) and its workshop leader is one of the PDTs. With the MTRC, the PDT and her team go to villages and conduct teachers' development courses. An oral report of the other DD, at IPD, suggests that this PDT has been very successful in designing and implementing this IPD project in almost all of the districts of MBAR. This PDT also delivers seminars for the certified and uncertified English teachers to improve their language proficiency and knowledge of methodology. The DD also said that monitoring of the project showed that the PDT had made considerable impact on the teachers in planning and conducting the lessons; in preparing resources, and in their relationship with the students. Student results have also improved since the MTRC initiative. The IPD annual report on education says that the most important and successful result achieved in education is the encouragement and increased motivation of the students. MTRC also succeeded in bringing in the school parents' committees [4], through allowing community members to borrow books and other resources and building trust through the regular contact. Along with the other trainers, the PDTs at IPD are preparing reading materials such as story books for the primary students. These books are very colourful and they are in three languages: Tajik (national), Shugnani (local) and English. The purpose for developing such books is to motivate students to read and to improve their language skills.

The PDTs in Osh Kyrgyzstan are also trying hard to achieve educational improvement. One of the PDTs from Kyrgyzstan reflecting upon his experience during our informal meeting said that while he was working with the AKES in Osh, he was responsible for planning and organizing professional development courses for the Aga Khan School (AKS) staff. During these courses they used the expertise of all the PDTs and VTP graduates. Their focus was on lesson planning, learning styles and critical thinking. These PDTs have conducted professional development workshops for Government schools in Osh as well. Another PDT said that she was working with the teachers in the area of methodology, trying to teach them child-centred learning approaches and also facilitating the AKS teachers in their everyday teaching practice.

These PDTs have developed a curriculum for all subjects taught at AKS. Some of the PDTs are working with the students and teachers at the Osh State University. They are bringing new methods, techniques and approaches to their classes; teaching the teachers and the students how to do research. Talking about their experiences the PDTs feel that IED has not only developed their content knowledge or methodology but it has changed their attitude towards the teaching/learning process and their behaviour towards their colleagues and students. They have became more open to sharing and have contributed to the change in the teacher culture of isolation.

One of the VTP graduates with whom I worked wrote in her reflection,

> IED was a high mount I climbed. Before IED I thought that I was a very good teacher and I was always trying to be isolated from the others. I was jealous if any other teachers' performance was better then me. After IED I came back totally changed not only because I improved my knowledge of pedagogy and methodology, but my attitude and behaviour towards my colleagues, my students and everyone around me. I became more sociable, confident and supportive to them.

This reflection shows that IED has helped its graduates develop subject knowledge and teaching methodology as well as social attitudes. These graduates as PDTs and visiting teachers have in turn attempted, often successfully, to help other teachers in the system develop more collegial relations with each other and improve their knowledge of the content and the methodology of teaching primary and secondary classes. They have worked particularly in the area of development of the teaching of English in the AKES schools. They have also begun, in a small way, to influence the teachers' professional development structures and culture and the curriculum.

Shortcomings

Despite the many achievements, noted above, there are still many areas where improvement is needed.

- Along with the successes, the PDTs face many challenges as well. Today the PDTs are doing a lot for professional development and school improvement, but they are spread out and therefore their work is not very visible.
- The PDTs are working with AKES at AKL, at IPD and at AKF, sometimes duplicating their efforts and not learning from each others' work. For example, the PDT at AKL has developed a curriculum for English language instruction for the primary classes, taking into consideration students' age level, the culture, content, context of the school and meeting all the requirements of the Concept of National Schools document in developing curricula and teaching resources. The AKL PDT worked very closely with the teachers and the students, conducting experimental model teaching and introducing the curriculum through a team teaching approach. To apply this

145

curriculum in the class for her students the PDT has done a small-scale study on 'How the curriculum works in the classroom. What changes do we need to make?' The commission of the Ministry for Education has approved this curriculum as well. Unfortunately, the PDTs at IPD have also started their work on the same thing without referring to the work already done. They could work with the already prepared curriculum and add something extra to it. Unfortunately they have spent a lot of time in duplicating the effort. This kind of duplication is happening a lot with the training material on methodology and pedagogy and development courses as well.

- The PDTs in the area are not able to support each other because they are overloaded and cannot get together and share their success or problems. They do not have time to go and observe each other while conducting workshops or seminars and to learn something more from each other. According to them, they are bound to their respective areas. Working in different institutions, although very close to each other in terms of distance in buildings, they feel isolated. At one of my meetings with the PDTs they said, 'The administration wants us to share with the other PDTs our experience but we are not able to do it. We do not get time during the day to visit and talk to other PDTs or observe what and how they are doing.'

- There is only a little support from the administration of the institutions the PDTs work in or from AKU-IED in further development of the PDTs. They rarely attend seminars, conferences or other courses. Sometimes the PDTs feel lonely and they give up. Working for three to four years with the same group of teachers, one PDT feels that 'the jar of knowledge and experience is empty.' Reflecting on her experience she adds,

for more then three years I was working with the same group of the primary school teachers in the areas of pedagogy, methods of teaching, child centred learning approach, curriculum, syllabus, lesson plan development, development and use of the no-cost, low cost recourses/authentic material etc. I conducted an English proficiency course for the same teachers. After my courses almost 85% of the teachers have attended VTP in Karachi and training courses in Bishkek Kyrgyzstan. To work with the same group was not more exciting and challenging for me after that. I had a feeling that the jar of knowledge and experience I had is getting empty but there were no opportunities for me to fill it again. Thanks to IED I was very confident in taking part in the English teachers' competition organized by the American Councils and won a scholarship to attend the three month development course in US. After I came I thought my jar is again full although there was nothing new for me at the sessions. But these sessions made me recall the knowledge that I have lost somewhere back in my mind.

Also just talking to teachers from different parts of the world one can learn a lot.

Another PDT during an informal discussion with me shared:

We know that our colleagues from the other countries are getting the chance to attend School Improvement Programmes (SIP) conferences; they conduct development courses in the neighbour countries and the same way they develop their knowledge. Unfortunately we have none of these opportunities.

- The M.Ed. graduates are playing an important role in the work towards improving the classroom teaching practice of teachers. The PDTs are the only people with the M.Ed. degree in the education institutions but neither the heads of the government education offices nor the administration of the institutions they work with pay enough attention to this.
- The PDTs work from 8 in the morning to 5 or 6 in the evening in their workplaces (the other employees work from 8 to 5) if they are not conducting courses. During courses they stay up to 8-9 at night. They have only one day off during the week. This is the only day they can be with their families and do something for the family. In addition their salary is very low which creates problems for them in their families. This is one reason several PDTs have left the education system for a better salary elsewhere.
- The PDTs working in the institutions do not get any leadership role (department leader) even though they have M.Ed. qualification. They get frustrated when a person with no such qualifications or even knowledge and experience leads them. This is another reason why they leave education.
- The PDTs who left their workplaces also say that nobody is interested in what they want to do or recognize the value of a M.Ed. or a PDT. Sharing his experiences during informal talk a PDT said that he wanted to be involved in research projects on professional development activities but the possibilities were zero, because the administration was not interested in this. The same PDT, talking about the salary, said that people with less experience and with no Master's degree were getting more salary than him. He concluded that 'The PDTs are also human beings and they need some intrinsic motivation as well. But the administration expects everything in the area of development from them, without any support.'

Recommendations for Improvement

- A meeting between a team of AKU-IED faculty members with government administrators and government authorities held in Khorog in the summer of 2002 helped immensely to change local perceptions and develop more understanding about AKU-IED's activities and about its graduates, both PDTs and the VTs. More such meetings are needed.
- We always talk of sustainability of professional development and of professional development as a continuing process. As mentioned earlier, the graduates from AKU-IED do not get enough opportunity to interact with the professionals within or outside Central Asia. There is a need for organizing meetings, seminars or conferences, or follow-up courses in the country or region as well as making it possible for the PDTs to attend such occasions outside the region.
- M.Ed. students should work together. This may become possible with the establishment of a Professional Development Centre in Khorog or establishing a team of PDTs at IPD.
- M.Ed. graduates need support in improving their economic conditions. Also these graduates have a very busy workload and almost no time for the family. Some of the M.Ed. graduates are living in rented houses and pay a lot of rent. The low salary packages are very significant in reducing the PDTs' motivation.
- M.Ed. graduates must have time and encouragement to do research on their own practice and on classroom teaching/learning processes. This is an important activity to learn and improve one's work. Not being able to do research will result in no learning for the PDTs and consequently for teachers they work with.

Notes

[1] The Aga Khan Foundation (AKF) is a non-denominational, international development agency established in 1967 by His Highness the Aga Khan. Its mission is to develop and promote creative solutions to problems that impede social development, primarily in Asia and East Africa. AKF is one of the departments of AKDN and was created as a private, non-profit foundation under Swiss law.

[2] Aga Khan Development Network (AKDN) is a group of development agencies working in health, education, culture and rural and economic development, primarily in Asia and Africa.

[3] The Aga Khan Education Service (AKES) Tajikistan is a private non-profit organization, a part of the Aga Khan Development Network (AKDN). It manages and supports many development projects around the world. AKES manages over 300 schools in the world. More than 50,000 students are enrolled in these schools in Pakistan, India, Kenya, Tanzania, Uganda and Bangladesh.

[4] The schools in MBAR have parents' committees. These committees support the schools in building a close relationship with the community through meetings, informal gatherings, and so forth.

References

Abdushukurova, T. (2002) Higher Technical Education in Tajikistan: Experience and Development Trends. Unpublished report, The Osimi Tajik Technical University. OSI Assistance Foundation –Tajikistan.

Aga Khan IV (1998) *Speech at the Opening Ceremony of the Aga Khan Lycée.* Khorog Tajikistan website. Available at: www.ismaili.net/timeline/98.html

Bruker, N. (2002) Secondary School: to perish or to be reborn? ASIA-Plus Information Agency (Dushanbe, Tajikistan). Available at: www.asaplus.tajnet.com

Case, F. (2002) Canadian Expertise Makes the Difference, *The Globe and Mail.* Available at: www.worldpartnershipwalk.com

Country Guide. The Times of Central Asia. Available at: www.times.kg/tajikistan/?pub.html

Encyclopedia: Tajikistan. Available at: www.infoplease.com/ce6/world/A0847665.html

Ismailova, L. (2000) A New School Year Started, *News in Brief. Asia Plus Information Agency* # 167(580). Available at: www.interviews.ru?Asia- PLUS/blitz/580.html

Jusenbaev, S. & Ryskulueva, F. (2002) *National Report. Higher Education in the Republic of Kyrgyzstan: current status and prospects.* Available at: www.unesco.k7/education/he/Kyrgyz/moec_kg_eng.html

Karim, G. (2003) Problems of Secondary School Education in Kyrgyzstan, *Central Asia-Caucasus Analyst.* Available at: www.cacianalyst.org/view-article.php?articled=1107

Kyrgyzstan Development Gateway. Available at: http://eng.gateway.kg/

Niyozov, S. (2001) Education in Tajikistan: a window to understanding change through continuity. Unpublished PhD dissertation, Ontario Institute for Studies in Education, University of Toronto.

Rashidov, A. (2000) *Education System in Tajikistan.* Country report. Available at: www2.unesco.org/wef/countryrepotrs/tajikistan/contents.html

CHAPTER 9

Developing Leadership and Management Capacity for School Improvement

MUHAMMAD MEMON, TIM SIMKINS, CHARLES SISUM & ZUBEDA BANA

I always felt that the majority of us are normally thrown into the field either by chance or circumstances ... we enter into our professional lives with hardly any relevant education, professional qualifications, and in some cases, even without basic skills. We are expected to learn along the way ... pedagogical leadership qualities are to be acquired through rigorous practice, not by scientific formulae ... like the artists, the head teachers must learn the habits of highly effective people, base their leadership on sound principles, and work ceaselessly to improve their art ... they have to acquire knowledge and practice, negotiate with the context and respond to day-to-day challenges of the school management affairs. (Quote from a head teacher's valedictory speech during graduation ceremony)

Context and Background

The quotation above comes from a school head teacher who had participated in an Advanced Diploma programme at the Institute for Educational Development at the Aga Khan University (AKU-IED) in Karachi, Pakistan. This chapter focuses on issues of leadership and management capacity for school improvement in Pakistan and beyond, through what has been learned from research and development at AKU-IED in cooperation with schools, both in Pakistan and in other areas of the developing world. It draws particularly on the experiences of the Advanced Diploma in Educational Leadership and Management and two research studies conducted jointly by faculty of AKU-IED and Sheffield Hallam University to understand the role of head teachers in secondary schools in Karachi. Where not otherwise stated, observations and claims arise from experience and findings of research studies, details of which will be provided later in the chapter.

The organizational and management structure of the education system in Pakistan varies from province to province. The majority of primary schools in the public sector do not have established head teacher positions because of financial constraints and their small size. Senior primary schoolteachers are designated as head teachers by providing them with some special allowance. However, they tend to focus more on their academic than management roles. Experience and observation suggest that they find it hard to maintain a balance between their academic and management roles due to a lack of role clarity and of adequate professional development. Secondary schools, similarly, are mainly managed by head teachers who are promoted on a seniority basis from among teachers, although a small number of head teachers are appointed through direct recruitment by the provincial Public Service Commission. The newly recruited head teachers in the public sector have neither management training nor experience of managing schools effectively. In contrast, the private sector mainly recruits its head teachers on merit rather than seniority, although the majority of them also do not have relevant management experience and training. Unlike primary school head teachers, secondary head teachers in the public sector tend to focus on management rather than academic aspects of their role, and this can also lead to an imbalance between their academic and management roles. The majority of head teachers, primary or secondary, in public or private sector, are deployed without any kind of induction or orientation. Thus, they only learn 'tricks of the trade' on-the-job through 'trial and error' methods to manage their schools. This has made them good 'fixers' rather than good 'problem solvers'. Moreover, the prevalent centralized and hierarchical education system does not allow them to go beyond the maintenance, compliance and conformity functions of their role. The head teacher quoted above acknowledges this situation.

Endorsing this analysis of the inadequacies of the school system's administrative and managerial capacity, the National Education Policy of Pakistan (Government of Pakistan, 1992) indicated, 'Substantial changes are required to be made in the administration of education to improve the efficiency of the systems' (p. 60). In the spirit of this statement, and realizing the importance of the role of educational leadership in managing schools effectively, successive governments of Pakistan have initiated a series of education reforms. However, no major breakthrough is evident for developing leadership and management capacity to improve the quality of education.

The Response of the AKU-IED

The AKU-IED was established with a mission to become and remain a leader in educational reform and improvement aimed at increasing the efficiency and effectiveness of schools and other educational institutions especially in developing countries (see Chapter 1 in this volume). Hence, AKU-IED is committed to building the leadership and management capacity of public and private school systems (including Aga Khan Development Network [AKDN]), through human resource development. In order to achieve this, the AKU-IED initiated a number of professional development programmes ranging from two months to two years in the area of teacher education and educational leadership and management. These programmes evolved as a result of the acknowledged needs of stakeholders including teachers, head teachers, and education officers/inspectors in Pakistan, Bangladesh, Kenya, Uganda and Tanzania, including Zanzibar. Research suggests that schools are unlikely to be successful in implementing changes effectively until key players have a shared vision about school improvement. The overall purpose of these programmes, therefore, is to promote a culture of pedagogical leadership, which invests in capacity building by developing social and academic capital for students, and intellectual and professional capital for teachers (Sergiovanni, 1998). He further suggests that: 'Pedagogical leadership develops human capital by helping schools become caring, focused, and inquiring communities within which teachers work together as members of a community of practice' (p. 37).

In order to develop schools as 'learning communities' or 'communities of practice', the AKU-IED offers the following programmes:

1. Master in Education – M.Ed. (Teacher Education) Programme. This is a two-year programme aiming at developing participants as exemplary teachers, teacher educators and effective researchers. The programme is offered to serving schoolteachers from public and private (including AKDN) sectors. The first programme was offered in 1994. On completion of the programme, graduates work with colleagues in their respective schools as Professional Development Teachers (PDTs). (See Chapter 3 in this volume.)

2. Certificate in Education (formerly known as a Visiting Teacher) Programme. This is a two-month long programme (240 contact hours) offered to serving schoolteachers from the above systems for improving their content knowledge and pedagogical approaches, including classroom management skills. The first programme was offered in 1995. This programme is developed and delivered by PDTs, which is one of the significant features of the programme. (See Chapter 5 in this volume.)

3. Advanced Diploma in Education (formerly known as Advanced Diploma in Subject Specialist Teaching) Programme. This is a one-year field-based programme (400 contact hours) offered to schoolteachers from the above systems who have acquired a Certificate in Education. The first

programme was offered in 1998. The purpose of this programme is to enhance teachers' pedagogical content knowledge and action research skills for becoming effective classroom practitioners.

4. Advanced Diploma in Education: Educational Leadership and Management (formerly known as an Advanced Diploma in School Management [ADISM]) Programme. This is a one-year field-based modular programme (400 contact hours) offered to serving and aspiring head teachers from public and private (including AKDN) schools. The first programme was offered in 1997. The purpose of the programme was to develop serving and aspiring head teachers as pedagogical leaders for enhancing the quality of education in schools.

5. Certificate in Education: Educational Leadership and Management (formerly known as a Certificate in Educational Management) Programme. This is a ten-week field-based programme (300 contact hours) offered to education inspectors, officers, serving and aspiring head teachers in and outside Pakistan. The purpose of the programme was to enable the participants to become effective pedagogical leaders for working with teachers on their professional development on-the-job.

All these programmes are considered to be important in their nature and purpose since they have contributed towards building individual and institutional capacity. However, the Advanced Diploma in Educational Leadership and Management programme, being longest in duration, is of special significance in creating leadership at the school level. AKU-IED's mission statement highlights explicitly the importance of pursuing effective school leadership and management by raising the level of competence of head teachers and other key school decision-makers. Effective head teachers do not just need technical skills; they should acquire emotional, intellectual, professional and managerial skills to manage their schools effectively. Therefore, professional development becomes paramount in developing head teachers in order to meet the increasing demands of their role.

Before discussing the evolution of the programmes in educational leadership and management, we will outline some of the issues that these programmes have been designed to address as indicated in existing literature from developed and developing worlds.

The Need for Building Leadership and Management Capacity through Professional Development Programmes

Literature on school improvement suggests that educational leadership plays a vital role in making education reforms successful. For example, de Grauwe (2000) argues that:

> Much research has demonstrated that the quality of education depends primarily on the way schools are managed, more than on the abundance of available resources, and that the capacity of

schools to improve teaching and learning is strongly influenced by
the quality of leadership provided by the head teacher. (p. 1)

Fullan (2001) considers capacity building to be an integral part of school improvement initiatives: without it, in his view, the desired results will not be achieved. Taking this notion further, Harris (2001) maintains that 'Capacity building is concerned with creating the conditions, opportunities and experiences for collaboration and mutual learning' (p. 261). Thus schools may not be able to improve until an adequate capacity is developed through collaboration and cooperation. Juma and Waudo (1999) suggest that institutionalization of learning and capacity building would not take place until the head teachers are trained.

School leadership and capacity building are not mutually exclusive. Hence, it becomes essential that the education system should promote school leadership by providing relevant exposure and professional development provision; otherwise the quality of education will not improve. Lack of education leadership in Pakistan seems to be one of the major contributing factors affecting the quality of education. Hoodbhoy (1998) indicates that the present education system is affected by the lack of sound management, leadership and governance principles. Memon (2000) argues that without effective school leadership schools would not become effective. This suggests a need for building leadership and management capacity in schools.

Consequently, professional development programmes for practising and aspiring head teachers are a growing feature of school systems in many developed and developing countries (Teacher Training Agency, 1998; Memon 2000; Hallinger, 2001; Tin, 2001; Wenchang & Daming, 2001; Wong, 2001). Preparing head teachers through developing their skills, competence, knowledge and attitudes for institutional capacity building will help them to move beyond 'perfunctory management functions' to the level of an effective school leadership. Ramsey (1999) reminds us that school leadership requires certain special abilities and that, while preparing programmes for improving school leadership, approaches should be developed enabling head teachers to become effective problem solvers and decision-makers. He maintains, further, that 'Good leaders routinely think ahead; plan in advance; try to forecast developments; play out possible, probable, and preferable scenarios in their minds; figure out where current conditions are leading; and anticipate how people may react to alternative courses of action' (p. 123).

Virtually all the available literature on school effectiveness and school improvement is drawn from the experience of developed countries and emphasizes the role of leadership, particularly that of the principal in achieving, maintaining and improving school quality. It proposes various models of leadership, but has been strongly influenced by more than 20 years' work on 'transformational leadership' (Leithwood et al, 1996) which places a strong emphasis on the role of leader in setting a vision for the school, typically focused around improved teaching and learning, and effectively inspiring and stimulating others in a commitment to the pursuit of this vision. Some international studies outside education have suggested that transformational qualities are seen as key aspects of 'good' leadership in most cultural contexts (den Hartog et al, 1999). In other words, unlike some other styles of leadership, they are not culture-specific. However, approaches to leadership that overemphasize the role of inspirational leaders are increasingly being challenged in the literature by models which emphasize more invitational and dispersed models of leadership (Stoll & Fink, 1996; Gronn, 1999). Furthermore, a number of writers about the education system of Pakistan and other developing countries have expressed considerable doubts about the degree to which head teachers either do, or might be expected to, act effectively as leaders in their schools (Ali et al, 1993; Warwick & Reimers, 1995; Memon, 1998). The reasons for this are various. One lies in the highly bureaucratic and hierarchical structures and rules which govern most school systems, especially those in the public sector. Another relates to the limited professional development and socialization experienced by most teachers and, indeed, by many head teachers. Yet another is associated with national cultures which may encourage dependency, autocratic management styles and aversion to risk (Hofstede, 1980, 1991).

Professional development programmes for school leaders and managers, we suggest, need to take account of the findings of research on school improvement, but they also need to recognize the importance of context and consider how far findings and recommendations which have emerged from research largely undertaken in developed countries can be translated to the very different historical, cultural and economic contexts of developing countries. This requires a thorough understanding of how head teachers and others behave in these different contexts, the reasons for this behaviour, and whether such translation is appropriate for all sorts of reasons, including ethics, western hegemony, and so on.

Developing Programmes in Leadership at the AKU-IED

Keeping in view the centrality of the role of head teachers in managing schools effectively, the AKU-IED started by conducting a series of monthly workshops for serving head teachers to develop their management and leadership skills and competence for improving schools. This led to the development of a tailor-made Advanced Diploma in Educational Leadership and Management programme. A programme development committee was formed, consisting of serving head teachers from public and private school systems including the Aga Khan Education Service, Pakistan, AKES, P along with AKU-IED faculty. The committee assessed the professional development needs of head teachers. The programme was delivered with the assistance of Sheffield Hallam University in the United Kingdom through two Higher Education Link Programmes funded by the United Kingdom

Department for International Development (DFID) and managed by the British Council, Karachi. The overall aim of the programme is to develop head teachers as 'pedagogical leaders'. The programme should contribute towards building leadership and management capacity for improving schools. The programme has the following major objectives for head teacher participants:

1. develop their analytical skills to reflect on their current roles and responsibilities in relation to effective leadership practices;
2. develop their understanding of their role as pedagogical leaders;
3. understand the use of information and communications technology as a tool for school improvement;
4. develop understanding about the dynamics of school effectiveness and improvement and the implications for overall school development;
5. develop skills and competencies for conducting action research for improving educational processes;
6. understand the notion of mentoring and develop their mentoring skills to work with staff in their respective schools;
7. understand the relevance and dynamics of school-community partnerships for making the school effective;
8. understand the notion of monitoring and develop skills related to performance indictors; and
9. develop a framework for school development plans based on the felt needs and future demands for their improvement of school performance.

Serving and aspiring head teachers of public and private school systems participate in the programme. A majority of the participants are female. The course participants are selected through rigorous admission process. This includes short-listing of candidates based on the selection criteria approved by AKU's Board of Graduate Studies followed by interview and writing reflections on the given management scenario.

The programme comprises 10 modules of 400 contact hours, of which 112 contact hours are assigned to a school-based practicum guided by the faculty during field visits. The programme has a flexible schedule; five modules are covered during the summer and winter vacations and the remaining five modules are offered through weekend sessions. Details of the modules are as follows:

- Reconceptualizing roles and responsibilities.
- Using information and communications technology.
- Conducting action research for school improvement.
- Developing pedagogical leadership.
- Developing effective leadership and management practices.
- Understanding professional development.
- Developing mentoring skills.
- Managing school community relationships.
- Monitoring and evaluating school performance.

- Developing action plans for school improvement.

Some Salient Features of the AKU-IED Programme in Educational Leadership and Management

As mentioned earlier, this programme is significant in the way that it deals with a group of professionals who are directly responsible for improving the quality of education in schools. This programme is linked to AKU-IED's other programmes in the area of teacher education and educational leadership that serve as a source of synergy for developing a 'critical mass' through creating the cultures of 'collaboration' and 'cooperation' required for capacity building (see Figure 5).

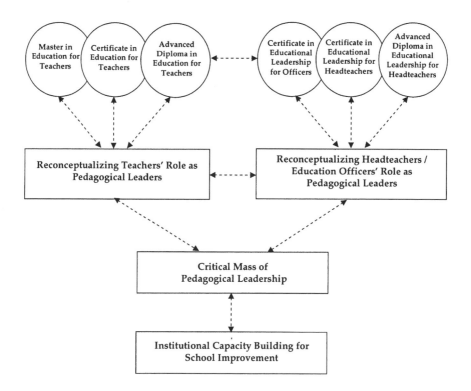

Figure 5. Capacity building through interlinked professional development programmes.

The overall aim of these programmes is to promote pedagogical leadership through developing shared understanding of school improvement strategies among the key players such as Board of Governors, parents, teachers and others who can contribute towards creating a 'critical mass' for managing change effectively in schools. One of the common features of these programmes is to develop critical thinking skills through reconceptualization of participants' roles as effective pedagogical leaders.

Particular features of the programme for head teachers are:

1. Course participants are provided with ample opportunities to unpack their management practices based on routines. Reconceptualization enables participants to examine their existing notions and practices of leadership and management and explore alternatives for enhancing their effectiveness as pedagogical leaders (see Memon, 2000).

2. Case studies, action learning, role-play, brainstorming, cooperative learning and group discussion are used as major instructional strategies in order to facilitate the course participants' learning.

3. Each module has a number of independent learning sessions in which the course participants are expected to discuss selected articles from the literature on educational leadership (for example, Bennis, 1989; Covey, 1990; Bolman & Deal, 1992; Goleman, 1995; Fullan, 1997; Sergiovanni, 1998; Leithwood, 1999; Memon, 2000; Fink & Resnik, 2001) and school improvement (for example, Barth, 1990; Fullan, 1997; Stoll & Fink, 1997; Harris, 2001) in their action learning sets. The readings are provided to them on day one of the programme. They are encouraged to make the best use of the library, computer and internet facilities. During independent learning time, participants are expected to meet and discuss their learning with their assigned tutors.

4. Course participants discuss issues related to school leadership and management practices in groups across the school systems and explore alternatives to improve these practices.

5. The programme has an in-built field-based component through which each participant is visited and shadowed at least three times by one faculty member during the programme to provide feedback for institutionalization of their professional learning.

6. The participants maintain reflective journals as a part of their programme requirement and share these with the tutors from time to time in order to seek feedback on day-to-day issues emerging in their schools. The reflective process of writing also helps them to seek alternatives in order to resolve their issues successfully and create a better management scenario in their schools.

7. The participants are expected to visit at least two school systems of their peers and learn from each other's experiences.

8. After completion of the programme, faculty members carry out school visits in order to check progress made by the participants in their personal and school improvement plans, developed as part of the final module. Here, faculty and participants engage informally in reflective discussions.

9. The faculty member plays a vital role as a 'critical friend' by providing constructive feedback to the participants. This has been considered as one of the main strengths of the programme as the participants feel that it

helps them to get professional support and guidance on-the-job in the application of new professional knowledge and skills.

All modules in the programme include a formal evaluation procedure.

The Associated Research Studies

The first piece of research involved an in-depth study of the roles of six Government and non-Government school head teachers using initial and follow-up interviews and the completion and analysis of diaries describing the demands, choices and constraints experienced in their roles (Simkins et al, 1998). This study identified three key sets of relationships which frame the ways in which head teachers have to manage schools. These are: relationships with their governors, including trustees or government education officers; relationships with parents, students and the community; and relationships with employees, especially teachers. We concluded that differences in the contexts in which head teachers work have significant effects on how they play their roles. In particular, those working in the Government school system (the majority of schools) and in the non-Government school system (operated both by trusts and by private boards) tended to respond in different ways to their differing contexts:

- Government head teachers worked within a governance regime dominated by relatively bureaucratic rules and structures whereas non-Government head teachers were subject primarily to the direct and personal influence of trustees and system managers.
- Government head teachers managed their teaching staff through direct supervision exercised through face-to-face contact and tours of the school. Non-Government head teachers, in contrast, operated delegated management through systems of middle managers and meetings with these.
- Government head teachers tended to see themselves as 'super-ordinates' and consider teachers as 'subordinates' whereas non-Government head teachers consider their teachers as colleagues and work with them for their professional development.
- Government head teachers tended to see the influence of parents as an interruption or a threat whereas non-Government head teachers saw parents positively as clients to be served.

These findings can be linked to differences in the ways in which Government and non-Government school head teachers manage their schools. In particular, Government school head teachers saw themselves as having considerably less freedom than did non-Government school head teachers to manage key aspects of their role related to curriculum, staffing, and relationships with parents and students. In part this arose from real differences in powers – for example, Government head teachers have no powers to appoint or dismiss staff and cannot create management structures differentiated by salary.

The second research study followed three graduates of the programme, using three interviews undertaken over a period of 12 months from their graduation to explore their experiences of attempting to implement change (Simkins et al, 2001; Simkins, Sisum & Memon, 2003). The study enabled us to explore in more detail how head teachers' personal efficacy is affected by the interplay between expectations generated by the national culture of Pakistan, the powers and accountabilities placed on heads by the school system within which they work and their own individual personalities and life histories.

These studies enabled us to gain an understanding of secondary headship in general as well as the interplay between these head teachers' roles and their experience of professional development provided for them by AKU-IED. This research data was further complemented by internal evaluations of the programme and by our own personal experience of working with the participants. Research findings suggest that national culture as an important variable has influenced leadership behaviour which is mediated by system and personal factors.

Impact of the Educational Leadership Programme on Developing Leadership and Management Capacity Building

Information gathered during visits made by faculty to all participants' schools throughout the programme, surveys conducted within the final module on school development planning and follow-up of the programme suggests a major shift in participants' thinking, attitude, behaviour and practice.

The majority of the graduates have introduced school-based professional development programmes to create a culture of community of practice. As one of the participants said;

> In fact, I kept trying to penetrate my previous limited notions on 'my role'. This showed how much ignorant I was to the task that was mine ... I had never conceptualised or seen my role as a head. Indeed I have lost the use of valuable time in many aspects ... I feel that I have played the 'informational leader' role, as I have merely been passing information to others, and that too in a manner not satisfying my conscience. (Quote from reflective journal of female head teacher from non-Government school)

Working with parents, staff, trustees and students to develop or revise school vision and mission statements has become common practice of Advanced Diploma graduates in Government and non-Government schools alike. A minority of head teachers also spoke enthusiastically about their team working with the PDTs and other AKU-IED graduates. Many head teachers have either started or improved their monitoring of teaching and learning in classrooms and giving feedback to teachers. It is evident from the school visits, that the head teachers now emphasize what makes a good lesson from the point of view of the learner, including the importance of clear lesson objectives, pace in lesson delivery, differentiation of tasks to match students' intellectual capabilities and acknowledgement of a variety of learning styles and student motivation. It is also evident that a majority of the participants have started working as pedagogical leaders. One participant, in her reflective journal, mentioned that

> A pedagogical leader is one who develops the students and teachers to empower and enhance their performance. I must be concerned with the social and academic benefit of my students and the intellectual and professional capacity of the teachers. I must try my level best to inculcate the habit of 'questioning'. We must have a quest for inquiry. To become a true pedagogical leader one needs to travel a long road. (Quote from reflective journal of female head teacher from non-Government school)

The development of more effective middle managers, particularly in their team leadership roles, has been the development target for some head teachers. Some schools have a sharper and more defined approach to school planning. There are signs of the head teachers developing their coaching and mentoring roles with staff. Production and management of improved learning resources has been a focus for others. For example one participant said:

> I began to realize how much time I have wasted in operational details which is nothing but a part of administration. I give topmost priority to the planning, organizing, execution, monitoring and evaluation. I feel that, as a pedagogical leader, I need to have vision, mission, commitment and insight into my role. (Quote from reflective journal of female head teacher from Government school)

During the programme follow-up visits by faculty, many head teachers from both Government and non-Government schools expressed the view that they had gained personally and professionally from the programme. Furthermore, many had attempted to introduce some changes in their schools to reflect the improvement agenda to which they had been introduced. However, there is considerable evidence that the ability of participants to translate management and leadership learning into sustained changes in practice in their schools was seen as heavily constrained by the contexts in which they worked. For example, one participant from a Government school told us, 'Actually I am free to do what I want, providing I do not go against the rule. The future development of this school is 100% my will', thus displaying at one and the same time both his sense of professional autonomy and self-belief to run his school as he wants but also understanding that there were limits imposed by his own and others' views of his role within a professional context.

During the programme we observed a practice of working together on common themes, sometimes within conference settings. On each occasion there has been a general acceptance that such joint sessions are very fruitful, as all parties can begin to develop a better understanding of how each group 'sees' the community of practice and to develop new ways of working together. As one participant said:

> We must be open to welcome ... and encourage others to learn from their experiences....As a head teacher I feel an inadequacy in myself. I must be willing to learn ... we have no business more important than getting totally and passionately involved in making our schools effective learning organizations. (Quote from the reflective journal of a male head teacher from a Government school).

Such cooperative activity, more regularly scheduled within the AKU-IED programmes, could increase the likelihood of successful team working on everyone's return to their school context. This has occurred within the programme framework as well as informally in many places, including the AKU-IED's social area, in head teachers' offices during school visits, and within the settings of several school improvement conferences. Further conversations also took place between individual faculty members and programme participants within tutorial sessions and module evaluation.

The participants' views and their practices suggest that the majority of them were able to develop skills such as team building, conflict resolution, participatory decision making, time management, mentoring, action research, conducting effective meetings, school development planning, mobilizing resources and reflective thinking, and so on. As one participant said:

> Prior to joining the programme I never asked myself questions such as: Why did I never sit down and question about my role?, Why did I behave with my teachers in an unprofessional manner?, Why did my personal disposition affect my professional life?, And why did I never put students' welfare and excellence at the heart of my profession? (Quote from a head teacher's valedictory speech during graduation ceremony)

The above reflections of the programme graduates provide us with some evidence that the graduates have already moved to new directions of improving schools. In particular, there has been a cross-fertilization of ideas and understanding and identification of mutual challenges faced by colleagues who are leading schools in the public and private school systems. The school visits, as part of the programme, have been a major determinant of this increased understanding. Comments received from the participants during the programme evaluation processes and also during the follow-up underlined how their involvement in a wide variety of teaching and learning approaches in the programme proved very powerful in challenging their own thinking and school practices concerning teaching, learning and leadership. The participants often commented on how their own school and their earlier teaching careers had been dominated by very didactic teaching methods and coercive styles of leadership. These views were further supported in the outcomes of our research, where specific questions were asked concerning participants' views on the strengths and weaknesses of the programme (Simkins et al, 2001).

Challenges for Developing Capacity Building for School Improvement

Despite the significant impact of the programme, our research findings indicate that the majority of head teachers experienced difficulties in sustaining change and improvement in their schools. At a general level in Karachi, from where most of the participants are drawn, the social, economic and political contexts of the schools in the public sector are seen by most of their head teachers to prescribe almost all that they might attempt in terms of school improvement. In the perceptions of head teachers interviewed in our research, the bureaucracy in the education department provides little in the way of practical, professional or emotional support for head teachers. Non-Government schools are often characterized by relatively distant Boards of Trustees. Both Government and non-Government school systems seldom give their head teachers any clear direction and many do not have a job description. Few people in positions of governance in either sector have extensive knowledge about education or what the purpose of a school might be beyond maintaining the status quo in society. Those who have participated in the programme have encountered difficulties such as lack of support from their school system, lack of professional autonomy, lack of resources, conflicting expectations of different stakeholder groups and a predominantly top-down directive management approach; the last of which is not exclusive to the Government system. Also, it is difficult to find any single or identical model or norm of collaborative culture in different schools because of the individual school culture.

Given these pressures and difficulties arising from the context of schools, the examples of school change described above must be considered indicators of some success. AKU-IED's 'critical mass' theory of school improvement is still based on the belief that collaboration will bring about the desired changes. However, our research findings and our experience of working with graduates suggest that although many head teachers have provided a platform for PDTs to form a culture of collaboration and cooperation in schools through working together on the tasks assigned by them, there is still a need for head teachers to consider themselves as an integral part of the whole process of team building and collaborative culture.

These considerations mean that, at this stage in the development of the programme, it is difficult to make any firm statements about the longer-term robustness of the changes in head teacher and school management practice which the programme has stimulated, or of the degree to which specific initiatives are linking into wider, whole-school planned strategies for improvement. Evidence from our research (Simkins et al, 1998, 2001; Simkins, Sisum & Memon, 2003) suggests that, for most head teachers, change is generally an incremental, even piecemeal process, and that the personal style that individual head teachers choose to adopt in leading and managing improvement varies considerably, as does the degree of quality, consistency and perseverance in their approaches. There is also some indication that many head teachers find it difficult to sustain even the more piecemeal changes, perhaps in part because they are just piecemeal but also because of the weight of constraints under which feel they must operate. The most successful examples of holistic approaches to change are found in the private sector schools where there may already be significant demand or encouragement and support for such changes and where head teachers' personal, and perhaps social, background gives them the motivation and confidence to lead change effectively. In her study Farah et al (1996) found that 'if the head is competent and also has a high status in the community, her [his] access to leaders and her [his] influence with other community members positively affects what she [he] can do for the school' (p. 146).

We should acknowledge that the difficulties of translating professional development experience into sustained school improvement are not unique to Pakistan. Some studies from other countries have shown how difficult it is to sustain improvements in school for any length of time (Stoll & Fink, 1996; Fink, 1997, 1999; Shaw, 2001). Nevertheless, the critical question for those considering the future planning of school leadership development at AKU-IED is how the current programme delivery can be made more effective, not just in aiding participants' to reconceptualize their head teachers' role and triggering the motivation for change, but also in determining their ability to translate that new thinking into practical strategies in their school communities that increase the chances of genuine school improvement becoming effectively embedded in their schools.

We noticed that, where examples of more robust change resulting from the programme were identified, these seemed to occur where either or both of the following two conditions existed. First, the local context of the school system and its community either encouraged initiative among its head teachers, or at least did not challenge a head teacher's right to act in an innovative way. And secondly, the head teacher had the personal qualities necessary to achieve change in difficult circumstances such as strong values and a clear vision, considerable self-confidence, a high degree of optimism about what is possible and the skill to work with and involve people, bringing them 'on board' in the change process. These are the characteristics typically attributed to transformational leaders, mentioned earlier. Evidence collected from interviews and school observations in our study sample of eight head teachers indicated just one clear example of such leadership.

Recommendations for Developing
Leadership and Management Capacity

Our research findings suggest that development work with head teachers would benefit by being much more focused on the professional and personal characteristics of the head teachers themselves, rather than simply on their acquisition of a body of school improvement knowledge and management techniques. Unless we give our head teachers time and opportunity to address what it means to *be* a head teacher leading change, what it *feels* like to be in such a challenging and at times isolated role, and how important it is to develop new models of working with others, then significant progress is unlikely.

Much of the work of AKU-IED, particularly the work on leadership development, is based upon conceptual models taken from North America and western Europe and yet the application of these concepts is taking place in a very different social, religious and economic culture. Rather than assert the appropriateness of pedagogical leadership models to Pakistan's schools, it may be better to explore how realistic it is as an aspiration for most head teachers working within systems that themselves often lack a clear embedded vision of educational purposes. There is a need to develop leadership approaches that respond at both philosophical and practical levels to the social, political and economic constraints within which school leaders must work. It is in the exploration of such issues and their development into indigenous practical strategies for school leadership and school improvement that perhaps the future programme, and similar programmes in other and differing cultural contexts, stand to make the most progress.

There is a need to give support to head teachers beyond the end of any professional programme. Head teachers need support to help them embed their new ideas, to develop and practice new roles and, at times, to be encouraged to show bravery over leadership decisions.

> I have learned a lot myself, but to implement, that is not easy ... I feel some pride in myself that I am more confident ... after giving a head teacher this type of course, if you don't support him, I am 100% sure that he will not change. (Quote from an interview from Government school head teacher)

One possible way of providing this post-programme support or mentoring for graduates would be to develop and utilize the capabilities of the growing number of more experienced school principals and head teachers who have been successful members of earlier cohorts and are now starting to make progress in the long haul of school development. Such support would be hugely strengthened if it were combined with more collaboration between this and other programmes at AKU-IED. The challenge here is for AKU-IED faculty to collaborate in designing and implementing programmes in ways that would have teachers, head teachers and education officers collaborate for school improvement. Support from the district education officers or the board of directors in the non-Government schools is necessary for the head teachers. We noted that those education officers who participated in AKU-IED professional development programmes were much more supportive and caring than others. Leadership and management development programmes must take account of the demands and constraints which particular school systems place on head teachers and others and of the consequent range of choices that are actually available to them (Stewart, 1982).

Conclusion

We can see that the findings from this research and developmental experience accord closely with what we quoted earlier from existing literature regarding doubts about the degree to which head teachers either do, or might be expected to, act effectively as leaders in their schools (Ali et al, 1993; Warwick & Reimers, 1995; Memon, 1998). The reasons offered, such as highly bureaucratic and hierarchical structures and rules which govern most school systems, especially those in the public sector, the limited professional development of head teachers, and a national culture which encourages dependency, autocratic management styles and aversion to risk (Hofstede, 1980, 1991), have all been borne out in this research. We can see that the role of leadership and management in schools is yet to be recognized fully in public and private school systems of Pakistan.

As de Grauwe (2000) indicated, the leadership role of the head teacher is critical and requires new non-traditional managerial skills. There is a need to focus on the personal dimension of leadership development, adopt a more integrated approach to such development within the individual school, and open up a debate on system constraints to school improvement addressing the issue of performance efficacy at a number of levels. The AKU-IED programme has been successful in providing participants with skills and competencies. However, the issue of educational leadership and management must be addressed in its real context for developing adequate capacity.

Our findings suggest that, while pedagogical and improvement-oriented leadership is not impossible in Pakistan, its emergence requires unusual circumstances and extraordinary personal qualities among those in leadership positions. Such circumstances and qualities may be quite rare, especially in the Government school system. Its emergence also requires development programmes that are sensitive to cultural context as indicated by Shaw and Welton (1996) and Shaw (1998). Since educational leadership and school improvement are inseparable, AKU-IED might valuably review *all* its programmes and ensure that leadership and school improvement stay as common threads across the programmes.

Lastly, although AKU-IED's programmes in general and its Advanced Diploma in Educational Leadership and Management in particular are designed carefully in line with school system needs related to school improvement, their overall impact is hampered by school systems' policies and plans and attitudes of their superordinates. The majority of head teachers seem to have been working in the situation portrayed by Cummings (1997) that

> training programmes are not guaranteed to have the desired impact if they are not accompanied by other changes which actually empower principals altering their status from that of last-line implementer of central decisions to first-line innovators of a flexible and responsive system. In the absence of empowering reforms, principals may consider the lessons shallow in that they are at the bottom of larger hierarchy and everything they initiate is ultimately subject to review. If they do well, they will be ignored. If they do poorly, they will be sacked. (p. 230)

It is clear that sustainable development has to address the wider systems within which head teachers work and AKU-IED must review development within this wider frame. This challenge is being tackled currently through work with education officers and administrative leaders in several regions of Pakistan. However, effecting changes to ways of thinking in a wider context and culture goes beyond the immediate scope of AKU-IED and takes us into human development at the national or international scale. The Aga Khan Development Networks provides opportunities for wider influence but the challenge will be to create or enable the governmental structures that encourage in-depth field-based development on a wider scale.

References

Ali, M., Qasim, A., Jaffer, R. & Greenland, J. (1993) Teacher Centred and School Based Models of Collegiality and Professional Development: case studies of the Teacher Resource Centre and the Aga Khan School Systems in Karachi, Pakistan, *International Journal of Educational Research*, 19(8), pp. 735-754.

Barth, R. (1990) *Improving Schools from Within*. San Francisco: Jossey-Bass.

Bennis, G. (1989) *On Becoming a Leader*. Reading, MA: Addison Wesley.

Bolman, L. & Deal, T. (1992) *Reforming Organizations*. San Francisco: Jossey-Bass.

Covey, S. (1990) *The Seven Habits of Highly Effective People*. New York: Fireside.

Cummings, W. (1997) Management Initiatives for Reaching the Periphery, in H.D. Nielsen & W. Cummings (Eds) *Quality Education for All: community-oriented approaches*. New York: Garland.

de Grauwe, A. (2000) Improving School Management: a promise and a challenge, *International Institute for Educational Planning Newsletter*, 18(4), pp. 1-3.

den Hartog, D.N., House, R.J., Hanges, P.J., Ruiz-Quintanilla, S.A. & Dorfman, P.W. (1999) Culture Specific and Cross-culturally Generalizable Implicit Leadership Theories: are attributes of charismatic/transformational leadership universally endorsed?, *Leadership Quarterly*, 10(2), pp. 219-256.

Farah, I., Mehmood, T., Jaffar, R. et al (1996) *Roads to Success: self-sustaining primary school change in rural Pakistan.* Study commissioned by World Bank, Islamabad.

Fink, D. (1997) The Attrition of Change. Unpublished doctoral dissertation, The Open University.

Fink, D. (1999) Deadwood Didn't Kill Itself: a pathology of failing schools, *Education Management and Administration*, 27(2), pp. 131-141.

Fink, E. & Resnik, L. (2001) Developing Principals as Instructional Leaders, *Phi Delta Kappan*, 82(8), pp. 598-606.

Fullan, M. (1997) *What's Worth Fight for in the Principalship: strategies for taking charge in the school principalship.* Toronto: Ontario Public School Teachers' Federation.

Fullan, M. (2001) *Leading in a Culture of Change.* San Francisco: Jossey-Bass.

Government of Pakistan (1992) *National educational policy.* Ministry of Education: Islamabad.

Goleman, D. (1995) *Emotional Intelligence.* New York: Bantam.

Gronn, P. (1999) *The Making of Educational Leaders.* London: Cassell.

Hallinger, P. (2001) Leading Educational Change in East Asian schools, *International Studies in Educational Development*, 29(2), pp. 61-72.

Harris, A. (2001) Building the Capacity for School Improvement, *School Leadership and Management*, 21(3), pp. 261-270.

Hofstede, G. (1980) *Culture's Consequences: international differences in work-related values.* London: Sage.

Hofstede, G. (1991) *Culture and Organizations: software of the mind.* London: McGraw-Hill.

Hoodbhy, P. (Ed.) (1998) *Education and the State: fifty years of Pakistan.* Karachi: Oxford University Press.

Juma, M. & Waudo, J. (1999) *An Inquiry into Head Teachers' Support Groups within the PRISM Project – Kenya.* Nairobi: Ministry of Education, Science and Technology.

Leithwood, K. (1999) *Changing Leadership for Changing Times.* Buckingham: Open University Press.

Leithwood, K., Tomlinson, D. & Genge, M. (1996) Transformational School Leadership, in K. Leithwood, Chapman, J., Corson, D., Hallinger, P. & Hart, A. (Eds) *International Handbook of Educational Leadership and Administration*, vol. 2. Kulwar: Rotterdam.

Memon, M. (1998) The Future of Head Teachers as Educational Leaders in Pakistan. Implications for Pedagogical Leadership, *Education 2000*, 3(3), pp. 23-28.

Memon, M. (2000) Preparing School Leadership for the Twenty First Century. Paper presented to the 13th International Congress for School Effectiveness and Improvement held in Hong Kong from 4-8 January.

Ramsey, R. (1999) *Lead, Follow, or Get out of the Way: how to be a more effective leader in today's schools.* Thousand Oaks: Corwin Press.

Sergiovanni, T. (1998) Leadership as Pedagogy, Capital Development and School Effectiveness, *International Journal of Education Leadership*, 1(1), pp. 37-46.

Shaw, J. (1998) Cultural Variations in Management Practices: an exploration of the management trainers' dilemma, *Public Administration and Development*, 18(4), pp. 319-342.

Shaw, J. & Welton, J. (1996) The Application of Education Management Models and Theories to the Process of Policy-making and Management: a case of compound cross-cultural confusion. Paper presented at the 8th International Conference of the Commonwealth Council for Educational Administration and Management, Kuala Lumpur, 19-24 August 1996.

Shaw, P. (2001) Critical Issues for School Leaders in Improving Schools. Paper presented to School Improvement Conference at AKU-IED, April.

Simkins, T. Garrett, V., Memon, M. & Nazir Ali, R. (1998) The Role Perceptions of Government and Non-government Head Teachers in Pakistan, *Educational Management and Administration*, 26(2), pp. 131-146.

Simkins, T., Sisum, C., Memon, M. & Khaki, J. (2001) Head Teacher Approaches to Managing Improvement in Pakistan Schools: lessons learned from case studies. Paper presented at the 14th International Congress for School Effectiveness and Improvement, Toronto, January.

Simkins, T., Sisum, C. & Memon, M. (2003) School Leadership in Pakistan: exploring the head teacher's role, *School Effectiveness and School Improvement*, 14(3), pp. 279-291.

Stewart, R. (1982) *Choices for the Manager: a guide to managerial work and behaviour.* London: McGraw-Hill.

Stoll, L. & Fink, D. (1996*) Changing Our Schools: linking school effectiveness and school improvement.* London: Open University Press.

Teacher Training Agency (1998) *National Professional Qualification for Headship.* London: Teacher Training Agency.

Tin, L. (2001) Preparation of Aspiring Principals in Singapore: a partnership model, *International Studies in Educational Administration*, 29(2), pp. 30-37.

Warwick, D. & Reimers, F. (1995) *Hope or Despair? Learning in Pakistan's Primary Schools.* Westport: Praeger.

Wenchang, L. & Daming, F. (2001) Principal Training in China: models, problems, prospects, *International l Studies in Educational Administration*, 29(2), pp. 13-19.

Wong, Kam-Cheung (2001) What Kind of Leaders Do We Need? The Case of Hong Kong, *International Studies in Educational Administration*, 29(2), pp. 2-12.

CHAPTER 10

Teacher Education and School Improvement: a case study from Pakistan

ANIL KHAMIS & SHAHIDA JAWED

Introduction

The Institute of Educational Development at the Aga Khan University (AKU-IED) Master's Degree made an explicit link between teacher education and school improvement via the M.Ed., as discussed earlier in this volume. There were, at the outset of the M.Ed., three objectives defined for the course participants that were the basis of the Aga Khan University's intervention in teacher education in Pakistan (AKU-IED, 1991). Course participants who were to be designated as Professional Development Teachers (PDTs) upon graduation were:

1. to become good pedagogues (exemplary teachers);
2. to undertake teacher education activities on behalf of the school and AKU-IED; and
3. to become change agents in school.

The M.Ed. programme has been described in detail in Chapter 3 of this book and so these details will not be repeated here. One important point to be reiterated, however, as it concerns the central point of this chapter and links to the 'teacher education for school improvement model' being promoted by AKU-IED, is that the key to any success the PDTs might experience in schools was thought to be the active participation and involvement of head teachers and educational managers (see also Chapter 9). They would, it was thought, encourage and support teachers to introduce new approaches to teaching and learning strategies employed in the classroom, and this point is well covered in the literature on teacher education and educational change (Goodlad, 1990; Zeichner & Tabachnick, 1991; Fullan & Hargreaves, 1991; Bacchus, 1996).

This chapter presents lessons from a case study, undertaken in a co-operating school, that illuminates AKU-IED's impact by studying PDTs' roles in school. The School A case study presents an analysis of the most remarkable elements in the process of change undertaken in the school based on the agency of the PDTs. With the oversight of the principal, two PDTs led the School Improvement Programme, supported by Visiting Teachers in the areas of science, mathematics, social studies and English. Within four years, the school had more than 20 of its 40 teachers participate in Visiting Teacher programmes at AKU-IED (see Chapter 5). The school culture, role and function of the principal and the pre-AKU-IED initiatives of the school emerge as important factors that affected the work the PDTs were able to undertake. The PDTs' main initiatives reflect the learning on the M.Ed., which relates to the expected outcomes of the original AKU-IED model as described above (AKU-IED, 1991).

The Cooperating School

The AKU-IED programme began by identifying cooperating schools from which students were drawn for the M.Ed. The cooperating schools were central to the development of a cadre of teacher educators, PDTs, in partnership with AKU-IED. The PDTs were then expected to initiate school improvement activities in the school as well as work as adjunct faculty at AKU-IED. The case study presented here serves to illuminate the impact of the AKU-IED intervention.

School 'A' is one of the 14 schools with which AKU-IED first entered into partnership in 1994. It is a private, not-for-profit school catering to a low-income population. It began as a community initiative aimed at poor and orphaned children from upcountry centres, many from the remote mountainous Northern Areas of Pakistan, who had no access to formal education. This school had a history of school improvement programmes pre-AKU-IED, targeting teacher development and quality of education.

School A now belongs to a registered child welfare organization committed to providing social, cultural and educational uplift to children from lower socio-economic backgrounds. Many of them are orphaned or from broken homes and are provided with accommodation in the school hostel. The school as a whole comprises three campuses. A boys' school campus and a girls' school campus, each of which has a primary and a secondary section, are located close to each other. A coeducational pre-primary section is also located on the boys' campus. A third campus, in different areas of the city has coeducational primary, secondary and pre-primary sections. Each school section has its separate administrative units with its own head and deputy head teachers

The first PDT graduated with the first cohort of AKU-IED M.Ed. in 1995. She was to return to the secondary branch of the boys' school after the two-year M.Ed. However, prior to resuming her duties her re-entry action plan (a requirement at the end of the M.Ed.) was reviewed by the school management. In response to the action plan, it was agreed by the schools heads of the three campuses that each should benefit from the professional and pedagogical expertise now being offered by the PDT. Consequently, the school reviewed its entire management structure resulting in widespread changes that affected the relationships among all three campuses and the boys' and girls' schools. The two most significant and far-reaching organizational changes were the promotion of the secondary head of the secondary section to the position of principal and the whole school establishment of the School Improvement Centre (SIC) in 1996.

The first change rationalized and legitimized the role of the principal which had until now been informal and without executive decision-making powers. Each school now reports to one principal who overseas the management, administration and educational standards of the three school campuses, including the work of the SIC, and reports to an honorary management board drawn from the community. The SIC was charged with the responsibility of enhancing teachers' professional development as its role in the new 'School Development Programme'. The first PDT was appointed as the directress of the SIC. The second PDT rejoined the school in 1998 and was offered the position of deputy director of the SIC.

Case Study School A

School Culture Pre-AKU-IED Intervention

Before 1995 there was a Balkanised culture in the sense that each of the eight schools worked in isolation and the heads reported directly to the school management committee. Teachers and heads had little interaction across the campuses, resulting in different curricular and teacher development provision as well as different salary scales and increments. The result was the school's inability to rationally plan its school development programme and incipient competition amongst teachers who would opt for transfers between schools, especially from the girls' school to the boys' school and from primary to secondary.

School Improvement through Teachers' Professional Development

The School Development Programme (SDP) was initiated in 1987 two years after denationalization of the schools.[1] The impetus for the SDP was from the work of the Aga Khan Foundation (AKF) and the Aga Khan Educational Services (AKES) which fund and run dozens of schools in Pakistan. Both are part of the Aga Khan Development Network (AKDN). School A is nominally included in the Network as it initially began work in the same parochial community; however, it has a completely separate management structure and does not form a part of the Network in terms of its finances and reporting. School A was invited to become one of the original AKU-IED cooperating schools in 1993, along with 13 other AKDN, private and government schools.

AKF and AKES had employed expatriate experts who devised improvement programmes based on school improvement and teacher education research conducted in Europe and North America (Bude, 1993; Black et al, 1993; Anderson & Sumra, 1994). Following these initiatives, the focus of the SDP at School A was on teacher development and improved curricula with the underlying belief that, until teachers are equipped with adequate content knowledge and pedagogical expertise, the quality of education cannot improve.

A strategy used to train teachers was to involve them in workshops conducted during the annual vacation. Various local teacher training agencies and individual experts were invited to conducted workshops. After a number of years of such workshops, it was recognized that these programmes were decontextualized since the invited facilitators were unfamiliar with local schools and the educational context in the country. AKES funding agency reports summarize that teachers' professional development efforts had not yielded significant benefits to students as teachers' own educational needs and other requirements were not addressed appropriately. For example, one participating teacher reflected, 'In spite of attending these professional development activities we don't even get any certificate and other facilities'. Not surprisingly, it emerged that there was very little uptake of the training provided and no effect was evident in teachers' classroom practices.

A further strategy to improve education in the school was the development of an English language improvement programme organized for teachers on Saturdays with a focus on learning grammar. The school had begun a drive to work in the medium of English soon after denationalization. Nationalized schools had been required to use the national language, Urdu, as the medium of instruction along with the provincial language (Sindhi). Mathematics and science were the first to be taught in English. The English language improvement programme was not sustained as teachers did not perceive its relevance to their teaching and the language workshops were considered an extra burden on teachers who were already overloaded with various tasks at school and had social and family responsibilities outside of the school.

Alongside the teacher development workshop programme, school heads were required by the school management to guide teachers in the implementation of a number of changes in the teaching methodology, syllabus planning, conducting examinations, admission policy and communication strategies with management, colleagues, students, parents and community.

Teaching and Assessment Process

Teaching is considered by most teachers in Pakistan, including those in School A's pre-AKU-IED intervention, as the transmission of information by the teacher to the student, and tends to be heavily teacher-centred. At the secondary level, the focus of the education is primarily on high stakes exam performance. Teachers, relying on the textbook, normally give lecture notes to students who are expected to memorize them with little or no attention given to understanding the content. Thus teachers have become textbook dependent and are overwhelmingly concerned to complete the syllabus so their students have at the least 'covered' the course content.

The AKU-IED's M.Ed. programme had established a number of conditions whereby course participants would be selected. First, the selection was of the school; that is, teachers could not directly apply for the programme unless supported by the school. Schools were also required to continue to pay the teacher's salary during the two-year M.Ed. and thereby not only invest in the development of the teacher but to take cognizance of the pressures on teachers to financially support their families. Applicants underwent a rigorous selection process undertaken by AKU-IED faculty which included observation of teachers' classroom practice and interview in addition to preset selection criteria to identify potential course participants.

When teachers in School A learned about the AKU-IED's M.Ed. programme, four teachers (one from the girls' secondary school and three from the boys' secondary school out of a total of some 60 teachers) put themselves forward as candidates. Most teachers could not afford the two-year time commitment due to family responsibilities. Ultimately, a teacher from the boys' secondary school was selected for the M.Ed. programme. She started the first M.Ed. programme in 1994 and went on to become the first PDT. A new teacher was appointed in place of this teacher.

The replacement teacher underwent a science Visiting Teacher (VT) programme in 1996 and was so motivated that she put herself forward as an M.Ed. candidate during the process of selection for the second M.Ed. When questioned what motivated her to undertake the M.Ed., she responded:

> [My] reasons to attend the M.Ed. programme were first the change I experienced in my perception of teaching and learning by participating in the VT programme in 1996. Because the VT programme provided a variety of exposure ... how the teaching and learning process should be. It created great motivation and eagerness to explore the other ways of enhancing the teaching-learning process. Secondly, before joining the teaching profession I had always dreamed of being a Master's Degree graduate but due to many reasons I could not achieve the target; the school provided me a golden chance to change my dream into reality. (PDT 2)

The PDT as Teacher, Teacher Educator and Change Agent

Upon the return of the first PDT in 1995, the school reviewed its school development policy. The new policy affected the administrative structure, role and status of (AKU-IED) qualified teachers, and remuneration and incentives were put into place to attract teachers to further professional training and development offered at AKU-IED and the increasing school-based provision being developed by the SIC.

A school-based teachers' professional development programme was initiated to be led by the PDT with oversight from the principal. Initially, the school chose to focus on enhancing the teaching and learning of science and mathematics after a needs analysis exercise conducted by the PDT. This was also the area in which the PDT had worked and had conducted action research with two other teachers during her M.Ed. study. An important aspect of the PDT's work plan was its foundation on action research and reflective practice. That is, the PDT consciously underwent and demonstrated an active learning process in which she taught a regular load, reflected on her practice and refined her efforts. This learning was then shared with selected colleagues at the school who were coached by the PDT. A further aspect of her plan was to work with those teachers who later attended VT courses at AKU-IED. The efforts of the PDT began to spread to different subject areas to both the boys' and girls' schools.

From August 1995 the PDT had started working with two science teachers in the boys' school. The teachers observed her teaching and discussed the lessons in open and frank exchanges. Gradually, they began to co-plan their lessons and team teaching emerged as a means to promote supportive and collegial relationships. During team teaching whichever teacher felt comfortable took the lead with others supporting and facilitating the students during the lesson. Teachers, working together, were given time by the school management to practice and reflect on their teaching and learning approaches, many of which were completely unfamiliar to them. Gradually the PDT's direct teaching role minimized as the co-teachers took on more of the teaching and planning as they grew in confidence and were motivated and supported to try new pedagogical approaches, such as more complex forms of group work, creating independent learning tasks, using library and locally available resources. By the end of the second year of the SIC the PDT's role was more one of facilitating teachers in different subject areas, promoting critical reflection, coaching, conducting demonstration lessons and initiating a school-based research agenda with her colleagues. The teachers who participated in the SIC professional development programme were granted free periods to work with their peers to plan lesson observations and to reflect and refine their teaching practices.

After the initial six months, when the work of the SIC had just started, the PDT had to report to AKU-IED to conduct a VT programme, a feature of a three-year post-M.Ed. contractual agreement of the AKU-IED with cooperating schools to share the PDT's time. The teacher development programme initiated at the school was disrupted during this period while the PDT was at AKU-IED on a full-time basis and spent only one day a week – Saturday – working with teachers.

During this time, in addition to working full-time at AKU-IED and with the responsibility to work at all three campuses, with teachers in the boys' and girls' schools exhibiting different attitudes and priorities with regard to the school and their own professional development, the pressure and strain to work with all interested teachers was too much for the PDT. All school personnel and the students, who began to question the different prevailing practices amongst teachers in the same school, felt this pressure and serious reservations were voiced and questions raised about the possibility to initiate and sustain school development, teacher professional education, and not least the workability of the school-AKU-IED 'partnership'.

The pressure resulted in much rescheduling and time planning of the PDT who continued teaching and mentoring in both girls' and boys' secondary schools – the first time one teacher had bridged both faculties. However, tensions developed at the girls' school because the PDT's approach challenged the existing culture. Traditionally the head teacher of this school had observed classrooms as an evaluator or inspector. She took the same approach towards observing the classrooms of those teachers who were working with the PDTs. This attitude put the teachers on the defensive and made the PDT especially uncomfortable at the girls' campus. Two factors can be discerned here. First, the head of the girls' school had not attended the heads' seminars held at AKU-IED to initiate and expose them to the pedagogical approaches being developed during the M.Ed. Second, the two campuses had existed as separate schools for a long time and had developed a closed community. The PDT, from the boys' school, was considered an outsider and a threat to the independence of the school and particularly the head. With the reorganization of the management structure, in 1996, the principal personally facilitated the PDT's work in all the campuses, which was significant in overcoming the resistance experienced initially by the PDT.

Lessons and Change

Many lessons are presented in this case study. Students showed great enthusiasm for the new approaches to teaching and learning, as did teachers who felt reinvigorated. One teacher commented how she was being forced to go to the library regularly and learn *'new things because the children's questions are so good'*. Whilst the change process has not been smooth nor has the support of all the teachers, significant outcomes are evident. The most significant outcome has been the impact on students' learning. Teachers, heads and the principal all agree that students demonstrate much more confidence, have improved their information processing skills resulting in asking 'better', more incisive questions, improved their communication and presentation skills, which are indicative of higher order thinking.

While new approaches to teaching were being introduced, the examination system had remained unchanged. This resulted in frustration concerning students' exam results and corresponding anxiety. Student exam results have actually been lowered since the start of the SIC's work which has been a point of contention between the principal, PDTs, and participating teachers on the one hand and certain heads and parents on the other hand. One student's testimony is illustrative:

> [I like] the teacher's teaching, I have started taking more interest
> and I enjoy it, but I am frightened to show my results to my
> parents because I have failed the examination and my father will
> beat me.

The obvious consensus arising is that there must be a match between the teaching and learning approaches in the school and the assessment process (paper-pencil test). At the time of writing this chapter the school has begun to pilot more effective and relevant testing during term time. The efforts of the school staff to make changes to the in-school term tests have met with parents' satisfaction thus far. However, the final province-wide examinations still cause great consternation to those leading the change. It is not surprising then that many in the school have not been motivated to adopt new practices.

Thus, the teachers were concerned that the new teaching and learning methods took too much time. This would make it difficult to meet their objective of 'covering' the syllabus on which the students would be examined at the end of the term. There was school-wide concern that the new teaching and learning processes and strategies did not match the assessment practices laid out by the provincial Ministry of Education, which relied on students having memorized the 'correct' answers.

Selection of teaching and learning activities were also problematic, for example, parents raised concerns that their children's notebooks did not have much writing in them and that the students seemed to receive less homework. Colleagues who were not involved in the teacher development programme expressed consternation that they continually had to shift the furniture back into rows and columns after another teacher had done group work with the class.

Upon the introduction of cooperative learning, the PDTs had come to rely on informal evaluation. With the passage of time, teachers began to come to rely on formative assessment as part of their teaching practice and reflection. When modifications were made by the school management upon the behest of teachers in the paper-pencil test (not the end of year examinations set by the Provincial Ministry of Education), the head of the girls' school resisted the changes although her campus teachers supported the changes. The PDT found solace in the words of the faculty who had taught her at AKU-IED,

> Don't worry about change: don't expect that the whole school will
> support you during the process of change. If your students are
> with you it means you are successful, let's start to work with them.
> Don't wait for change at the whole school.

Three years after the AKU-IED intervention more than 60% of the teachers in School A had been trained in the VT programme and a second PDT has graduated from the M.Ed. programme. This increase in professional human resources led to management and pedagogical changes suggested by teachers themselves and facilitated by the principal. For those unable to access AKU-IED Visiting Teacher Provision (that is, Urdu, Sindhi, *Islamiat* teachers for which AKU-IED does not have programmes), a system of 'pools' or departments was created whereby language teachers work with English language VTs and the PDT and similarly *Islamiat* (religious education) teachers are pooled with social studies VTs and the PDT.

With these developments, including management and organizational changes, the focus and work of the PDTs evolved. They engaged in less classroom teaching and spent more time in classroom-related activities (observation, team teaching, and demonstration) with teachers and planning teacher development programmes, including in-class development strategies targeting teaching-learning approaches with an aim to improve students' learning outcomes.

The following are in evidence as successes of the AKU-IED model and whilst the pedagogical leadership can be attributed to the PDT, she, herself, acknowledges that the inspiration for her work is her continued association with AKU-IED:

- The school developed a mass of professionally developed teachers who viewed their teaching practices critically.
- The establishment of school-owned, planned, and delivered in-service programmes aimed at the development of all teachers.
- The availability of in-house professional development teachers who have teacher education expertise.
- The establishment of a mutually beneficial relationship with AKU-IED whereby the school engages in research and development of its school improvement model.
- Teachers acknowledged for their improvement efforts financially.
- Creation of a collegial teacher culture in which all teachers are involved through systematic and rational processes.
- Teachers themselves demanding their share of the available professional support rather than professional development being thrust upon them.
- Students reporting greater satisfaction with the teaching and learning available in school.

The first PDT describes the successes of the AKU-IED intervention:

> Since 1995 we have observed a lot of successes related to teachers'
> professional development as well as students' learning, such as:
> development of confidence in teachers and students; teachers
> reflecting on their own classroom practices; students especially
> raising questions rather than remaining silent in class; teachers
> wanting to go beyond the textbook rather than totally relying upon
> it. The whole staff are busy in identifying innovative ideas for
> teaching because now students don't like the teacher to be doing
> all the talking in the class.

Challenges

However, many challenges still confront the school where most children come from poor and difficult family backgrounds. For example, in each class there are widely different ability groups. Teachers continue to face the challenge of providing individual attention and equal learning opportunities for all students. A notable point is that students from impoverished homes and backgrounds do not perform well academically and are consistently below average; teachers have struggled to show significant progress with these children. This has been identified and acknowledged as unacceptable to the school and raises important questions as to the ability of the school to cater to all children. The PDTs and teachers have met and are determined to initiate a dialogue with the concerned families to identify the underlying reasons and causes for students' performance and wish to work towards meeting children's educational needs in accordance with their family and home circumstances. The PDT remains hopeful that such challenges will be overcome and this is further testimony to the efforts of the PDTs to continue to learn and play the role of educational change agents to reach all those who are in the school.

The challenges faced by the school can be categorized into two areas with regard to school improvement and teachers' further professional development:

- The workload facing PDTs, pool heads and teachers is quite heavy and has impinged on non-school related activities and personal time. The first PDT felt initially that when the second PDT joined the school, her workload would be reduced. However, all those who are actively involved in the change process find themselves extremely busy.
- Initially the first PDT was involved in all areas related to school improvement including management in which the PDT was not trained. This has inevitably led to the PDT spending more time on administrative and management tasks when her time could be more profitably spent on teacher education and development.

In summary, it is clear that the PDTs' efforts via the SIC have spread to all the campuses and, in particular, inside the classrooms. Over a period of three years, the school's culture has evolved from being isolationist to more collaborative. The above-mentioned challenges have been exacerbated by the high annual teacher turnover rate of between 10-15%. This remains, in the school, the major obstacle to further teacher development and impinges on the school development plans; interestingly, the average turnover rate of AKU-IED trained teachers in the school is comparatively much lower at 3.5%. There are several reasons that have been identified by the school that yields this high turnover rate: change of residence due to marriage; a heavy workload; use of Saturdays for teachers' professional development activities; and better remuneration elsewhere – possibly outside the teaching field. No doubt this has been disruptive to students, parents, and the school and especially the PDTs who have had to keep training and inducting new teachers into the school's improvement model. The consequence has been that less attention is then given to teaching and learning improvements in the classroom and from ongoing development work.

Conclusion

This case study illuminates the applicability of the teacher education model and its appropriateness to teacher professional development needs as exhibited by the PDTs in this case study. That is, both PDTs exhibited and manifested their learning as pedagogues, teacher educators and change agents. As has been the case in this school, and this outcome is corroborated by evidence from other case studies of cooperating schools (Khamis, 2000), PDTs found greater professional satisfaction if perceived as teacher educators and change agents as opposed to only classroom-based teachers.

This finding has implications for the AKU-IED M.Ed. programme. The salient point is that, if the M.Ed. continues to emphasize change agency as a key role, then either (i) the requisite skills in planning and management of organization change will need to be developed; and (ii) roles PDTs are expected to play in schools will need to be carefully considered. The evidence to date suggests that PDTs aspire to play a school leadership (principal/head teacher) role or to become teacher educators at the tertiary level. Both these aspirations encourage PDTs away from classroom-based roles. With the dearth of qualified teachers and the even greater lack of postgraduates in the school system, it is understandable that PDTs have been urged to move away from the classroom by the school management itself.

Notes

[1] All schools in Pakistan were nationalized in 1972 upon a decree of the military government. In 1985, Pakistan returned to civilian rule.

References

Aga Khan University – Institute for Educational Development (AKU-IED) (1991) *A Proposal to the AKU Board of Trustees.* Karachi: AKU-IED.

Anderson, Stephen E. & Sumra, Suleman (1994) *Evaluation of the School Improvement Program: Aga Khan Mzizima Secondary School, Dar es Salaam.* Geneva: Aga Khan Foundation (AKF).

Bacchus, M.K. (1996) The Role of Teacher Education in Contributing to Qualitative Improvements in Basic Education in Developing Countries, in B. Brock-Utne & T. Nagel (Eds) *The Role of Aid in the Development of Education for All,* pp. 134-160, NASEDEC conference, University of Norway.

Black, H., Govinda, R., Kiragu, F. & Devine, M. (1993) *School Improvement in the Developing World: an evaluation of the Aga Khan Foundation Programme.* SCRE Research Report, no. 45; DFID Evaluation Report EV545. Edinburgh: Scottish Council for Research in Education.

Bude, U. (1993) *Field-based Teacher Development Programme: a monitoring exercise in Northwest Frontier Province, and a Review of FBTD Activities in the Northern Areas of Pakistan.* Bonn: German Foundation for International Development (DSE).

Fullan, M.G., & Hargreaves, A. (1991) *What's Worth Fighting For: working together for your school.* Toronto: Ontario Public School Teachers Association.

Goodlad, J.I. (1990) *Teachers for Our Nation's Schools.* San Francisco: Jossey-Bass.

Khamis, A. (2000) The Various Impacts of The Institute for Educational Development in its Co-operating Schools in Pakistan. Unpublished Ph.D. thesis, Institute of Education, University of London.

Zeichner, K.M. & Tabachnick, B.R. (1991) Reflections on Reflective Teaching, in B.R. Tabachnick & K.M. Zeichner (Eds) *Issues and Practices in Inquiry-oriented Teacher Education,* pp. 1-21. Philadelphia: Falmer Press.

CHAPTER 11

School Improvement:
a case from Bangladesh

YASMEEN BANO & SULTAN MAHMUD BHUIYAN

Teachers' professional development plays an important role in school improvement. Teachers equipped with sound subject knowledge, better pedagogical skills and with necessary pedagogical content knowledge can effectively facilitate children to learn by creating meaningful learning opportunities for them. According to Barth in Law and Glover (2000), 'Probably nothing in a school has more impact on students in terms of skills, development, self confidence, or classroom behavior than the personal and professional growth of their teachers' (p. 238). There are various ways to facilitate teachers to grow professionally and in-service teacher education is one of the effective ways to do so. This study describes an in-service teacher education programme undertaken by the Aga Khan Education Service, Bangladesh (AKES, B) mainly for the teachers of Aga Khan School, Dhaka (AKS, D) in collaboration with the Institute for Educational Development at the Aga Khan University (AKU-IED), Pakistan. The background of the programme and the model used for teacher education, and strengths, challenges and issues related to the model are also discussed.

Background

AKS, D is a coeducational and English medium school, which was established in 1989 with only 80 students. It follows the GCE Ordinary and Advanced Level Curriculum. At present it is nurturing over 1000 young people with the support of 106 teachers. It caters for education from playgroup to A level. Why did the school feel the need of having a school-based professional development programme? The answer lies in the fact that quality of education is at the heart of all AKES, B activities in order to achieve its vision, namely to make the school a centre of excellence. The aim of the school enumerates that, 'The Aga Khan School is a caring and nurturing educational environment in which every student is provided with the opportunities to develop artistically, emotionally, intellectually, morally, physically and socially to his or her full potential' (Rehman & Bhuiyan, 2001). In order to achieve this, a group of competent teachers was essential who can facilitate children's learning process with its professional skills. AKES, B believes that the quality of education can be enhanced by providing opportunities to teachers for professional growth and in this regard AKES, B started a collaboration with AKU-IED. Initially the school sent two teachers for the Master's in Education programme and two for the Visiting Teachers Programme (VTP) [1], to AKU-IED, Pakistan. Later on it was realized that intensive professional development of the teachers cannot be done by sending the teachers to AKU-IED because of high cost, problems of substitute teachers in the absence of the teachers gone for training and a very long period required to complete the basic professional development of most of the teaching staff. Meanwhile in 1998 AKES, East Africa started an in-service teacher education programme in Kenya in collaboration with AKU-IED. The programme was named the VTP-Nairobi Model. It was a modified form of AKU-IED's VTP with a large field- based component. The idea was picked up by the AKES, B also as it seemed feasible because of the presence of two Professional Development Teachers (PDTs) at the AKS, D. Several visits and negotiations between AKU-IED and AKES, B evolved a further modified model for the VTP and was named the VTP-Dhaka Model. So far two VTPs have been conducted, that is the VTP-Dhaka Model 2000 and 2001 for the professional development of 44 AKS, D teachers. Basically the programmes were designed for the teachers of AKS, D but in 2000, three teachers from India and in 2001, two teachers from the two other educational institutes of Dhaka also participated.

The VTP-Dhaka Model

Structure

The Dhaka Model was designed keeping in mind that teachers' routine teaching schedule did not get disturbed because of the in-service teacher education programme. For this purpose the whole programme was divided into the following three components:

- *Component I.* It was a three-week component held in the school's winter vacation. The main emphasis was to help the participating teachers to reflect upon their existing beliefs and practices of teaching and learning so that the process of reconceptualization about learning and teaching could be initiated in them. The teachers were also exposed to some interactive ways of learning and teaching, learning theories, ways of assessing students' learning, questioning skills, classroom management, lesson planning, and so forth.
- *Component II.* It was a five-month field-based component from January to May. During this component the teachers worked in their own schools according to their school timetable to practise new ideas learnt

during component I. This component emphasized on putting theory into practice. To provide the support to the teachers, PDTs and the principal observed their lessons and conducted feedback sessions according to a set schedule. The teachers were also provided with the support for lesson planning and trying out new teaching strategies in their classes as per their needs. Five seminars were also conducted during this period in order to provide the teachers with an opportunity to share their successes and challenges and to learn some more new ideas.

- *Component III.* It was also a three-week component conducted in the summer vacations. During this component the teachers were exposed to some other interactive ways of teaching and learning in the light of the needs identified during components I and II.

Features of the Dhaka Model

There are certain characteristics which make the VTP-Dhaka Model a different model from the other models of VTPs. Some of these features may be found in the VTP-Nairobi Model as well.

- It was a collaborative model, namely a model that evolved with the partnership of a school and a university. The PDTs of Bangladesh and a coordinator from AKU-IED faculty worked together to design a programme according to the needs of AKS, D teachers. It was not a university-designed model for a school, rather it was a model designed by the school with the support of the university. This approach enhanced the ownership of the programme among its users and made it need based.
- It was a very contextualized and need-based model for the teachers of a particular context. The designers (PDTs) of the programme and the participants of the programme were from the same school context; they knew each other, were aware of the strengths and weaknesses of the school and knew both the needs of the students and the teachers. These commonalties were quite helpful in making the programme contextualized.
- It was a generic model, namely a model designed to cater for the needs of a variety of teachers in terms of teaching subjects and subject levels. Though it was named as the Primary Education VTP, the teachers of the pre-primary school, secondary school, O level teachers and A level teachers also participated in it besides the teachers of the primary school. In AKU-IED based VTP models, subject areas guide the design of the programme. For example the content of VTP Science caters to the needs of only science teachers. In the VTP-Dhaka Model, pedagogical strategies and ideas were at the forefront. The content selected for the programme was quite generic in nature and focused on the basic pedagogical knowledge, skills and attitude which it was

185

necessary for all the teachers to know like the stages of child development, cooperative learning, questioning skills, classroom management, lesson planning, and so forth. While discussing any of the ideas, links were made to various teaching levels and the subjects. In some cases after having an introductory session for a strategy or theory, participants were divided according to their teaching subjects and classes and then they did an in-depth study as per their teaching needs in order to make sense of it.

- It was a field-based and reflective model. It had a large field-based component in which the teachers got enough opportunities to implement their learning in a real classroom situation under the support of PDTs. This was the strongest feature of the model as it helped the teachers to internalize the new ideas as well as initiated the process of change in a supportive environment. Component II provided the teachers and the PDTs with enough opportunities to reflect on their successes and challenges and as a result of this ongoing reflection, ideas were modified to make them workable in the classes. This ongoing reflection was also very useful to plan component III in the light of the emerging needs of the teachers.

- It was a cost-effective and capacity building model in various ways. Most of the material resources required for the programme were generated from the school and in turn the resources developed during the programme were included in the school's resource collection. Most of the programme implementation team was also from the school. The team for conducting the programme comprised a Coordinator from AKU-IED, two PDTs of AKS, D and 3-4 school staff members as Support Faculty. In VTP-Dhaka Model 2000, the senior and experienced teachers were selected for this role and in VTP-Dhaka Model 2001, four graduates of VTP-2000 were identified for this role. In this way not only human resources were identified from the school but they were groomed as well to work as resource people in the future.

If we look at the above-mentioned features, one main thread can be picked up which generated all these features and that was the involvement of the school in the whole process right from idea conceiving stage to the evaluation of the programme. The major role taken by the school, made it possible to make the programme need based, reflective and flexible. Based on the experiences of the VTP-Dhaka Model, it can be argued that perhaps the school-based in-service teacher education programmes can play a more effective role in school improvement as compared to university-based in-service teacher education programmes.

Impact of the Programme

The impact of the VTP-Dhaka Model can be studied in various dimensions such as the impact on the teachers, children, PDTs, the school as a whole and the impact for AKU-IED, and so forth. A vast research study needs to be done in order to explore all the above-mentioned dimensions in detail. However, the responses of the teachers in the final evaluation questionnaire, classroom observations, informal talk with PDTs, teachers, school principal, and so forth have made it possible to draw a few conclusions about the impact of the programme.

Impact on the Teachers

The majority of the teachers shared that they had enhanced their confidence a lot as a result of attending the programme. This enhanced confidence helped them to develop a good self-concept about themselves. Their responses and PDTs' observations showed that the teachers had become more confident for planning lessons and using new teaching strategies. The following are some of the responses of the teachers about the impact of the programme in terms of enhanced self-concept:

- I am now confident and proud of being a teacher.
- Now I can accept others' opinion easily with respect.
- I feel myself more capable of thinking.
- I have become assertive and positive about my teaching and learning.
- I can evaluate and analyse myself.

Several teachers shared that they had become more organized for their classes by planning lessons properly such as:

- The programme made me proactive and organized before the lesson.
- Now I have a clear concept of what, why and how I am going to teach my children.
- The programme has organized my thoughts.

Several teachers shared that they were more comfortable and competent for using various teaching strategies and approaches and handling the students in their classes. A few examples of such responses are:

- I am more skilled now.
- Selecting activities will be no problem for me.
- Project work will be done more systematically now.
- My lessons have become more student centred and lively.
- I can manage group work well using cooperative learning.

Impact on PDTs

Informal talk with PDTs, and their reflections, revealed that the programmes helped them to enhance their own understanding of various concepts. Getting ready for teaching teachers and supporting them in the field pushed the PDTs to think more critically and to broaden the schema of their own understanding for various pedagogical aspects. Since the programme was school based, PDTs had to take care of several administrative aspects of the programme also and it helped them to learn how to be more organized and systematic. These programmes also made PDTs think very critically about several important issues related to adult learning such as how to develop a good relationship with very senior colleagues during the programme as facilitators, how to enhance patience while facing criticism from colleagues, how to practise what is being preached by them, and so forth. Reflections and deliberations on these issues helped the PDTs to grow themselves as more effective teacher educators.

Impact on Children

It is very difficult to make any conclusion about the impact on children but based on the classroom observation and teachers' views it can be said that the children have become more active learners in the classrooms as they are given opportunities for group discussions, making presentations, raising questions, presenting arguments, and so forth. The students have also enhanced their skills for working in groups and to be creative. All these things have enhanced students' confidence and interest for learning as some teachers stated that they had far less complaints about students' absences from the school.

Challenges

The following are a few major challenges related to VTP-Dhaka Models 2000 and 2001.

The biggest challenge of the programme was one of its strong features, namely to deal with a very heterogeneous group in terms of teachers teaching different levels and subjects. The team tried to present the ideas in a way that every one could benefit but still the teachers of O levels and A levels felt that their needs were not met very much. It was also very challenging for the team to put the ideas according to the needs of various teaching levels. For example, O level and A level teachers wanted to have more in-depth discussion on the requirements and needs of adolescents and ways to tackle their problems while pre-primary teachers were interested to know more how children in years 2-4 learn and what were their needs. The teachers also wanted to discuss a few concepts from their subject content areas but it was very difficult to do this because of having a variety of teachers. Facilitators were also not competent for some of the subjects like Accounting and Business Studies. Though the team helped the teachers to use various resources like the Internet, the library, and so on, in order to explore more about their own subject areas but there was still the need to cater for the individual needs of particular teaching levels.

Some ambiguity in the role and responsibilities of PDTs posed challenges for both for PDTs and the teachers. PDTs were assigned classes to teach even when the field- based component of the programme was going on. It was very challenging for PDTs to manage the assigned routine classroom teaching together with all the activities of the VTP for about 23 teachers. This ambiguity affected the programme in the following two ways.

1. Most of the time PDTs remained busy in the assigned routine classroom teaching and with the activities of VTP. They could not get time for their own growth through reading recent literature, searching the Internet, collaborating with their colleagues for better planning, carrying out small scale research, and so forth. It was very important for PDTs to refresh themselves so that they could meet the needs of a context-based VTP. When PDTs work at AKU-IED they just concentrate fully on the planning, implementation and reflection of the programme and it brings creativity and effectiveness in their work. Working in a school environment with the routine responsibilities was challenging.

2. In component II of the programme, support of PDTs for the teachers plays an important role. In both the VTPs in Dhaka that support was given through four classroom observations conducted by PDTs. After each observation, the teachers were provided with an opportunity to discuss the strengths and areas for improvement of the observed lesson with PDTs. It was observed that the teachers needed more help than a few classroom observations during their field-based component. They needed a mentor to work with them. They needed a person who could make formal observations of classes, who could sit with them in their planning time to act as a catalyst for generating new ideas, a person who can scaffold them in the classes when they take a risk of trying out a new idea. The teachers also felt the need of more support as they mentioned it while responding to the evaluation questionnaires for components II and III. A few of such responses are as follows:

- There should be unannounced/sudden/surprised/ informal observation besides formal observation by PDTs in component II.
- More observations are required.
- Teachers will learn more by teaching with an expert.
- More PDTs are required so that they can provide us more help and feedback to our reflections and lesson plans.
- 'Here' PDTs could not provide that much support because of their other school responsibilities as well.

Implementation of the new ideas in a real classroom situation was a big challenge for both PDTs and the teachers. The following were the special situations which imposed challenges for them:

1. Since a few teachers were selected from each section of the school, namely Senior, Junior and Primary, therefore some teachers from each section got an opportunity to attend the VTP and some did not. As a result of this selection approach, when the teachers returned to their schools, they faced challenges in working with those of their colleagues who did not

have this exposure. The challenge became severe in the light of the fact that in some school sections teachers of various class sections were expected to do the same planning for teaching in order to give similar experiences to all children and to maintain the similarity in written work. It was difficult for the teachers to make their colleagues understand the new techniques/ideas because they themselves were at the learning stage and not ready to coach others. The teachers themselves suggested that it would have been better if the programme was planned for the teachers of a particular section.

2. In the school, the process of professional development started from the teachers. Though the Principal and the Vice-Principals attended some sessions as observers no professional development was planned for them as such. When the teachers started applying their learning in the classes, the support, which was required in terms of supportive infrastructure, was not in place. In general, the school management was quite supportive to teachers to facilitate them to implement their learning but there was a need to bring certain changes in school policies and general practice in order to facilitate the process of change. For example, teachers' workload was kept the same as it was before though the expectations were raised high. They were now supposed to use library and computer laboratory resources, develop their own resources in the form of teaching material, plan lessons, write reflections, share with colleagues, and so on. To fulfil all these new expectations they needed time and they were not facilitated in this area. As a result teachers became quite exhausted and at times they questioned the applicability of all the new ideas learnt in the school in terms of available time. There were some other issues also which could have been addressed by the management like creating time for sharing, creating space for storing newly developed resources, reviewing teachers' workload, correction of work policy, and so on. Perhaps if the management had been well aware of the dynamics of change process and had a deeper understanding of school improvement, they could have reflected on all these issues in order to support their teachers.

Issues Related to School Improvement

The VTP-Dhaka Model was a part of the school improvement effort. If we look at this model in a broader perspective in order to see its impact in the long run for school improvement, we find certain issues surrounding it. The Dhaka-Model for the professional development of the teachers, presents a model of in-service teacher education which was part of the school improvement initiatives. The school wanted to bring a change in the 'chalk and talk' method of learning and teaching by making the classes more student oriented, interactive, collaborative and inquiry based. The main issue was that the planning for the teacher education programme was done thoroughly but the planning of this innovation was not done as a change process for school improvement. The aspects of implementation, institutionalization, sustainability, and so forth were not thought out carefully before the beginning of the programme. The major issue is the sustainability of the impact of the professional development in terms of changed classroom practices. The school embarked upon the programme without establishing a proper academic support system for the follow-up and support for the graduates of the programme. Though the two PDTs are in the system, in the absence of proper role and status they are not in a position to do the follow-up. After the completion of the VTP-Dhaka Model 2000, the graduates were not followed up in any way. In the absence of a proper professional/academic support system, the teachers may fall back to their old practices. It raises the issue of continuity also. How will the school provide further opportunities to the teachers to continue their professional development? How will novice teachers be inducted in the system in future? How will ongoing academic support be provided to them?

The challenges surrounding the model raise important issues about school improvement such as whether the process of school improvement should start with the extensive professional development of the teachers or must it start with the development of a basic framework/model for school improvement? Should the professional development of teachers come first or should the professional development of school management be at the top? Is it more effective to think about the aspects of follow-up and sustainability of change after the change starts or it is more appropriate to think about these issues and structure them in the planning before the initiation of change? To respond to the needs of the various school systems, should AKU-IED's role be limited to facilitate the process of professional development of the staff or should it be broader in order to support the systems to develop basic frameworks and think of various aspects of follow-up and sustainability before initiating a change?

Note

[1] The Visiting Teacher Programme is a short teacher education programme of AKU-IED. It is an eight-week course conducted at the university campus.

References

AKU-IED (2000) *Visiting Teachers Programme. Dhaka Model 2001. Report on Component I*. Karachi: AKU-IED.

Law, S. & Glover, D. (2000) *Educational Leadership and Learning: practice, policy and research*. Buckingham: Open University Press.

Rehman, K. & Bhuiyan, S.M. (2001) School Based Professional Development: a Bangladesh experience. Paper presented at SIP Conference 2001 in Dhaka.

CHAPTER 12

School Improvement: a case from the Northern Areas in Pakistan

GULZAR KANJI & TAKBIR ALI

General Background

The Northern Areas of Pakistan with their rugged, rocky and breathtaking mountain scenery, snaking rivers and mighty glaciers, have recently emerged from isolation after the Pakistan and Chinese governments completed the building of the Karakoram Highway in the early 1980s, linking Pakistan to China. Criss-crossed by the mountain ranges of the Karakoram, the Hindukush and flanked by the Himalayas on the eastern side, this rough terrain with some of the highest mountain peaks in the world, consists of numerous fertile valleys sustaining small communities, whose livelihood mainly depends on agriculture and livestock. Lack of good roads and transport facilities has resulted in communities generally remaining isolated for centuries. The exact figure for the population is not available for the Northern Areas; however, according to the Pakistan government's estimate in 1996 it was approximately 1.6 million. The majority of the population is Muslim and consists of Sunni, Shia, Ismaili and Nurbakhshi communities (King & Mayhew, 1998, pp. 36-37).

Educational and Professional Development Context

In the Northern Areas – as in the rest of Pakistan – teaching is a poorly paid profession, which is not highly regarded by the local communities. In order to improve the status of teachers and the quality of teaching and learning both the government and the Aga Khan Education Service in the Northern Areas began to train hundreds of teachers through their Field Based Teacher Development Programme (FBTDP) which was initiated by the Aga Khan Education Service in Pakistan in the early 1980s.

The Aga Khan Education Service, Pakistan (AKES, P) is a non-governmental organization (NGO), which owns and manages 123 primary and secondary schools, mainly in the Gilgit and Ghizer districts. Although they were set up primarily for the education of girls they have more recently become coeducational. Parents generally prefer to send their children to these schools because their medium is English, unlike the government schools where the medium of instruction is Urdu. Other NGOs such as the Naunehal and Hunza Education Resource Project (HERP) as well as many private and army institutions complement the government provision for schooling.

The Institute for Educational Development at the Aga Khan University (AKU-IED) has also played a significant role in the professional development of teachers from the Northern Areas by training several experienced teachers as Professional Development Teachers (PDTs) through their M.Ed. Programme, and through their eight-week long Visiting Teacher Programme (VTP) based in Karachi (see Chapters 3 and 5). At the same time, AKES, P has taken a major initiative in conducting additional programmes for teachers, such as the Learning Enhancement and Achievement Programme (LEAP) for the improvement of communication skills in English. In the government sector, the Northern Areas Education Programme (NAEP) has focused on teacher development, management training for heads and communities and production of new curriculum materials. This has been made possible through financial and technical aid from the World Bank, Department for International Development, UK (DFID) and the British Council (United Kingdom [UK]).

The Establishment of the Professional Development Centre in Gilgit

In order to improve further the professional development of teachers in the Northern Areas, the AKU-IED and the Aga Khan Education Service set up a partnership which culminated in the establishment of the Professional Development Centre, North (PDCN) in Gilgit in 1998. The purpose of PDCN was stated thus in the original proposal which was developed by AKU-IED and AKES, P:

> The core function of the PDCN would be professional
> development of teachers who are already in service. Supporting
> functions would include management training of school heads and
> middle and senior level educational managers, curriculum
> development and research.

The PDCN set as its goal the development of strategies and initiatives which would build up a critical mass of well-trained and effective trainers, teachers and educational managers at primary and secondary levels, in the government, AKES, P and private schools, bearing in mind the needs and opportunities of female teachers. From the outset the PDCN began to develop strategies and approaches which were context related and innovative, which would improve the quality and standards of student outcomes and which would enable the team to try out and test new ideas, evaluate these and also attempt to influence policy. Thus the PDCN established a range of activities such as monthly educational forums, management programmes, regular meetings on gender issues, and short courses on primary education and library skills; the field-based Whole School Improvement Programme (WSIP) became the central feature of the PDCN's activities. The academic team at the Centre comprised five Professional Development Teachers (PDTs) who were trained by AKU-IED, an experienced head teacher and former HMI (Her Majesty's Inspector) of schools from the UK, and a programme coordinator from Canada who already had the experience of leading the Language Enhancement Achievement Programme (LEAP) in the Northern Areas of Pakistan. As mentioned above, their remit was to achieve the programme goals with the help and guidance from various faculty members at AKU-IED, who visited the Northern Areas for short periods of two to three weeks to support and enhance the PDCN programmes.

What is ?ADD 'THE' Whole School Improvement Programme?

The whole School Improvement Programme (WSIP) is an approach to enhance the quality of teaching, learning and student outcomes, which enables the external motivator – a Professional Development Teacher (PDT) in this instance – to focus on a school as a learning organization and a community of practice. In order to improve classroom practice, it was recognized that many traditional structures and systems would need to change concurrently, and that the head, the staff and the community would need to work together to ensure that new ideas and practices were tried out, adapted and internalized by them. Various research studies carried out, for example, in the British context by Hopkins (1996) and Stoll and Fink (1996), have shown that the interrelationships between different areas of school improvement have a critical role in enhancing or constraining student learning and outcomes. The main areas addressed concurrently in schools by the PDCN are as follows:

- leadership and management;
- the quality of teaching and learning;
- curriculum and staff development;
- community involvement;
- students' behaviour and emotional development, and health education;
- accommodation and resources for supporting learning (see Appendix).

Centre-based and individually focused training in the Northern Areas over the past decade has not significantly changed the traditional practices in schools partly because the head teachers and the educational providers did not support the returnees in implementing new ideas and initiatives, and partly because the political and cultural undercurrents as well as professional jealousies within schools hindered them from initiating changes and improving their schools. According to House (1981) it is important to consider the impact of cultural, political and technological aspects on institutional improvement because these undercurrents are instrumental in enabling innovations either to succeed or to fail. In an unsupportive school climate, the newly gained skills of teachers are quickly eroded and the status quo is re-established. In Hargreaves's view (1994, p. 436): 'First, there is little significant school development without teacher development. Second, there is little significant teacher development without school development'. He argues that these two propositions challenge the more simple view that improved schools result from improving individual teachers.

This is not to say that all centre-based and individually focused training is fruitless. Rather, it could be very productive if schools took on the role of learning communities and became more receptive to new ideas and practices. Therefore, the PDCN team attempted to influence positively the interplay between the cultural, the technological and the political aspects (House, 1981) of the project schools by being a part of the school life as it was lived, and by focusing on the whole school as a unit of training. The strategy of treating each project school as a unit of training was based on the PDCN head's experiences of school inspections in the UK and the ideas gleaned from other researchers such as Fullan (1992), Hargreaves (1994) and Stoll and Fink (1996), who argue that greater success is achieved in improving schools if the institutional development and individual teacher's professional development go hand in hand.

How does the Whole School Improvement Programme Work?

The WSIP has a school-based focus for a period of at least one school year requiring two Professional Development Teachers (PDTs) to work with class teachers for two-person days a week in the first year, followed by less intensive support in the second year. As mentioned earlier, the PDTs are highly experienced and skilled trainers with a sound knowledge of educational theories and practice gleaned from their experiences and from the M.Ed. Programme at AKU-IED. Keeping in mind the realities of classrooms and the knowledge base and beliefs of teachers, PDTs help teachers maximize the available human and material resources to improve the quality of teaching and learning. They attempt to develop good practice through collaborative work, team teaching and activity-orientated learning. Additionally, a workshop is held every week after school hours to enhance teachers' professional knowledge and skills. The schedule of workshop topics includes: principles of children's learning, classroom organization and methodology, behaviour and discipline, health education, curriculum development, enhancement of some content knowledge, and improvement in examinations and assessment practices. Through these workshops it is intended to establish a culture of regular staff meetings, the purpose of which is to institutionalize regular professional/academic dialogue amongst teachers and heads. This is the most difficult challenge in terms of changing the deeply embedded egg-crate-like culture of schools (Hargreaves & Fullan, 1992, p. 220), where teachers teach within their own boundaries. The programme is not only designed as a vehicle for implementing effective practices but also as a research tool for examining the project schools' effectiveness as organizations, and the quality of the support structures and procedures of the educational systems which manage these schools.

The Programme

In the first year of the programme, 14 primary schools were selected: four in Hunza, four in the Ghizer valley and six in Gilgit. The size ranged from approximately 90 pupils to 200. The staff generally consisted of a teacher-in-charge and four to eight assistant teachers. In the primary schools, hardly any support staff such as secretaries, cleaners or caretakers were employed, with the result that all administrative work and maintenance had to be done by the staff and the local volunteers. Furthermore, because the teacher-in-charge or the head had a full timetable of seven or eight periods a day, neither of them was able to do justice to either the teaching load or other responsibilities such as meeting parents or collecting fees or supporting other teachers in their classrooms. It was in this very challenging context that PDTs worked alongside teachers and attempted to improve their practice.

The Role of Head Teachers

During the pilot phase of WSIP the training team quickly recognized that improvements in the area of teaching and learning, curriculum and staff development, resourcing and student behaviour required commitment and support from head teachers, who were instrumental in setting the cultural climate of their institutions. Since WSIP did not provide sufficient management and leadership training for heads, it was decided to involve AKU-IED faculty in conducting an additional, field-based programme – Certificate in Educational Management (CEM) – concurrently with WSIP for head teachers (see Chapter 9). The two programmes together seemed to have a greater impact on school improvement than either programme on its own. CEM brought about an attitudinal change in the majority of head teachers, who became bold enough to question and criticize the prevalent management and teaching practices in their schools. As other research studies have already demonstrated, the quality of leadership emerged as the most powerful factor in bringing about improvements (Farah, 1996; Memon, 2000). It was also found that the female heads in the project schools were more willing and flexible in adopting new ideas than their male counterparts, regardless of the systems they belonged to. The three most successful schools

197

in the project had female head teachers. The most successful school, which had the least material resources, and most untrained teachers, had the advantage of a young enthusiastic head with a vision and an ability to motivate the staff, parents and the community in taking on new approaches.

Teaching and Learning in WSIP Schools

Not unlike a minority of head teachers, a small number of teachers in the project schools benefited only marginally from the various opportunities offered by WSIP. There was great variation in an individual teacher's willingness and endeavour to learn more about his/her profession and in turn to improve the quality of teaching and learning in the classroom. The team came across different types of teachers in the project schools. Many teachers and head teachers welcomed new ideas enthusiastically, and put them into practice – ideas such as making low-cost materials in the form of zigzag books for reading or making displays of children's work or collecting nuts and seeds for counting or cutting cardboard shapes to demonstrate say, the concept of fractions. The heads became bold enough to observe teachers and proffer advice. Unforeseen problems arose when teachers and heads tried to initiate group work or stop using physical punishment particularly because the children were unused to such ideas. But these problems helped many participants to seek solutions. This group of professionals tended to display a positive attitude towards new challenges for their own learning as well as students' learning. In one instance, a head took the students into his confidence by explaining to them why the school had stopped beating them and what was expected of the children. He also devised a system of cards, which were given to the children for good behaviour. Other heads changed their timetables to create longer periods for practical work or created resource and library areas to store and retrieve materials or added sports activities to their timetables.

The second group, on the other hand, showed a lukewarm attitude towards new ideas and efforts to change. They put into practice new methods or ideas in the presence of the PDTs; but as soon as the external support and follow-up discontinued for whatever reason (for example, a PDT missing one school visit or not giving time to that particular teacher), they reverted to their old routines of rote learning and chalk and talk. The third group of teachers, who balked at new ideas and practices, were generally cynical, disillusioned and full of complaints against individuals and educational systems. Variations in teacher attitudes had a significant impact on student learning. Where teachers showed enthusiasm and support for new ideas, the students also responded with enthusiasm and commitment. The training team had the most difficult task of influencing the negative attitudes of teachers in order to create a critical mass of like-minded staff, who would continue with improvements after the team's departure. One major difficulty was in shifting teachers from chalk-and-talk approaches to doing practical work, for example, in the areas of numeracy or science. Because this kind of approach required planning and collection of materials, some teachers felt that it was too time-consuming for them. A story was recounted by a PDT about a teacher who continued to remain glued to her chalkboard despite several demonstrations by the PDT in the use of teacher-made games and practical activities created from waste materials. The PDT was beginning to despair when the teacher asked the PDT to bring her a cardboard box. The PDT beamed and thought, 'What a break through!' The following week, armed with boxes and other materials, the PDT approached the teacher's class and gave her the boxes. Upon seeing the boxes, the teacher picked out one and said, 'Thank you. This will be just right for making a parcel for my things.' The PDT was astounded at the response of the teacher, but continued to struggle on to bring about small improvements in her class.

Curriculum and Staff Development

In an educational climate where teaching is driven by textbooks and examinations, teachers perceive coverage and rote learning as the major ways in which to deliver the National Curriculum, although ironically, hardly any teacher has ever possessed, let alone seen the National Curriculum document. Thus the weekly workshops, which covered topics such as classroom management and organization, teaching of subjects such as mathematics, language and science, and developing assessment tools, encouraged the heads to work with their teachers. These workshops opened up opportunities for sharing information and generating an academic dialogue between heads and teachers. In one project school, for example, the head and the teachers continued to meet on the school premises during occasional holidays to plan together and make materials. Gradually teachers began to give time to planning and preparation in many project schools. With the aid of the PDTs, the teachers began to produce low-cost materials in order to promote more activity-based teaching and provide practical experiences for children. This particular innovation also led to the development of resource rooms and resource corners in the schools. In the lower primary classes, for example, PDTs helped with the collection of natural materials such as stones, sticks, nuts and seeds, flowers, leaves, bones, fur and feathers to strengthen conceptual development in the areas of numeracy and environmental education. Teachers also used cartons, boxes, newspapers, food packets, old fabric and plastic materials to make charts, pockets, books, drawings and flash cards. A purpose-made 'Teacher's Bag' was given to each member of staff filled with essential materials, such as scissors, glue, sticky tape, pins, crayons and pencils, marking pens, rulers, string and other useful materials to improve teaching and learning opportunities. One teacher commented, 'Without the bag and the materials we have got in our bags, in my view, a teacher is not complete.' A head teacher was moved to say, 'I view this bag as a teacher's weapon, as important as a gun for a hunter.'

Making materials, however, was not as difficult as changing the length of some periods from 35 minutes to possibly an hour in order to allow students sufficient time to carry out practical activities. The routines seemed to have been cast in concrete in the minds of heads and teachers. Persuasion and demonstrations by the PDTs ultimately resulted in changes in the length of some periods in most schools.

Another major innovation was the introduction in all project schools of the mobile library system. This required PDTs to select 50 information and story books for each school from the PDCN library to develop a reading culture and to inculcate the habit of reading amongst teachers and students beyond the textbooks. Teachers were also encouraged to enrich the content of the textbooks by using information books and stories. Again transporting the books proved easier than getting the schools to create library periods or incorporate additional material in their lessons. The change was brought about after much patience and perseverance on the part of the trainers. This particular innovation has had a significant impact on the attitudes of teachers and pupils alike in opening up the secondary world of imagination and engendering interest in information materials beyond textbooks.

Community Involvement

One of the six areas of development, as mentioned earlier, was the involvement of parents and the local community in the life of the school. While the local community had often played a significant role in raising funds and constructing school buildings, they were not encouraged to be involved in their children's learning. The parents bought school uniforms and textbooks, paid monthly fees and expected schools to give daily homework to their children. This was where the schools and parents drew their boundaries. The mothers' responsibility was generally to remain at home to attend to household chores, raise children and do agricultural work. PDTs, therefore, sought to enhance parents' participation by creating Mothers' Committees in schools to address such issues as homework, health education and cleanliness, students' behaviour and social development. This was seen as the beginning of a long road to getting mothers involved in understanding what their children did at school and how they could help them at home. Within a short period of time, mothers' gatherings at most schools became a regular event. Commenting on the mothers' responses, one head teacher said,

> Given the grim realities of the context, initially I thought that
> motivating the mothers and attracting them to school would be an
> impossible task since our females who work as housewives are
> illiterate, ruled by men, have no say in the use of household
> budget and are overloaded with household chores. But my
> judgement turned out to be wrong. If we plan well and work hard,

we can arouse parents' interest in their child's education and get from them whatever support we want.

Because the home environment and social attitudes do not promote gender equity, schools seemed to be the most appropriate places to foster an understanding of gender issues. PDTs consciously gave leading roles to girls in mixed-gender classrooms during activities, and placed girls in the front rows of classes. They also brought gender aspects to the fore in workshops by frequently giving lead roles to female teachers in discussions, lesson planning and teaching. They celebrated 'mothers' day' in schools, and established a pattern of home visits to build up women's confidence and to involve mothers in different activities in schools.

Pupil Behaviour, Health Education and Social Development

Health education, cleanliness and social development were addressed through the workshops and through PDTs' practice in the classrooms. Although cleanliness improved and pupils began to take responsibility for various tasks, the problem of physical punishment remained because it is deeply embedded in the culture of the communities. In an authoritarian culture, students often lacked confidence to interact with either the teachers or their peers. PDTs did manage to bring about small changes through the creation of an interactive teaching environment, the introduction of practical activities, opportunities for discussions and the use of appropriate questioning techniques during lessons.

Accommodation and Resources

Many project schools suffered from a severe shortage of classrooms. Furthermore, they did not use the available space effectively. Frequently, the training team had to face the problems of having the nursery and class 1 sitting outside the school building in extreme weather conditions, often on bare, dusty and rock-strewn ground with no furniture and no surfaces to write on. PDTs challenged this established practice that hardly anyone had tackled before and succeeded in enabling the schools to rethink their use of space and other resources, particularly in relation to the youngest pupils in the schools. PDTs also enabled teachers to make useful aids such as pegs out of broken furniture for hanging students' bags, or shelves to store materials and books.

Benefits to PDTs and Institutions

PDTs felt that they were able to apply their newly gained theoretical knowledge to real classroom situations thereby reviewing and refining it, and transforming it into procedural knowledge. For them it was a unique context in which they could demonstrate how different methods influenced teaching and learning, how practices could be changed and how problems could be solved, particularly by attending to the interplay between the political and cultural attitudes of staff. PDTs helped the heads to address many policy-related issues such as the supply of teachers and educational resources, and to show the policy-makers that these issues impacted on the quality of teaching and learning. PDTs not only engaged in a whole range of self-initiated activities in schools but also dealt with unexpected events and emergencies (for example, what to do with a child suffering from cholera, typhoid or diarrhoea, or how to maintain cleanliness during such epidemics). They also mentored teachers, did demonstration lessons, co-planned and co-taught lessons, cleaned classrooms and washrooms jointly with teachers, helped with behavioural problems, found appropriate books and information for the teachers, and made and used low-cost materials for teaching purposes. WSIP had clearly demonstrated that the quality of teaching and learning improved significantly when several aspects of school life were addressed at the same time, and when the head and staff jointly acted to examine critically and improve policies and practice.

Outcomes

Fullan's observation (Fullan, 1985, p. 396) that 'change takes place over time' was borne out again and again during the programme. One year is but a short period of time for schools to show significant improvements, particularly in examination results. However, improvements recorded by the training team were as follows:

- 9 out of 14 schools made changes in their timetables to create library periods and also double periods for practical work.
- In 10 out of 14 schools the system of one-teacher-one-class was introduced in the nursery and class 1.
- Standards of cleanliness improved in all schools. In 5 schools, the heads gave up their own offices or shared the space to accommodate pupils without classrooms.
- Most heads began to visit classrooms during lessons, and teachers also planned in advance at least a couple of lessons a week.
- Students developed greater confidence in their interactions with others.
- Benefits of the mobile library were evident in student enthusiasm and usage of books both by teachers and students.
- The education providers were beginning to pay greater attention to the suggestions made by PDCN. For example, they had begun to ensure that washrooms were available in all schools. They also began to provide more educational resources to schools.
- PDTs learnt that each school was a complex organization with its unique culture and that school improvement demanded a range of skills from them such as forward planning, flexibility, listening to the voices of teachers and pupils, patience, good communication, resourcefulness,

problem solving, conflict resolution, sound knowledge of the curriculum and above all, a sense of humour. They not only talked about school improvement, but they also *lived* it.

- Combination of CEM and WSIP accelerated improvements in schools.

Challenges

A major issue for PDCN is how to combat the weak infrastructures of the educational systems, which impact negatively on the work of the schools. Issues related to poor accommodation and resources, lack of maintenance, frequent absences of staff, inadequate staffing and poor support and monitoring structures. If these issues are not addressed effectively, then no amount of training will bring about significant and lasting improvements in schools. Other major issues such as poor content knowledge of many teachers, lack of management skills of head teachers, and low level of community involvement also need to be addressed.

Although small successes were evident in the programme, many challenges seemed formidable and as daunting as the mountains in the Northern Areas. Despite the feelings of frustration and despondency at times, the training team continued to work with zest and a sense of humour. Rosetta Marantez Cohen's comments confirmed the team's view that the quality of innovations was critical for success, that the innovations were not easy to implement, and that they needed to be seen in their proper perspective. Reflecting on her involvement in a three-year project called Quest, she writes:

> Taken together, then, there is nothing glamorous or even clear-cut about the modest reforms, which emerged over the course of the 3 years of Quest's existence. Though successes have occurred (e.g., teachers becoming renewed and revitalized, students becoming tolerant of one another), the day-to-day work of reform is still a complex, ambiguous morass of gains and losses, successes and defeats. Change, when it happens at all, happens slowly and incrementally. It follows no a priori plan, emerging instead as a patchwork of theory, personality, and compromise. (Cohen, 1995, p. 3)

References

Cohen, R.M. (1995) *Understanding How School Change Really Happens.* Thousand Oaks: Corwin Press.

Farah, I. (1996) *Roads to Success: self-sustaining primary school change in rural Pakistan.* Karachi: AKU-IED.

Fullan, M. (1985) Change Processes and Strategies at the Local Level, *The Elementary School Journal*, 85(3).

Fullan, M. (1992) *Successful School Improvement.* Buckingham and Philadelphia: Open University Press.

Hargreaves, D. (1994) The New Professionalism: a synthesis of professional and institutional development, *Teaching and Teacher Education*, 10(4), pp: 423-438.

Hargreaves, A. & Fullan, M. (1992) *Understanding Teacher Development.* New York: Teachers College Press.

Hopkins, D. (1996) Towards a Theory for School Improvement, in J. Gray, D. Reynolds, C. Fitz-Gibbon & D. Jesson (Eds) *Merging Traditions: the future of research on school effectiveness and school improvement*, pp. 30-51. London: Cassell.

House, E.R. (1981) Three Perspectives on Innovation, in R. Lehming & M. Kane (Eds) *Improving Schools: using what we know*, pp. 17-41. Beverly Hills: Sage.

King, J. & Mayhew, B. (1998) *Karakoram Highway.* Hawthorn, Victoria: Lonely Planet.

Memon, M. (2000) Improving Schools through Educational Leadership Programmes in Pakistan. Paper presented at the 13th International Congress for School Effectiveness and Improvement: global networking for quality education, Hong Kong, 4-8 January.

Stoll, L. & Fink, D. (1996) *Changing Our Schools.* Buckingham: Open University Press.

APPENDIX

Improving Opportunities for Children to Learn

Quality of Teaching and Learning

Teachers have high expectations of pupils' achievement. They have clear objectives, lesson plans and evaluation procedures. They use appropriate textbooks, displays and resources for teaching and learning. Children are active learners and do sustained work. They are highly motivated, eager to learn and show initiative.

They take risks and are not afraid to make mistakes.

Leadership, Management and Administration

Head Teacher has a clear vision for the school and high expectations. HT communicates effectively, demonstrates instructional leadership, supports teachers and visits them in class, shares responsibility, provides for staff development, manages finance, plans ahead and keeps good records, works collaboratively with parents and community.

Curriculum Development and Staff Development

National Curriculum is enriched by the use of relevant resources and information. The curriculum is broad, balanced, relevant and matched to children's needs and experiences. It is challenging. HT and teachers organize regular in-service training. They constantly endeavour to improve their knowledge and skills.

Community Participation

Parents and community are involved in the work of the school. They co-operate and collaborate with Headteacher and teaching staff. Parents are involved in their children's learning, and policymaking.
Parents and community share their skills with teachers and children.
School organizes regular meetings and classes for the community.

Building, Accommodation and Resources

School environment is well maintained, inviting and attractive. It is effectively used. Resources, including the library, are adequate and easily accessible. There are good displays of children's work and other materials.
Children and teachers take pride in their environment and maintain high standards.

Social, Moral and Spiritual Development of Students and Health Education

Standards of students' behaviour and discipline are exemplary. Students are well behaved, cooperative and keen to take responsibility. Students and teachers collaborate, and show respect towards each other and all members of the school community.

CHAPTER 13

Problems of Teachers' Re-entry in Schools after In-service Education

RAZIA FAKIR MOHAMMED

Introduction

This chapter reports a research study of how mathematics teachers who had participated in an eight-week in-service Visiting Teacher (VT) mathematics education programme, organized by the Institute for Educational Development at the Aga Khan University (AKU-IED) in Pakistan, implemented their learning in their classrooms. As the researcher in this study, I engaged in two phases of research. In Phase 1, I adopted an interpretative stance in a phenomenological tradition to understand the teachers' classroom implementation of their learning following the course they attended. Evidence from Phase 1 showed that teachers alone were not in a position to accelerate their improvement within existing school and systemic constraints. A need emerged from the teachers to establish a collaborative relationship between myself and them for development of teaching in the context of the classroom. I, therefore, extended this research from a study of teachers' implementation strategies to a participatory study (Phase 2) of processes involved in supporting teachers' learning and classroom implementation. In this chapter I report only from Phase 1.

A new role in the classroom, in the context of the Visiting Teacher Programme (VTP) at AKU-IED derives from the literature that suggests characteristics for teaching mathematics according to a child's psychological and social perspectives of learning in the classroom (for example, Cobb & Steffe, 1983; Cobb et al, 1991; Jaworski, 1994). This perspective suggests that a mathematics teacher's primary responsibility is to assist in the learners' cognitive restructuring and conceptual reorganization through providing opportunities for social interaction in mathematical tasks that encourage discussion and negotiation of ideas to help them develop conceptual understanding. The instructors on the VT course in mathematics education focus on the conceptual shift in the practice of teachers from traditional to innovative methods: helping children to develop their thinking and to become responsible individuals within society, and also to assume responsibility for their own learning. They encourage the course participants (VTs) to hypothesize, argue and seek patterns while rationalizing rules and facts, and implement new ways of teaching in classrooms in a cooperative environment. The aim of this approach is to promote VTs' conceptual understanding of mathematics so that they will, in turn, promote their students' conceptual understanding in mathematics classrooms. I designed my research to follow up with some of the teachers who had resumed their teaching after attending the course. This chapter documents and discusses the practical reality, and the challenges and concerns of teacher adaptations to their new role in the context of schools in Pakistan emerging from Phase 1 of the study. Participants in Phase 1 of the study were five teachers, from different government and private schools. They had attended secondary mathematics Visiting Teachers (VT) courses in 1998 or 1999 at AKU-IED. Two of these schools had Professional Development Teachers (PDTs) and the others had VTs from other programmes in different subject areas.

Methodology

The data collection in Phase 1 of the research (from mid-September 1999 to early December 1999) mainly involved field-notes from classroom observation and audio-recorded conversations of my pre- and post-observation meetings with the teachers. The first research meeting with each teacher involved a lengthy conversation about the teachers' learning experiences in the VT course at AKU-IED. The subsequent meetings involved classroom observations and follow-up interviews or conversations. The language used in conversations between the teachers and the researcher was Urdu; the teachers' explanation in their classrooms was also in Urdu, therefore data was collected in Urdu in this study. Analysis was a process of organizing and managing the data regarding the teachers' practice and issues in their classroom after attending the course; and of explaining and understanding this data from the teachers' perspectives (Moustakas, 1994). Analysis began by working on each teacher's data as a whole, including all the field-notes and transcriptions relevant to the teacher in the first phase of my research. I grouped the relevant statements or actions, which were explaining similar aspects of teaching or developing teaching in the classroom. I reviewed the organization of my data critically, reading and rereading it several times. By use of the constant comparative method, in a grounded theory perspective (Glaser & Strauss, 1967), several themes were identified.

Overview of Teachers' Perceptions and Practice

From the conversation in our first meetings it became evident that all five teachers were aware of the usefulness of the new methods of teaching they had experienced in the VT Programme and were motivated to improve their teaching. The teachers believed that students could learn better if a teacher provided them with opportunities to learn mathematics practically and related mathematics to daily life. The teachers liked the collaborative environment at AKU-IED, where mutual dependence was a norm and they did not feel a sense of failure or of inadequacy. The way they experienced themselves as learners at AKU-IED helped them to reconceptualize their roles as mathematics teachers in their respective schools as each of them was motivated to bring change in their classroom practice.

However, from my observations regarding their practice it appears that the major criterion of success in their lessons was emphasis on students' right answers to teachers' mainly closed questions. Teachers acquired all their information, for teaching a topic, from the textbook. A topic was especially important for them if it was expected to be included in the examination. Their teaching was mainly focused on the completion of the exercises given in the textbook. The teachers would provide the students with a formula and solve problems on the board. The students copied down or listened to the teacher or gave answers to the teacher's mainly closed questions. I have chosen a representative piece of teaching from my field-notes and presented it in Figure 6.[1] The topic of the lesson is 'ratio', in Class VII.

In my observations of the teachers' practice, I saw little evidence of the characteristics of a teacher's new role discussed at AKU-IED and based on the mathematics education literature: for example, teachers making sense of the students' thinking in terms of listening to what students say and debriefing their answers; encouraging classroom activity and student involvement; discussion of mathematical ideas by students, and between teacher and students, in an interactive learning environment (for example, Cobb et al, 1991; Jaworski, 1994). I observed that teachers in both government and private school contexts were always in a rush, running from class to class, with a heavy load of 'corrected copies' (students' notebooks).

Teachers' Problems

From my analysis of the conversation regarding inconsistency between the teachers' practice and their stated beliefs, based on their participation in the VT Programme, the following themes were identified.

School's Expectations

The teachers' conversations suggested that in their schools, either government or private, they considered themselves to be a means of carrying out school routines, bearing the workload and accepting the limitations and orders of their school authorities. The teachers perceived that the characteristics of a good teacher are those of being regular and punctual in all the tasks given by the school authorities as their appraisal would depend on their annual performance report.

1 T	You know that the symbol of ratio and proportion is different. Read the question.
	The teacher pointed to a student and asked him to read aloud the question from the text book.
2 S	The ratio between ages of Ali and Ejaz is 3 and 4 and Ejaz and Anwar is 2 and 3. What is the ratio among the ages of three of them?
3 T	Who is younger than whom and who is older than whom?
	The students did not answer the teacher's question. The teacher turned to the board and wrote the following information.
	Ratio between Ali and Ejaz = **3:4**
	Ratio between Ejaz and Anwar = **2:3**
	Continuous ratio**?**
	After writing the information, he turned to the students.
5 T	Would you tell me the method to find the solution
	The students were quiet.
6 T	In your book a method is given which is called 'N method'.
	The teacher turned to the board, and asked again what was the ratio between Ali and Ejaz. One of the students gave the answer which was 3 and 4. Then the teacher wrote the student's answer on the board. He asked another question about Ejaz and Anwar's ratio and wrote in the following manner,
	Ali: Ejaz: Anwar
	$3 \quad 4$
	$2 \quad 3$
	The teacher linked the quantities with the arrows as it is shown above.
7 T	A figure of 'N' is formed so this method is called 'N method'. We need to multiply numbers linked by arrows to find the answer. For example we will multiply 2 and 3, 2 and 4, and 3 and 4.
	The teacher asked more questions while solving the above example, e.g. what would be the product of 3 and 4, what will you get when multiply 2 by 4. The students answered correctly and the teacher wrote their answers. After that the teacher multiplied the numbers and, by relating them with arrows, wrote **6: 8:12**.
8 T	Do you know a table which can divide 6, 8 and 12?
	One of the students replied that it was '2'. The teacher simplified the result further.
9 T	3:4:6 is our answer. Now all of you please copy down the question [solution].

Figure 6. Representative piece of teaching.

For the government school teachers, the most important issue was the physical set-up, namely, the poor condition of classrooms, lack of resources, large numbers of students in a class, authority of the school management in decision-making regarding their teaching subjects, pressure of workload and low level of students' thinking. A top-down form of decisions, inspections and increasing workload diminishes the teachers' confidence in their ability to improve and minimizes possibilities of learning, as one of them said:

> At IED, we had the opportunity to work together. In school,
> teachers do not have time to talk to each other. We see each other
> at teatime. Teachers are always in a rush for going from one class

to another class....The students are mostly irregular, and if I make groups the next day the students would complain that the group is incomplete as someone else is absent ... . I have 62 girls in one class, correction of their note books, preparing test papers, recording numbers in report cards, is my responsibility. I have other classes also. If we make a little mistake, in counting the student marks, the head teacher immediately calls a meeting. You do not know how much pressure we have.

The private school teachers appeared to be responsible for testing their students regularly in order to get better results in their final examination. One of them said:

We have regular monthly tests, class tests besides four terminal exams. We have to complete, correct, and revise students' work in order to make them able to pass the coming 'exam'. Again preparation of results [which includes correction, counting and grading] is all the time with us. I take copies with me to my home and spend my bedtime in checking. The school is very strict in timely checking of children's work. The school expects us to be regular, punctual and attentive to each student in order to get good results. I do not have time to relax. Have you ever seen me at leisure?

The private school teachers did not mention, explicitly, any problem of getting resources. However, new ways of teaching learned at the AKU-IED required time and professional support to teach a topic and the teacher could not always afford such time and support.

The school provides materials if we need them. I can make photocopies of work sheets. We have many books in the library and I often use them. Some topics are very difficult and I don't have ideas about how to teach them in new ways. Then I teach in my own way ... . If I find that I am behind in completion of the syllabus as compared to my colleagues, I teach directly from the book. It is not possible to allow students to participate actively all the time.

My analysis suggests that, on the course, the teachers became aware of the importance of applying their new learning for the enhancement of the children's learning in the school. They were with like-minded, supportive people and at the AKU-IED they never felt alone or insecure. Contrarily, in the school environment the teachers practised traditional methods of teaching as they did not have a similar facility of support and expectations by like-minded people at the school.

Lack of Moral Support

After attending the course the teachers wanted the school's support or encouragement to try out innovations such as group work or focusing more on questioning in order to incorporate these approaches into existing classroom routines. They needed a vote of confirmation of their new thinking from the school environment in which they worked. For this purpose they shared their action plans (developed at AKU-IED) with the head teachers. They looked for other colleagues and the school management, who could think, believe or act like they had experienced at AKU-IED. However, they did not receive encouragement; everyone was pursuing routine traditional teaching practices:

> When I came to my school I shared my action plan with the head teacher and she told me that I would not be able to perform accordingly. And it was true.

Referring to his meeting with the head teacher after resuming teaching, one teacher said:

> Instead of listening to me (about my learning at IED) my head teacher said, 'I want a treat from you for your certificate from the Aga Khan University' ... Nobody there had a similar perspective of teaching such as I had developed at IED. And after a few weeks I locked my files in a cupboard and resorted to the routine way of teaching.

Evidence shows that the teachers after the course were insecure in their thinking in schools. They re-entered the schools with new thinking but in a familiar pattern of activities in the culture of schools the teachers appeared to be highly routine-bound. The private school teachers had a fear of losing their jobs and survival in the school, because teaching was also a major source of earning for them, and all their efforts were therefore directed to satisfying the school's needs and expectations.

I quote one private school teacher's comments here. Though she said that she was joking, I now feel that it indicates a real problem. She said:

> if my 'correction' will not be completed in time, my school will kick me out. Do you think that IED would then feed my family?

My analysis is that new thinking and re-entry is perplexing and both cultural and moral support is required in putting new vision into practice. The teachers alone are not in a position to accelerate their improvement within the existing school and systemic constraints. This also results in teachers' adoption of a non-risk form of teaching, low motivation for improvement and discouragement by an authoritarian culture of school. As one of them said:

> Do you think two months' training is enough? There is nobody from IED who comes to school and asks us about problems and work after the VT course.

The teachers' re-entry into their school after the VT phase was a difficult period in rationalizing their learning into a different social setting which had different aims, agenda and expectations from AKU-IED. They needed moral and professional support in order to align their new thinking in the school context. Thus, it was easier to resume their previous role in school, as that role had already been accepted by the school from their many years of teaching experience. In addition to that, traditional teaching was the way teachers could work on their own.

Self-imposition

The teachers' conversations indicated their conformity with their former experiences of learning and teaching mathematics traditionally and its pervasiveness in the school context. For example, one teacher said that she was comfortable in teaching through the traditional method:

> I teach according to the way my teachers taught me ... I like the traditional way of teaching because it is easy and I do not know another method.

The teachers assumed that if they were to start thinking about their AKU-IED learning in the classroom practice, they would not be able to satisfy the school syllabus and preparation for examinations.

> The new way of teaching should be right from the primary school. The students' basic concepts are very weak. If I commit myself to this basic work, how would I manage to complete the syllabus?

The teachers did not have time or motivation to think about their practice on their own during or after their teaching time in the school:

> There are other visiting teachers in school and I do not think they are applying the VT. Everybody is in routine. They think that if they are satisfying the school's needs, why they should give themselves problems.

The new methods of teaching learned at AKU-IED demanded time, support and effort and were incompatible with the school expectations:

> The IED environment is far away from the real situation of school; IED's methods negate the applicability of its philosophy in school. IED provides relaxation in timing and luxury in resources and satisfies all basic needs, which was quite in contrast to the school where teachers have difficulty in getting a chair or a glass of water.

However, none of the teachers was directly stopped by anyone from effecting change in terms of their decisions to adopt new methods of teaching. The teachers were decision-makers regarding how the subject matter, imposed by the management in the form of a prescribed textbook, was taught.

> We know that we have to complete the textbook, nobody tells us how and what, but we know it. Sometimes they ask us to choose important exercises and finish the syllabus.

The evidence indicates that teachers viewed the lack of external support as an obstacle – a constraint in applying their new learning in the classroom. They were not explicitly aware of their responsibility or potential in developing their teaching practice. They had seen their school limitations as insurmountable problems and the solution of those problems was out of their reach. In addition, the teachers' previous experiences were recognised by the existing culture of schooling in Pakistan. The schools assessed them according to their efficiency and proficiency in helping students to get results and complete and revise the textbook as many times as possible; which means that their previous teaching was very much accepted by the context as well as approved by themselves. One of them asked me:

> Is it all applicable in this situation? If you were allowed to work here would you be able to maintain the quality of thinking and work you all do at IED?

It is important to recognize here that teachers alone were not in the position to improve their teaching. They did not seem to be aware of their own self-resistance in developing their teaching.

Interpretations and Expectations

I found an issue of difference between the teachers' interpretations of their learning and the course expectations. For example, the teachers, who believed in active involvement of students and thought their teaching practice to be in line with the AKU-IED principles, were really changed teachers according to their own views. In the case of some teachers, their students worked in groups for sure – they were *sitting* in groups – but the group work was not promoting students' deeper understanding of mathematics as hypothesized at AKU-IED. For example, one teacher, who arranged group work, viewed the purpose of group work in the following way:

> I explained everything, then completed the exercise [the teacher solved each question] and gave questions for practice to work in groups. You can understand how much work I have to do.

The outcomes of group work were limited as there was no evidence that the group discussion contributed to the students' understanding of the topic. In a physical set-up of a group, either the students would solve questions individually in their groups according to the teacher's method or help their friends to apply the teacher's method in solving questions or explain what the teacher asked them to do. Although, the teachers used the terminologies of group work, open questions, practical aspects of mathematics, use of concrete materials, and so forth, they did not discuss the meaning or substance of all the mentioned terms, and it seemed that they did not think about how these approaches would contribute to students' learning.

Discussion

Because of my experience of being an instructor in the VT programme, I knew that the teachers' mathematical misconceptions (such as concept of an angle, ratio equations, and so on) were discussed in the course in a very detailed manner. However, there was no evidence of the teachers using that experience of mathematics in their classroom when students' misconceptions were apparent. Why did the teachers not apply their learning of mathematics in teaching? Why did the teachers' perceive IED's perspectives of teaching in this limited way? Were such ideas and approaches not applicable for the teachers' needs, in the ways they were introduced to the teachers? Why does such a conflict exist? This could be an issue of a difference of expectations between teacher and learner, 'didactic tension', as Mason (1988) called it. It could be said here that the teachers had got the shell (the names of strategies and methods) but not the pearl (understanding) inside it. What might resolve this conflict?

The teachers' practice, in accordance with the school's expectations, reveals the problems of teachers' adaptations of behaviour with respect to authority or culture, as well as transference of the teachers' learning from one culture to another culture. The university course took the teachers away from all the problems they faced in schools and provided them with a new experience of learning in a relatively luxurious environment. It could be seen as an unintentional and gentle imposition on the teachers, who had had opposite experiences of working/learning previously. My analysis is that an imposition, either strict or gentle, resists change in understanding but quickly appears in the change in behaviour and in words. At the university the teachers had resources, opportunities and encouragement to try out new ideas with professional support which extended their thinking in relation to modifying their teaching practice. However, the school expected them to complete the syllabus and shaped the teachers' practice according to its expectations. The teachers' behaviour in two different environments points to the influence of the nature of two contexts in making or breaking their efforts of developing teaching. This also identifies the conflicting expectations of different environmental conditions in believing, at AKU-IED, and practising change, at school. Thus, the difference between two cultures of teachers' learning and practising reaffirms teachers' confidence in deeply held experiences of traditional teaching of mathematics and their consistency with the culture of school. Teachers' practice, therefore, appears to be resistant to change, no matter how effectively a university course engages them in new methods.

The conflict could also exist when there is a big difference between the teachers' (in this context the instructors of the VT programme) expectations and the learners' (the teachers) expectations and the instructors' philosophy of teaching and the teachers' theoretical perspectives. The instructors of the VT programme encouraged the teachers to develop a perspective of teaching similar to theirs, so that the teachers could introduce change into their classrooms. The instructors provided an environment for the teachers so they would not only learn mathematics but also the process of learning mathematics in an interactive learning environment. These expectations could be seen as a substantial and sudden difference from the teachers' previous experiences, thoughts, perceptions, environment and experiences to the new one in the short period of the course. They were situated in a powerful culture that had a heavy influence on their thinking and actions. A question arises as to whether it is possible for teachers to grasp new concepts (mathematics and mathematics teaching) in a limited time at AKU-IED, with no continuing support in their school. The teachers themselves were not secure in fulfilling those expectations. It is therefore not surprising that they remembered some terminologies without an in-depth understanding.

The teachers had difficulties rationalizing two roles. One role was based on their tacit perception of being a teacher, completing the textbook and preparing students for examinations. The second role was to enable the students to be actively participating in their learning according to the teacher's new understanding. Limited time and support did not allow them to reflect on the implications or gain insights. Some teachers thought both roles could not be fulfilled by a teacher at the same time. Some tried to adopt both perceptions but were not able to fulfil them in order to enhance students' learning and the issue appeared in the form of didactic tension.

Thus, the teachers' teaching was in the tradition of the school and society with little influence from their learning at the course. These teachers were traditional teachers but also appeared responsible adults. A lack of support and a culture of practising routine in schools had discouraged them from continuing change in their practice. The teachers' saying that 'nobody could understand our problems', or 'there was nobody from IED to care for our learning', all showed that these teachers were discouraged by their schools as well as ignored by the university in their further improvement. At the initial stage of change, teachers needed consistency between their learning and contextual expectations and support; the school had its own limitations, aims and agenda and the teachers expected continued support from AKU-IED, which was not available. Under the unfavourable conditions of the school, although desirous of teaching according to course ideology, they just kept their wishes to themselves.

A Way Forward

From the discussion above, it can be assumed that any proposed change in teaching should address areas such as school policy, teachers' working conditions and resources, innovative curricula and improvement in teacher appraisal structures (as discussed in Day, 1999; Kelly, 1999). The question remains: what are the implications for teachers who are struggling for change in schools in the context of Pakistan, where bringing changes at a policy level is an ambitious goal? The teachers' issues confirm that change cannot flourish in a vacuum. Teachers, isolated from support and within conceptual and contextual constraints, see the school as an authority figure, teach for the right answer and explain rules, rather than discussing the reasoning behind them.

Several questions emerge for the community of teacher educators: can teachers achieve any improvement, if the culture works against the teachers' improvement? How can teachers maximize their learning capacities if their self-esteem is low? What can be the nature of teacher education in these circumstances and limitations? How can we, as teacher educators, liberate teachers from the imposed constraints of schools in their contemplation of change? In order to respond to these questions I will refer to one of the teachers who said: 'We need an environment to "push" [drive] us.' Evidence from Phase 2 of this study also demonstrates that a highly supportive and trusting relationship between a teacher and a teacher educator is of benefit for teacher education, and for research with the teachers in Pakistani schools (Mohammad, 2002).

It is important to recognize here that teachers' engagement in an in-service course is necessary and, potentially, a powerful part of the continuing professional development of in-service teachers; however, leaving teachers unsupported in school and expecting them to be change agents cannot bring about improvement in practice at the beginning of this journey to change. Teachers' professional development is restricted rather than extended, fragmentary rather than coherent, while they feel isolated within their constraints and view the course as a one-shot professional learning event.

Note

[1] I have translated into English all transcripts and quotations from teachers from the Urdu in which they were spoken and recorded.

References

Cobb, P. & Steffe, I.P. (1983) The Constructivist Researcher as Teacher and Model Builder, *Journal for Research in Mathematics Education*, 14, pp. 83-94.

Cobb, P., Wood, T. & Yackel, E. (1991) Assessment of a Problem Centred Second Grade Mathematics Project, *Journal for Research in Mathematics Education*, 22(1), pp. 3-29.

Day, C. (1999) *Developing Teachers: the challenges of lifelong learning.* Norwich: Falmer Press.

Glaser, B.G. & Strauss, A.L. (1967) *The Discovery of Grounded Theory.* London: Weidenfeld & Nicolson.

Jaworski, B. (1994) *Investigating Mathematics Teaching: a constructive enquiry.* London: Falmer Press.

Kelly, A. (1999) Education or Indoctrination? The Ethics of School Based Action Research, in R. Burgess (Ed.) *The Ethics of Educational Research.* London: Falmer Press.

Mason, J. (1988) Tensions, in D. Pimm (Ed.) *Mathematics, Teachers and Children.* London: Hodder & Stoughton.

Mohammad, F.R. (2002) From Theory to Practice: an understanding of the implementation of in-service mathematics teachers' learning from university into classroom practice. Unpublished doctoral dissertation, University of Oxford.

Moustakas, C. (1994) *Phenomenological Research Methods.* London: Sage.

CHAPTER 14

Affecting Schools through a Health Education Initiative

TASHMIN KASSAM-KHAMIS & SADIA MUZZAFAR BHUTTA

Introduction

Health is inextricably linked to educational achievements, quality of life, and economic productivity. By acquiring health-related knowledge, values, skills and practices, children can be empowered to pursue a healthy life and to work as agents of change for the health of their communities. (Dr Hiroshi Nakajima, Director General WHO, 1997; see Nakajima, 1997)

Since the 1950s it was acknowledged that to learn effectively children need good health (WHO Expert Committee on School Health Services, 1950). Research shows that malnutrition as well as parasitic and other infections in primary school age children cause low school enrolment, high absenteeism, early drop-out and poor performance (Pollitt, 1990; Levinger 1994). When health is defined more broadly as a state of complete physical, mental and social well-being rather than merely the absence of disease (WHO, 1978), the health benefits of education are easily established. School has a direct effect on the self-esteem and health of its staff and students (Hopkins, 1987; Sammons, Hillman & Mortimore, 1994). This positive effect is particularly significant for girls who as future mothers are more likely to seek prenatal care earlier, give birth to healthier babies and bring them home to healthier environments. In fact, the single most important determinant of a child's health is believed to be its mother's level of education (Das Gupta, 1990; Arya & Devi, 1991). For example, mothers who have attended even one year of schooling are more likely to have their children immunized (WHO, 1996).

The evidence of the close relationship between health and education supports the drive for promoting health in schools to combine the goals of 'Health for All' and 'Education for All' through the Global School Health

Initiative (WHO, 1996). This initiative for Comprehensive School Health Promotion integrates three areas in the school, which usually work separately, into one health programme, namely the school environment, school health education and school health services, hence the term 'comprehensive' (WHO, 1996, 1997).

In 1997, the Institute for Educational Development at the Aga Khan University (AKU-IED) conducted a study to identify the need for school health programmes in Pakistan (Hawes & Khamis, 1997). This concluded that while the education policy of Pakistan identifies health and physical education as a part of primary schooling, it is only attended to in a token way; school staff and parents desired health promotion as a necessary part of their children's education and confirmed that not enough was done in the schools in this regard. In 1998, as a follow-up of the needs analysis, AKU-IED, in partnership with Save the Children (UK) and the Child-to-Child Trust (UK), began an action research project entitled, 'Health Action Schools' to develop prototypes or models of health promoting schools in Pakistan. This chapter will focus on the effects of teachers' training in health education, and children's participation in promoting health, on the school and its community.

Health Action Schools in Pakistan: an overview

Some 40 schools were initially visited as potential pilot health action schools and five were selected using the following criteria:

1. School Head and or the Principal expressed interest and enthusiasm to try out the project.
2. Teachers and students wished to take on the programme.
3. Schools represented different socio-economic and educational contexts.
4. Schools were within reasonable reach of the AKU-IED (within an hour by car).
5. Schools were willing to interact with each other when possible to share ideas and act as a support to each other.

The selected pilot schools consisted of three schools of low socio-economic status, one of high socio-economic status and one of middle socio-economic status. Three of these schools were mixed and there was one boys' school and one girls' school.

The implementers of the health action programme were the schools themselves, initially through the teachers. AKU-IED inputs into schools were confined to teacher development through training, monitoring and the distribution of resource materials for lesson planning and teaching. No additional textbooks, audio-visual materials or other costly financial inputs were given to the school as this would endanger the possibilities of sustainability in schools with limited resources.

Each school appointed a health co-ordinator, from amongst the teachers, to manage the programme and committed to 30 health education lessons per year (or 10 lessons per term over 3 terms) taught either as a separate weekly subject or through finding time within other carrier subjects, for example, Science, Social Studies or Language. Thus on average at least one health lesson was taught each week. Moreover, each school designed and implemented its own 'School Health Action Plan' (SHAP) based on local health priorities and needs of the children. In the SHAP teachers identified an overarching health theme for each term under which health education topics were identified. For example, in one school under the theme Hygiene, topics on oral health, safe stools and food hygiene were taught for lower primary, middle primary and upper primary classes respectively. In addition co-curricular and environmental activities were defined to promote health beyond the school to the community. For example, under the Hygiene theme the term activity in one school was a Neighbourhood Cleanliness Campaign or a drama for the community on Safe Clean Water. Therefore, the initiative incorporated health education within the timetable and management structures of the schools without requiring significant reorganization of teaching time or syllabus coverage.

The method used to teach health was different from what teachers were used to in other subjects. It required teachers to teach a health topic over a sequence of activities or series of steps that linked learning in school with action at home. This helped children think and make decisions about health and encourages teachers to promote understanding and life skills on health issues. The particular approach to teaching health introduced in the five health action schools was the *Child-to-Child approach* (see Figure 7).

This approach promotes the following principles (Bailey et al, 1992):

1. Children's participation in their learning is crucial.
2. To link what children learn now with what they do now.
3. To link what children do in class with what they do in the community.
4. Health Education is not taught in one lesson and then forgotten but is learnt and developed over a longer period of time.
5. Health Knowledge is translated into Health Action.
6. Children can become health promoters in their communities.

Teacher training was the first step in the implementation of the Health Action Schools (HAS) pilot schools. Teachers were first exposed to the six step approach during the introductory Child-to-Child training which usually lasted two-three days. In a series of training sessions with support follow-up in school, the six step approach was translated into a 'topic' or unit plan in order for teachers to plan a sequence of activities on one health topic so that a minimum of four lessons (approximately 40 minutes each), with homework in between, were spent on each health topic. This was intended to help teachers move away from the idea that a health topic can be taught in one lesson. Teachers set KNOW (knowledge), DO (behaviour and action) and

FEEL (attitudes and life skills) objectives. This enabled children to go beyond knowledge to taking action and changing behaviour. Teachers then planned a lesson or homework on each step.

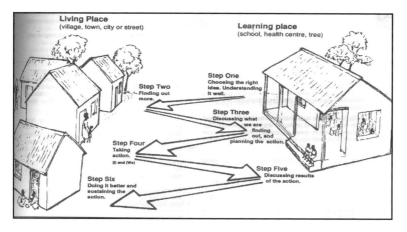

Figure 7. The Child-to-Child approach.

Our experience in Pakistan (Khamis, 2000) suggests that the Child-to-Child approach has helped teachers to:

- Promote more children's participation in the classroom.
- Use active child centred methods in order to promote understanding.
- Be more outward looking in their teaching by linking learning in the classroom with experiences at home.
- Move away from teaching health in one lesson to planning a series of lessons on one health topic.

We have also found that health education helps teachers improve their teaching methods, *even in subjects other than health*. It appears that as health is personal and related to daily living, teachers find it easier to teach health in a child centred way, involving children in their learning and relating health to life at home. Once they have gained confidence by trying out the new teaching methods in health they are able to use the same methods to teach other subjects. The following sections in this chapter will describe in more detail how health education has worked as a lever of change and the factors that have led to this success.

Health Education: a vehicle to school improvement

Success in health education proved to be a step towards school improvement. This section will discuss the impact of the health programme on teachers and children.

Children learn and have fun at the same time when we teach health. More children come to school on the day when health is taught. (Head Teacher, Government School)

Impact on Teachers

In the beginning of the project it was observed that in most of the pilot schools teachers were inclined to use rote learning in the classroom. Lesson planning, children's involvement in the teaching/learning processes and talking about their teaching practices were rather alien, especially to teachers in government schools. Through workshops, school follow-up and lesson observations, teachers became more open to discussing their practices, sharing experiences and asking critical questions to improve their own practices. There was evidence of teachers not only using active methods like storytelling, pictures and puppet shows in their health lessons but also when teaching other subjects.

I learnt how to tell stories by story mapping in the health sessions ... but now I use story-telling strategies in other subjects too. (A Private School Teacher)

This is the first time I have used puppets in my teaching over the last eight years and the children really enjoyed it. They were all listening. (A Government School Teacher)

When asked why they chose to teach health education teachers responded that they saw benefits in the programme for themselves and their own families as well as for the children they teach (Carnegie & Kassam-Khamis, 2002).

I have been inspired to be meeting a need of children. That's why I teach health – to create an awareness in children on how to care. I have also learnt more about health which benefits my own children and family and neighbourhoods this also motivates me. For example, I can now give First Aid to my own children or to others in the school, even if the nurse is not around.

I had never imagined children can do so much, making toys for younger children. I was surprised by how children were able to make poems on health issues. The children amazed me – how much data they would collect from surveys. I thought they would only collect information from their families, others would not give them but the children received a positive feedback from the community. The response has been positive from everyone so the process survives. (Former HAS Health Coordinator, now Deputy Head, Private Boys School)

Impact on Children

The project encouraged and increased children's participation in the classroom and in promoting health, through linking the school with the home. Children developed better communication and inquiry skills by having to finding out more from home or from other classes in the school, about a health topic discussed in their class. They were involved in formulating survey questions, collecting data, and planning health action on the basis of survey results.

The following quote illustrates how children enjoyed being involved in the health lessons.

> I like my health teacher because she is very kind and she gets angry rarely, only when we make noise. The most important thing I like about her is that she involves us in discussion during the lesson, while the other teachers usually just teach us the lesson. When our teacher teaches us a health topic she asks us to gather information and we make graphs....I really liked some of the health topics because the teacher used pictures. For example, she drew a picture of a dining table with different foods on it. It was very good and I remember it. (Student, Private Boys School)

The external evaluator of HAS's comments below show the health programme helped to make the classrooms more inclusive of girls and significantly enhanced their participation (Carnegie & Kassam-Khamis, 2002, p. 51).

> I have visited many co-educational schools in Pakistan where the girls are virtually invisible, huddled at the back of the class. It was therefore a joy to see the head teacher, who initially appeared very conservative, direct about 70% of his lesson to the girls. When he asked a question, boys would fling up their arms, while the girls raised a discreet finger. Yet he noticed these hesitant fingers and coaxed the girls to respond to the class. These are the small, but highly significant beginnings of helping girls to become active participants in classroom learning, not just statistics for the register. Later, in a role play, a girl took a key role as the doctor, the figure of authority. The photo below indicates how confident and happy she felt in this role. (External Evaluator on visit to the Rural Government School)

Teachers reported changes in the health behaviour of children, including an increased number of children bringing boiled water to school, children bringing healthier food in lunch boxes and a decrease in the number of accidents in the school. We specifically documented changes in the health knowledge and self-esteem of children. Our findings on these two aspects are discussed below.

Children's Health Knowledge

Both mid-term and end of term external evaluations of the programme found that there had been an improvement in children's health knowledge skills and behaviour. This was further confirmed by our own pre- and post-tests on health knowledge and self-esteem (Khamis, 1998; Gibbs, 1999; Carnegie & Kassam-Khamis, 2002). Examples of health knowledge questions included how to make Oral Rehydration Solution; how long to boil water for safe drinking; how to prevent coughs and colds; the diseases prevented by immunizations, and so forth. Figure 8 compares the percentages of correct answers to health knowledge questionnaires in the pre- (baseline) and post-tests of students tracked from each school (1998 vs. 2001). An increase in health knowledge is seen in all schools (chi-squared tests) but this is statistically significant ($p < 0.05$) only in the poorest government rural school.

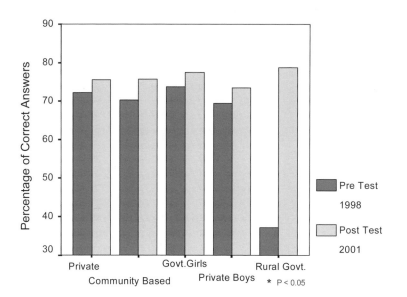

Figure 8. Comparison of health knowledge.

There appear to be three possible reasons for this marked improvement in the government schools as compared with private schools.

225

- Use of mother tongue to teach health education probably helped children from the Urdu medium schools to understand the health messages better than those children who had been taught health education in English, by teachers often not proficient in English themselves.
- Health was taught as a separate discipline rather than integrated or 'carried' through another subject such as science and social studies. Teachers often did not have the skills to integrate health within other subjects but were better able to focus on health concepts when health was taught as a separate subject.
- The whole school was involved in the health education programme. In most schools health education was targeted to selected classes only and in these schools we see less improvement both in health knowledge and self-esteem. However, where the whole school was involved in health education and promotion children's self-esteem and health knowledge was markedly increased.

Children's Self-esteem

Increasing children's self-esteem was an anticipated outcome of the HAS intervention. A validated self-esteem questionnaire for over 8-year-olds in primary schools used elsewhere (see the Lawseq questionnaire in Lawrence, 1996) was adapted and translated to assess the self-esteem of HAS children as there was no tool to assess self-esteem which has been developed and tested in Pakistan. Before the pilot project began the questionnaire was administered with children aged over 8 years and the same children were tracked after three years for post-evaluation.

Figure 9 shows a statistically significant improvement (t-test, $p < .05$) in children's self-esteem in the rural government school after three years of the health programme and a greater increase than the other three schools, in the community-based school. (In fact in one school we see a slight decrease in self-esteem, though this is not statistically significant.) This may be due to the fact that only in these two pilot schools (government and community-based), a one teacher to one class relationship exists. This is where a teacher has children for most of the time in a day and would have more chance to enhance their self-esteem because they know and understand the children better than a teacher who just stays with a class of children for an hour in the whole day (Lawrence, 1996). In the beginning of the project the chalk-and-talk method was prevalent in most schools and in some schools teachers even used the stick whilst teaching. Over the project period gradual improvements have been observed in the way teachers teach. No school teacher in any of the HAS pilot schools now uses the stick in the classroom and children have been seen to be more involved in the teaching/learning process through active methods. Use of chalk and talk to teach was much less prevalent in all schools. In the rural school during baseline data collection children were too shy to even go up to the blackboard to write their names. By the end of the project not only were children happy to teach others through drawing pictures on the blackboard but they were seen to be both asking questions and answering teachers' questions, a sign of their growing confidence. As is supported by the final evaluation, more impact is seen in the smaller, poorer schools and thus perhaps greater gains are to be made where lower starting points exist (Carnegie & Kassam-Khamis, 2002).

> In measuring impact and identifying potential constraints to implementation, it is concluded that the greatest gains can be made in small, poorer resourced schools in rural areas or close-knit urban communities. (Final HAS Evaluation, Carnegie & Kassam-Khamis, 2002)

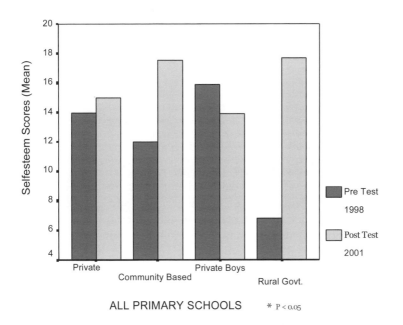

Figure 9. Comparison of self-esteem.

Factors that have Led to a Change in Teaching and School Improvement

In this section we try to identify the factors that have led to school improvement and teachers teaching better.

Partnership and Ownership:
the dynamics of a school-university partnership

The HAS project was clearly owned in each setting by the school even though it was initiated by the university (AKU-IED). Teachers often highlighted the prestige in being involved in a pilot programme that was watched by others. They mentioned to the mid-term reviewer that they enjoyed visitors from the university and abroad asking them questions and 'learning' from their experiences. They also enjoyed being partners in the research project with a well-respected university. They saw personal gains in exposure to the AKU-IED's professional development courses as well as its resources – sometimes to the detriment of the school as through this teachers were more marketable and were able to move on to better jobs. Teachers also saw a direct benefit as a result of the support received from AKU-IED for their teaching, such as in lesson planning, health content materials given and professional development sessions.

> I like the way the HAS project has evolved all these 3 years, completely involving the concerned schools. As a result, the whole project was quite 'tailor made' for us. (Head Teacher, Private School)

Needs-Based and School-Based Teacher Education

After initial workshops in each school, to expose head teachers and teachers to the idea of becoming Health Action Schools and the Child-to-Child methodology, the HAS team began conducting workshops according to the specific needs of the teachers in each school. Imagination and flexibility were the main tools in modifying and adapting training inputs to match the realities of each school and classroom and be responsive to the needs of individual teachers.

A school-based model of training was designed for government schools teachers who were reluctant to attend training held at AKU-IED, which required them to travel to IED after school hours. The school-based training sessions were conducted during school hours for not more than two hours at a time once a week for over four to six weeks. The training was based on a health topic to be taught by the teacher during a particular week. The lessons were observed by the IED-HAS team. This school-based training and follow-up in government schools resulted in regular teaching of health issues and the use of active methods in the classroom.

> I think we learn much more from trainings and support that happen in our school. It is practical and contextual and we learn that promoting health is possible in our own resources. When trainings happen in IED we come, we note but we don't do. (Class 5 Teacher at Rural Government School)

Child-to-Child Methodology: linking school and community

> For the first time our school is lice free! Although we have an anti-
> lice campaign every year, this time I think it worked because of
> our approach. It was different. We were not telling children and
> parents what to do. The children understood the problem and
> found the solution themselves. I think it was the Child-to-Child
> six step approach that did it. (Private School Teacher)

The objective of the Child-to-Child approach is to enable children to become
health promoters in their communities. For example, through this approach,
HAS children have reported that they have helped their parents refrain from
unhealthy habits like smoking and eating chalia/pan (beetlenut).

> My father used to chew pan a lot but when we discussed in the
> class about the bad effect of chalia and pan on health ... it helped
> me to convince my father stop chewing pan and I am proud of
> that. (Student from a Private School)

The Child-to-Child approach was used to encourage teachers to use methods
that promote understanding, help children to think and take decisions about
health, and link health learning with action, This approach advocates that
health topics are not taught in one lesson but covered over a series of lessons
(four to eight periods). Through this sequence of activities children initially
recognize the health problem and study it well by relating health issues with
their own homes and communities. It was observed that teachers slowly
moved away from being prescriptive about healthy behaviours (for example,
TELLING children they MUST be clean) to helping them UNDERSTAND
WHY healthy behaviours were important.

> With the Child-to-Child approach the students are learning based
> on their past experiences which is more effective. (Community-
> Based School Teacher)

Once teachers became more confident in the use of active methods they were
convinced of what children CAN do rather than cannot do.

> Even children who are usually dull and lazy take an interest –
> probably because they are involved. Initially I thought teaching
> health in this way would be a lot of work but the children are also
> working with us so we do not find it a burden, we enjoy [it].
> (Government School Teacher)

Fun Active Method Enhancement Sessions:
helping teachers through short but sustained support

A particularly popular model of HAS training was called FAME (Fun Active
Methods for Education). These two-hour school-based sessions were

requested by teachers, who selected a specific method from a 'menu'. The sessions were open to all teachers, not just health teachers.

> I feel the FAME sessions really made me use and generate new methods in my teaching. I had heard of and learnt about these methods before – stories, puppets, pictures, SMART objectives, but FAME made me practice them, how to do them. And I did them in health and then automatically I started to use the methods in other subjects. For example, I started using stories in teaching farming in social studies because I noticed children listened more. They were more involved and attentive and participated more. (Teacher, Private Boys' School)

These sessions on different teaching methods like storytelling, puppets, dramas, effective use of blackboard, discussion and questioning, group work, pictures, surveys and games were designed to help teachers use active methods not only for teaching health but all subjects (Khamis & Shivji, 1999). Teachers were observed using the material and methods in their own teaching and voiced the benefits for their children.

> Simply using pictures can enhance thinking, observation, speaking, writing analysis and discussion skills of children. (Community School Teachers)

> I never knew that puppets can be made so quickly and used effectively in the classroom. Shy children participate in it ... they don't have to show themselves. (Private School Teacher)

The importance of these FAME sessions in improving teaching/learning was commented on by both external evaluators. This is of enormous significance and indicates that for some teachers the HAS programme is providing an effective school-based form of 'Teacher Training' (Gibbs, 1999).

The Role of Head Teachers

The role of head teachers as the key people is crucial in initiating and sustaining any change. The heads were central at all stages from the 'entry negotiation' till the end of the Health Action Schools (HAS) project. Heads were involved in the pre-launch workshops because without them taking the ownership of the project sustainability would have been fragile. Where head transfers were frequent (rural government school and community-based school), little health education took place and, when it did, teaching was poor with little participation by the children. As new head teachers had not bought into the programme from its initiation there was little understanding or ownership of it or recognition of its importance. Teachers were therefore neither encouraged nor supported to be innovative with the curriculum to include health topics. However, in schools where head teachers had chosen to be part of the project, and were familiar with and supportive of the HAS initiative, not only did health teaching happen but teachers were also seen to involve children more in the lessons. In the two double shift schools, the private boys' school and government girls' school, we saw head teachers taking the initiative to expand their health programmes to the girls' and boys' shift schools respectively. In the private school, where the head had been with the programme, from its start, the programme was extended to include the middle and pre-primary section classes.

School Follow-up

The HAS team observed that without school support the professional development courses did not bring change in the classroom. Much time was spent in school follow-up by the IED-HAS team sitting with teachers, encouraging them to read material, setting objectives and planning and observing lessons. One important outcome of school follow-up was that teachers began to plan health teaching in groups, sharing and learning from each other. This became a powerful professional development activity.

The IED-HAS team developed their own monitoring and tracking strategy, which focused on tracking individual teachers and observing all of the lessons on one topic. Verbal feedback as well as documentation followed observations to track progress. This tracking strategy not only enabled teachers to improve their teaching methodologies but provided guidelines to the HAS team for planning the next training course or FAME sessions based on their needs. This link between training content and impact in teachers' classroom practice resulted in teaching development.

> We need an initial 2-3 day orientation but then training should
> happen through lesson observations and school support and
> monitoring. This supports us in our teaching at the time we are
> teaching it. (Teacher, Private Boys' School)

Conclusions

Health education is a key determinant for quality education. Through this research programme we have seen that the health promoting school and Child-to-Child approach create an enabling environment to help teachers teach better and encourage greater participation by children, which in turn enhances their health knowledge and self-esteem. However, the involvement of the whole school in the programme is important rather than just particular target classes.

Two factors enable uptake and success of the programme. Firstly, the support of the head as the main gatekeeper to the school is crucial. Where the head does not support the intervention even committed teachers are unable to bring about any change. Secondly, the language of instruction for effective health education needs to be the mother tongue.

Each school develops a different health programme based on its own contextual needs, resources and realities. Hence the model cannot be replicated but expansion can occur through adapting lessons and applying these to build on particular strengths of existing programmes. This has already occurred through self-identified expansion programmes that have approached HAS to help bring health education in schools. Examples of this can be found in the Northern Areas of Pakistan (Water and Sanitation Extension Programme); Afghan refugee transit centres in Karachi (FOCUS and Aga Khan Education Services); Afghan camps in Peshawar (Save the Children); and community supported schools in rural Sindh. In addition health education modules and courses are now offered on IED's teacher education programmes to expose course participants to the area of school health promotion.

Finally, in contexts such as Pakistan where it is necessary to scale up in order to meet the national needs for school health promotion, human resource intensive approaches, such as that described in this chapter, are not realistic. Other strategies of supporting teachers in the school such as appropriate curriculum materials and teaching aids must be provided to support teachers. The HAS team at IED is in the process of publishing contextually relevant and sensitive materials which are based on research findings of the project and start with where teachers are at. The larger external context of schools must also be engaged to support health education in schools. The IED-HAS programme has attempted to do this through policy dialogues and sharing knowledge and resources with local and national partners.

References

Arya, A. & Devi. R. (1991) Influence of Maternal Literacy on the Nutritional Status of Preschool Children, *Indian Journal of Paediatrics*, 58, pp. 256-268.

Bailey, D., Hawes, H. & Bonati, G. (1992) *Child to Child: a resource book*. London: Child to Child Trust.

Das Gupta, M. (1990) Death Clustering, Mother's Education and the Determinants of Child Mortality in Rural Punjab, *Population Studies*, 44(3), pp. 489-505.

Carnegie, R. & Kassam-Khamis, T. (2002) *Quest for Quality. Final Evaluation of HAS*. Unpublished report. Karachi: AKU-IED.

Farah, I. with Mehmood, T., Jaffar, R. et al (1996) *Roads to Success: self-sustaining primary school change in rural Pakistan*. Karachi: AKU-IED.

Gibbs, W. (1999) Mid Term Review Report of Health Action Schools. Unpublished Report. AKU-IED: Karachi.

Hawes, H. & Khamis, T. (1997) *Proposal to Develop Health Action Schools in Pakistan for AKU-IED and SC (UK)*. Unpublished. Karachi: AKU-IED.

Hopkins, D. (1987) *Improving the Quality of Schooling*. Lewes: Falmer Press.

Khamis, T. (1998) Traditional Health Beliefs and Customs of Pakistani Primary School Children, *SCN News, United Nations Systems Forum on Nutrition*, 17, pp. 29-30.

Khamis, T. (2000) A Steady Climb on the Six Steps to Health, *Child-to-Child Newsletter*, pp. 2-8.

Khamis, T. & Shivji, F. (1999) Fun Active Methods Enhancement Manual. Unpublished Report. Karachi: AKU-IED.

Lawrence, D. (1996) *Enhancing Self Esteem in the Classroom.* London: Paul Chapman.

Levinger, B. (1994) *Nutrition, Health and Education for all.* Newton, MA: Education Development Centre and United Nations Development Programme.

Nakajima, H. (1997) *Promoting Health through Schools.* A report of WHO expert committee on School Health Education and Promotion, Geneva.

Pollitt, E. (1990) *Malnutrition and Infection in the Classroom.* Paris: UNESCO.

Sammons, P., Hillman, J. & Mortimore, P. (1994) *Characteristics of Effective Schools.* London: Office for Standards in Education.

World Health Organization (WHO) Expert Committee on School Health Services (1950). *Report on the First Session.* Technical Report Series 30, Geneva: WHO.

World Health Organization (WHO) (1978) *Report of the International Conference on Primary Health Care, Alma-Ata USSR.* Geneva: WHO.

World Health Organization (WHO) (1996) *Promoting Health through Schools – the Global School Health Initiative.* Geneva: WHO.

World Health Organization (WHO) (1997) *Promoting Health through Schools.* Technical Report Series 870. Geneva: WHO.

CHAPTER 15

The Teaching of Research in a Teacher Education Programme

IFFAT FARAH & NELOFER HALAI

The Task Force that recommended the creation of the Institute for Educational Development at the Aga Khan University (AKU-IED) in Karachi, Pakistan called attention to the absence of reflection and inquiry in teacher preparation programmes and the lack of research-based knowledge about teaching and learning in Pakistan and other developing countries. The proposed AKU-IED programmes, particularly the M.Ed. in teacher education, were expected to improve this situation by integrating reflective practice across all courses and modules and by including a research component. The Task Force [1], advised that the research component in the M.Ed. should be based both on the prior experience of the course participants (CPs) and on their future roles as school-based teacher educators. It also recommended an emphasis on qualitative research methods because 'it accommodated greater cultural flexibility and consistency with current educational practice' (AKU-IED, 1991). This chapter will describe the evolution of the research component in the M.Ed. and discusses critical issues confronted in the process of preparing teachers to engage in academic research. We, the authors of this chapter, are faculty members who have participated in the development and teaching of the research component over 10 years. Writing this chapter has been an opportunity to share reflections on our experience and on more general issues of the teaching of research. However, to ensure that our analysis and interpretations of the issues were shared we sought feedback from faculty colleagues and some former students.

Developing a research course is generally challenging (Rouhani, 1999; Page, 2001); developing a research course in our context has been particularly so. Almost all CPs of the M.Ed. programmes have been teachers who have had little or no experience of conducting research or utilizing research knowledge. A tracking study of the IED's M.Ed. graduates

(Siddiqui & Macleod, 2003) showed that not all of them become school-based teacher educators and very few engage in research after graduation. Within this context we have constantly grappled with questions such as what should be the purpose of teaching research to our students. Should all CPs, regardless of their interests, aspirations, and future needs, learn to do research anyway? Why should we teach research? What should we teach? How and how much should we teach? In the rest of this chapter we describe the development of the research component within the M.Ed. programme and our continuing struggle with these questions.

The research component in the first M.Ed. programme consisted mainly of a research-based dissertation carrying 15 credits (out of a total of 70 credits) and conducted after completion of course work. During their dissertation year, students in small groups read about particular research approaches and made a presentation on these in weekly seminars and some faculty led seminars on research methods were conducted during their visit to partner universities.[2] Some modules such as those in Mathematics and Social Studies engaged students in small-scale classroom action research. The dissertation required CPs to design, carry out and report a relatively small-scale research study. Following task force recommendations, the IED seemed to favour qualitative research methods. Consequently all dissertation research projects employed qualitative research methods. Almost all CPs conducted action research so that they themselves might try out a new teaching strategy or study the process of supporting one or more teachers to learn a new teaching strategy. At the end of the M.Ed. programme, the CPs gave feedback on the dissertation process. They strongly recommended that more attention be given to the teaching of research methods during the programme. Participants felt that they had been inadequately prepared to conduct the research for their dissertations and to learn from the process.

In response to students' feedback and recommendations received from external evaluators, some changes were made in the second programme. The teaching of research methodology was formalized by including a three-week segment on research methodology during course work. This was given a weighting of five credits, raising the total credits for the research component from 10 to 15. The three weeks on research methodology were integrated within a module titled Research for Teacher Learning and School Improvement. This integration reflected a belief that research is learnt best as you engage in it within a relevant content area. Students read about and had class discussions on various aspects of doing and assessing qualitative research. They were helped to formulate researchable questions in the areas of school improvement and teacher learning, to collect and analyse data, and report their research in a paper submitted at the end of the now extended course. The research papers were assessed for knowledge and understanding in the area of school improvement and teacher learning as well as on their understanding of research methodology. Student feedback on this programme brought forth several issues and problems. First, while students appreciated the input and the opportunity to engage in a small research project before the dissertation, they felt overwhelmed by input on two other 'heavy content areas' coming at the same time. Second, their openness to learning from the process of conducting research was negatively influenced by the assessment procedures. The marks carried by the single assignment, assessing understanding of research methods as well as teacher learning and school improvement, and the limited time available for reflecting on and learning from the research process were also concerns for both the faculty and students. Third, students found the readings on research paradigms and theoretical issues in qualitative research extremely difficult in terms of the ideas presented and language used in them.

The research training component was restructured as a result of this feedback. A separate course on qualitative research methodology was developed with the aim of preparing students to conduct their dissertation research using qualitative designs. The course introduced the underlying assumptions and principles of qualitative methodology and engaged students in tasks such as developing research questions, conducting qualitative interviews with their colleagues or other teachers on campus, doing observation exercises, selecting and justifying the sample and methods of data collection for particular questions. Simpler introductory readings on qualitative research were assigned. Students were encouraged to develop the work done in this course into a dissertation proposal. This was very clearly a general and introductory course. The faculty teaching it expected that students could go on to learn a particular method such as action research or case study during the planning and conduct of the research project for their dissertation.

Students seemed to find this 'how-to-do research' approach helpful in preparing better, or at least making them feel better prepared, for the dissertation task. However, duration of the module, namely three weeks, was still considered too short for the purpose. Other issues also began to emerge. There were faculty concerns about students' ability to read, understand, and use published research papers and about the exclusive focus on qualitative methodology. Faculty members recommended that the course should be expanded to address these. In response, a seminar series was included in the second year of the two-year M.Ed. where faculty were invited to present their own research, particularly explaining the research design. The seminars were useful to some extent although some faculty continued to feel the need for more input to help understand and, to some extent, use quantitative methods. The demand for more preparation before the dissertation continued to be made. For the faculty offering the research module, teaching both theoretical underpinnings and principles and processes within a short time was, to say the least, extremely challenging. On the one hand, they felt that unless students understood the basis for the different methodologies they would be unable to design and conduct good quality research; on the other hand, they were acutely aware that the students did not have the educational background to develop this understanding in the relatively short available time.

The next M.Ed. programme included a new non-credit module called Educational Inquiry in its first year. This module aimed to develop an understanding of the significance of inquiry in education, and to enable CPs to become critical consumers of educational research within both qualitative and quantitative paradigms. While the aims and objectives of this module have remained the same over the past 10 years, new components have been introduced such as some basic statistics for use as tools in the analysis, organization and processing of data. To further alleviate concerns about the exclusive focus on qualitative research methods in the credit-bearing course, some input on quantitative research was included in the module. However, feedback from students confirmed faculty fears that to cover both qualitative and quantitative approaches in the limited time was a very ambitious undertaking. The approach being currently taken is to offer Educational Inquiry (an introduction to research paradigms) as a credit-bearing course in the first year of the programme. Plans are also being discussed to allow students to make a decision about the kind of research they wish to engage in by choosing either a qualitative or a quantitative methods course in the second year. The purpose of developing two separate courses for two full semesters will be to provide the time and focus needed to understand a particular paradigm better.

These developments of the research courses in the M.Ed. programme show a shift from an initial focus on classroom action research to a broader view of general educational enquiry. The initial aim was to prepare teachers and teacher educators to study their own practices or to conduct research for the improvement of classroom practice. The shift was towards the more generic course work to prepare educationists, located inside or outside schools, who can conduct research on broader educational issues. There was also a shift in the view about learning how to carry out research. The first few programmes reflect the view that one learns research mainly by doing research (thus the mini studies during certain modules and the dissertation). The later programmes suggest or assume that one can learn about research practice from theory and others' experiences prior to engaging in research. Commonly, research methods courses combine the two by requiring some research project within a research methods course (Glesne & Web, 1993). The separation of the research project and fieldwork (done during the dissertation) from the taught course has contributed to an increasing perception, particularly among students, that the dissertation is the opportunity to demonstrate what has already been learned in course work rather than being itself an opportunity to learn. This has resulted in an almost exclusive focus of the CPs on the dissertation output itself rather than on the process.

The Dissertation

All students in the M.Ed. programme are required to submit a research-based dissertation. From the students' perspective this is a most important and high status activity for several reasons: it carries 25% of the total credit hours; it is seen as the culmination of the M.Ed. programme; and it may facilitate access to a Ph.D. programme. Although students have read about, discussed and practised various parts of the process of doing research (for example, formulating a research question and carrying out an interview and observations), the dissertation research is their first experience of engaging in a research study largely independently, and of writing an extended research report. They face difficulties in making decisions and having to rationalize and justify every decision. They also find it hard to believe that they should learn from the research process as they experience it and write about this learning in their dissertations; their assumption is that the dissertation should tell the corrected and sanitized process. Other difficulties are in transforming their findings into knowledge (putting discrete findings together) and in accepting that the knowledge they create through research is legitimate knowledge. Students feel more comfortable supporting their claims with the literature they have read than with the data they have collected. The dissertation process, along with the M.Ed. programme in general, creates a struggle for the students between new views of knowledge, processes of knowing and the culturally salient concepts about what is valuable knowledge and how it is acquired (from authority normally symbolized by the book). This later form of knowledge (often seen as given, authoritative and unquestionable knowledge) has been learnt from schools and from society in general. As one of our graduates said quite expressively, 'as teachers we never feel that we can generate valuable knowledge, we are recipients of knowledge from authority. The systems leave very little room for us; there is a sense of powerlessness' (personal conversation). This issue is discussed further in Chapter 16.

Another significant challenge is posed by the difference in perspectives of the teacher and the researcher. McIntyre (1997) pointed out that teachers are not trained to be researchers so that 'it seems unreasonable to demand of teachers that they be researchers as well as teachers, when the expertise required for the two activities is so different' (p. 132). The CPs are teachers and bring their identity, perspectives and moral values with them. Most courses in the programme expect students to review and refine their perspectives but not necessarily to set them aside. The research component seems to require such a setting aside. In a paper about the problems of preparing educational researchers in a doctoral programme, Labaree (2003) points out that the professional practice of researchers is sharply different from the professional practice of teachers. Teachers have a normative and moral perspective and are concerned with solving problems, and doing what is best for the students. They often find it difficult to discard this perspective and adopt a researcher's analytical perspective, concerned with understanding what is happening and why it is happening first. In Labaree's experience 'this reluctance often leads students in education doctoral programmes to shift the discourse about educational issues from what is to what should be, looking for practical solutions before explaining the problem (Labaree, 2003, p. 18). We have similar experiences in the M.Ed. programme. The CPs are often unable to make the analysis and understanding of a phenomenon their primary concern. Their immediate response to data is a critique of what they have seen or heard and recommendations to fix the situation. This difference in perspectives does not suggest that teachers cannot or must not engage in research. In fact there are very strong arguments for why they should. Cochran-Smith & Lytle (1993) for instance argue that teacher inquiry can make a very significant contribution to the generation of knowledge about teaching, learning and classrooms. That contribution can be useful for the teachers' own practice, for the practice of the immediate community of teachers and for the larger community. Teachers can bring a 'truly emic, or insider's perspective that makes visible the ways that students and teachers together construct knowledge and curriculum' (p. 43).

A majority of the students find writing the dissertation in English a very daunting task. However, often, it is not only a matter of not knowing the language well enough. Other academic skills such as the abilities to think and conceptualize, to seek connections, synthesize and analyse are difficult for many students. These skills are not part of the repertoire of the majority of participants at the time of entry to the course. While they improve during a year and a half, problems at various levels of severity still exist. Inadequate skills of writing in English and a perception that they must adopt a rather stereotypical, *classy* academic style (Becker, 1986) often lead students to adopt a writing style which is difficult to follow. The dissertation has to be delivered within a given amount of time and the challenge is both to learn about research and about writing research. These, of course, are closely connected tasks particularly if one is doing qualitative research (Glesne & Web, 1993; Labaree, 2003).

The successful completion of a research project typically needs several kinds of expertise. These include: (1) expertise in the substantive areas of the research; (2) expertise of selecting and using appropriate methods; (3) expertise in knowledge of the context in which the research is conducted; (4) personal experience; and (5) expertise in effectively presenting the findings and conclusions (Sandelowski, 1998). Our experience of students' dissertation writing shows that while lack of one or more of the above skills may create problems, it is the bringing together of all of these to the process of completing the research project that poses the major challenge.

Despite all these difficulties, students' feedback suggests that they greatly value the dissertation as an opportunity to synthesize what they have learned over the entire M.Ed. programme. Although such feedback is encouraging for the faculty and the programme, we need to clarify better the purpose of teaching research and the specific learning outcomes of the dissertation process. Research-related outcomes are rarely directly evident in the students' work after graduation and most graduates have not engaged in research after programme completion.

The faculty also acknowledges the value of the research methods course and the dissertation. However, there is continuing discussion and debate about the purpose and nature of the research component. Should the research component be a necessary input in the preparation of professional teachers? Do teacher educators or educational managers require the research component? Should the research component be provided only for only educational researchers and future scholars? Surely we cannot have one response for all CPs given the different roles they might take on after graduation. According to a recent proposal future M.Ed. programmes will offer a compulsory course in educational inquiry. Beyond this course, students may opt to prepare further as educational researchers by taking another research methods course and completing a research-based dissertation or they may choose to carry out a development project in a classroom, school or school system, and write a report on the outcomes of the project.

Notes

[1] The task force recommendations were guided by a paper written by a faculty member of a partner university.

[2] CPs in the first programme were sent to the two partner universities, Oxford University in the United Kingdom and the University of Toronto in Canada, for nine weeks towards the end of the second year. The purpose of the visit was to study teacher education and school improvement in a different context and to use the library resources at these universities. Since the IED library resources at that initial stage were minimal, students were asked to conduct the literature review on the topic of their dissertation while they were at the partner universities.

References

AKU-IED (1991) *A Proposal of AKU Board of Trustees: first Task Force report*. Karachi: AKU-IED.

Becker, H.S. (1986) *Writing for Social Scientists*. Chicago: Chicago University Press.

Cochran-Smith, M. & Lytle, S. (1993) *Inside Outside: teacher research and knowledge*. NewYork: Teachers College Press.

Glesne, C. & Web, R. (1993) Teaching Qualitative Research: who does what? *Qualitative Studies in Education*, 6(3), pp. 253-266.

Labaree, D. (2003) The Peculiar Problems of Preparing Educational Researchers, *Educational Researcher*, 32(4), pp. 13-22.

McIntyre, D. (1997) The Profession of Educational Research, *British Educational Research Journal*, 23(2), pp. 127-140.

Page, Reba N. (2001) Reshaping Graduate Preparation in Educational Research Methods: one school's experience, *Educational Researcher*, 30(5), pp. 19-25.

Rouhani, S. (1999) Partnerships in Research and Supervision in South African Higher Education, *Journal of Practice in Education for Development*, 4(1), pp. 35-42.

Sandelowski, M. (1998) The Call to Experts in Qualitative Research, *Research in Nursing and Health*, 21, pp. 467-471.

Siddiqui, N. & Macleod G. (2003) Tracking Graduates of AKU-IED's M.Ed. Programme: the classes of 1999, 2000, and 2002, in A. Halai & J. Rarieya (Eds) *Impact: making a difference. Proceedings of an International Conference*. Karachi: AKU-IED.

CHAPTER 16

Key Themes and Issues in Educational Development: a critical perspective on the IED model

IFFAT FARAH & BARBARA JAWORSKI

Introduction

The chapters of this book have traced a story of educational development involving changes in professional practice, and in schools and systems, through the work of one institution, The Institute for Educational Development at the Aga Khan University (AKU-IED) in Karachi, Pakistan. Chapters so far have dealt with a variety of focuses and locations of IED work, and together highlight the considerable complexity of what has been involved. In this final chapter we emphasize what we consider to be key elements in this complexity.

In the first section of this chapter, we remind readers, briefly, of 10 years of history in IED development, introducing key terminology relating to people, processes and practices in the IED model and its operation, ending with a framework within which we can address issues. We follow this with what we believe to be two key areas of issues central to development in and beyond the IED: partnerships in educational development, and theory and practice in learning and teaching. Finally, we address impact in IED and its related systems, and raise questions for future development and research.

Ten Years of Development at and through the IED

The IED is both a Professional Development Centre (PDC) and an Institute in a University (the AKU). It has duties therefore related both to developments in learning and teaching, students and teachers, schools and systems, and to academic achievement within a university setting. It was built alongside a complex of schools in order to emphasize its role as a PDC, although it was also expected that high academic standards would be achieved consistent with a university of international standing. It is important therefore to consider two areas of development within the IED model; those related to development of schools and school systems associated with IED (many regarded as 'collaborating' schools); and development of programmes related to furthering knowledge of learning and teaching. The IED 'model' is first and foremost about the former, but in attending to the latter, the IED found itself drawn towards academic structures and away from the professional areas that are at the roots of development. Here we see a tension that manifests itself in a range of issues on which this chapter will focus. At the time of writing, two further PDCs are in operation, one in Northern Pakistan and one in East Africa, and a new IED is planned in East Africa. Experience and research will show how the tension between the academic and the professional plays out in this expanded and expanding institution.

Work at IED builds on models of school/university partnership developing from experience in other parts of the world. The basic model (we refer to it as The IED Model) involves the idea of the Professional Development Teacher (PDT) acting within both school and university to enable the development of other teachers and promote more effective teaching in the school context. PDT education is through a two-year Master's Degree Programme (M.Ed.) delivered at IED and grounded in practice through local partnership schools. Chapters 3 and 4 have discussed the principal features of this programme and issues that it raises for the IED and its partners. The M.Ed. programme insisted on a high level of academic achievement, but this was not necessarily consistent with achieving a high level of practical awareness in relating theoretical learning to issues in the field. The programme had to grapple with tensions between theory and practice.

Any partnership school has one or more PDTs. These are teachers of the school, educated in the M.Ed. programme, who have returned to the school to take up new roles. For example, they might be expected to develop their own teaching as exemplars or models *for* other teaching and teachers, and to work *with* other teachers to enable them to develop their teaching practices. These returning graduates are also expected to conduct courses at IED for teachers from their own and other schools. It is expected that course participants will develop an understanding of subject and pedagogy to support their development in school. Although the M.Ed. programme provided the academic background for this work, exemplified in school practice, it became clear that PDTs needed to develop practical expertise related to such new roles. Various chapters have elaborated these needs along with ways in which involvements in other programmes (for example, teaching in the Visiting Teacher Programme - see Chapter 5), or participation in the WSIP (Chapter 12) have gone some way to providing further education for PDTs.

In the model, development of other teachers in partnership schools arises through joint work between teachers and PDTs. Some of these teachers attend Certificate in Education (formerly Visiting Teacher) programmes taught mainly by PDTs at IED, and more recently at Professional Development Centres in the field. Programmes vary from an eight-week, university-based model, located at the IED (Chapter 5), to more recently developed field-based models which combine theory-based sessions (seminars and workshops) with ongoing teaching in teachers' own classrooms. These later models originated in the field (for example in Nairobi, East Africa; see Chapter 7) and one version has been introduced at the time of writing at the IED itself. Certificate programmes are taught or supported directly by PDTs, and indirectly by IED faculty who provide support to the PDTs. Thus we see teacher learning taking place alongside PDT learning, and the two are inextricably related (as Chapter 5 shows).

For teachers who have achieved their Certificate in Education and wish to undertake further study, IED offers an Advanced Diploma Programme, a one-year field-based study in one of five subject areas (English, mathematics, science, social studies or primary education). In the Advanced Diploma, teachers continue to teach in their schools, and are supported by PDTs and IED faculty to engage in special school-based activities and to attend short intensive periods at the IED. They produce a portfolio of work throughout the year and report on a small-scale inquiry into aspects of their own teaching and students' learning.

The IED model of school-university partnership can thus be seen to have developed from university origins, through M.Ed., Certificate and Diploma programmes to school classrooms in which teachers and PDTs learn side by side. The success of the IED model in terms of teaching development depends crucially on relationships between teachers, PDTs, and IED faculty and the support they receive from schools. Very early in these programmes, experience and research showed that the cultures of school, educational system and wider society influenced crucially what was possible outside the university seminar or workshop. The PDTs, fresh from their M.Ed. programme, returned to their schools eager to activate their M.Ed. learning. However, despite the power of new knowledge and theoretical motivation, most of them had little power within these educational systems. Other teachers, returning from the Certificate Programme, had even less power. The new knowledge also acted as a barrier to development when those in managerial positions within schools, lacking understanding of PDTs' roles and perceiving PDTs as a threat to their authority, resisted PDTs' attempts to fulfil their new roles in the school context. Even those principals who supported IED's work, and were genuinely motivated to improve teaching, were often at a loss to know how best to use their returning PDTs. IED's early recognition of these problems led from short, ad hoc meetings, seminars or workshops to the fully fledged Advanced Diploma course for principals and head teachers that is now in operation. As Chapter 9 indicates, the IED model has developed to include school leaders who need to understand the educational principles of the model and ways in which teachers, with their support, can enable the model's success. However, again, and unsurprisingly, there are many issues influencing the outcomes of teacher–principal relationships. Principals have both power and responsibilities that affect what teachers are able to achieve, and often the factors influencing the exercise of power are at odds with the principles of the model. Chapter 9 shows that such issues are central to head teacher development and hence to school development.

Further in the developmental story, we find that larger education systems often constrain the schools in taking initiatives for change. We refer here to curriculum and examination systems, expectations of stakeholders (for example, head teachers, parents, politicians, and so forth); to societal values related to education, and to cultural norms related to social practices. We see that attempts to bring changes related to students, teachers, and classroom processes are ineffective unless they pay attention to the wider sociocultural setting in which classrooms are located and to the people with power who could legitimately change (see, for example, Mohammad, 2002). The IED model, most recently, has reached out to some of the people with such power, including education officers and administrators at local, provincial and national level, often, encouragingly, at their request. Meetings and workshops led by IED faculty have introduced new ideas and principles for management and leadership practice and followed this up with support to develop and enact new leadership roles in the field. These levels of application of the model, as yet, have fledgling status, so it is hard to address whether they are proving effective. However, one encouraging factor is that regional government agencies in Pakistan are seeking IED assistance to support development in their regions based on what they see already in operation.

From its beginnings, IED had worked closely with faculty members from two partner universities (PUs), Oxford and Toronto. Resulting from recommendations of the first task force (see Chapter 1), partner universities were chosen to exemplify aspects of the model on which IED was based and were intended to support IED in its growth. Partner university faculty joined faculty at IED in planning and delivering programmes and conceptualizing development. Although much that is positive has resulted from the collaboration (this book is one example), there have also been many issues to address in this partnership, some of them discussed in Chapter 2.

The IED model has developed layers of learning and human relationships that include teachers, principals and educational managers. The school can be seen as a central unit and the PDT as a central actor working for teaching development supported by principals and managers. Of course none of this school development can take place without development at the IED itself and learning by the partner university faculty who collaborated with IED. IED faculty members have had to learn the practicalities of implementing the IED model, through experience, personal reflection and research into the developmental issues these programmes have revealed. Many have needed further education in the theoretical principles which underpin the model and in international research that explains or elaborates questions relating to experiences at the IED. Partner university colleagues had to develop knowledge and awareness of sociocultural factors in order to perceive how theoretical ideas and principles to which they were committed could be used in the educational settings in which the IED operates. Doctoral programmes at partner universities have provided opportunities for IED faculty to conduct research into the IED's developing systems alongside their own academic enhancement. Through supervision of such research, as well as their own involvements in the field, PU faculty have themselves grown in understanding of developmental issues. Increasingly, stronger and closer relationships between members of all these groups have come to be seen as central to the development of educational knowledge and practice.

In reviewing the IED story, we see four main stages of IED development over the years, Conceptualization, Implementation, Outcomes and Evolution, as follows:

- *Conceptualization*: From its first task force onwards, IED has engaged at a conceptual level with ideas and issues about its aims to achieve and how they should be translated into practice. That practice is not only within the IED itself but also in activity in schools and classrooms and the wider educational context. There have been two further task forces in IED's 11-year history, each of which has reviewed achievements and suggested directions for further development.

- *Implementation*: Implementation has gone hand in hand with conceptualization in a complex reflexivity in which reflection, a key theoretical element in IED operation at all levels had led to review of concepts and deepening of understandings about the educative processes in which IED is engaged. Thus programmes have been designed, tested in the field, redesigned, and so on. Evaluation has been incorporated in all programmes, leading to clearer knowledge about processes and practices which inform future progress and suggesting ways of addressing or circumventing problems.

- *Outcomes*: Outcomes can be seen most obviously in terms of people whose professional lives have changed in profound ways as a result of new knowledge, know-how, and ways of thinking. Less tangible is the IED *identity* and characteristic modes of educational engagement that have emerged from conceptualization and implementation. Since this book has focused, necessarily, on conceptualization and implementation in the early phase of IED's evolution, we do not attempt to discuss impact in any great detail. However, we believe that a critical review of outcome and impact must be the topic of future work.

- *Evolution*: Reflexive cycles between conceptualization and implementation over time form an evolutionary pattern in the IED's progress. By this, we mean that as all the people concerned in IED practices and their development address issues and deal with challenges resulting from implementation of initial concepts, then change gradually takes place. The first task force focused on school improvement, through the development of a critical mass of teachers, and school-based teacher development. The broad approach included notions of clinical teachers acting as mentors; reflective practice in learning, teaching and development; and university–school partnerships for promoting development of teachers and teaching. The implementation of these notions challenged IED to realize and resolve tensions between university and school, between school-based and school-focused models; between development of critical mass and development of the whole school, between individual capacity and system capacity or lack of it, and between teaching of subject content and teaching pedagogy. An evolutionary process involving implementation, review, reflection, and response to emerging needs and challenges was set forth and resulted in more stable relationships between theory and practice. We focus below on some of the key issues and challenges in this evolutionary process: one purpose of this chapter is to try to make sense of these issues and look critically at ways in which the IED and its partners are addressing them. We do this with reference to some of the associated theory, research and experience that inform the debate, and end with some reflection on issues fundamental to future progress.

University–School Partnerships and Teacher Development

The first task force recommended that

> AKU [the Aga Khan University] should found an Institute for Educational Development (the IED) dedicated to the improvement of teaching and teacher training and to the development of educational research focused upon those tasks and upon the needs of Pakistan ... [The Institute] should articulate its work in and through real setting in real schools (hence the insistence upon the concept of the professional Development School or Centre, drawing explicitly upon the metaphors of medical education and the teaching hospital. (AKU-IED, 1991, p. 7)

This recommendation was inspired by new approaches and initiatives in initial and in-service teacher development in the USA and the United Kingdom where disappointments with the outcomes of educational reform efforts, dissatisfaction with initial teacher education, and new understanding and research knowledge about teacher expertise led various individuals and groups to advocate a closer link between teacher education and schools.

Partnerships between schools and universities (where teacher education had traditionally been located) were proposed to enable renewal of school capacity and redesign of initial teacher education (Holmes Group, 1986; Goodlad & Sirotnik, 1988; Goodlad, 1990). Such partnerships were established in the USA in and through the idea of Professional Development Schools (PDS) which were to provide clinical preparation and practice (much like the role of hospitals in medical education) to student teachers under the supervision and mentoring of clinical teachers (designated as such because of their teaching experience and expertise). Participation in PDS activities would provide the opportunity for clinical teachers to develop as teacher educators skilled in sharing expertise and guiding student teachers' understanding of effective teaching. Clinical teachers would collaborate with university based teacher educators to develop and teach university courses. An important goal for such collaboration was to professionalize teaching through the creation and application of new knowledge in the classroom (Holmes Group, 1986).

Similar ideas were tried out in in-service education through such initiatives as the Schenley High School Teachers Centre established in the Pittsburgh school district. This centre was located within a comprehensive high school and was staffed by outstanding and professionally committed teachers who served as Clinical Resident Teachers (CRT) and who both taught in the Schenley School and participated in Teacher Centre activities. These included the conduct of eight-week- long programmes for teachers from across the school district. These visiting teachers were replaced in their classrooms by replacement staff from the Teacher Centre. Describing the Schenley programme and its impact, Bickel and colleagues state that

> The CRT experience underscores the value of involving teachers
> in reform efforts, particularly when influencing the performance of
> teachers is the major goal. This experience demonstrates the levels
> of professional skill and commitment that can be tapped within
> the teaching force, without having to lose the power of good
> teaching in the process. (Bickel et al, 1987, p. 13)

At about the same time as these initiatives were taking place in the USA, school–university partnerships in initial teacher education were also starting to develop in the United Kingdom. One example was the Oxford Internship Scheme, based at the University of Oxford, Department of Educational Studies (OUDES). The term 'internship' was borrowed from medical education in which trainee doctors undertake hospital internships to gain relevant professional experience. At Oxford, the interns were participants in a one- year professional course for secondary schoolteachers. From the first days of their course interns were associated with a school in which they spent initially two days per week, increasing to five days for a substantial part of their year. Here they supported the work of experienced teachers and taught pupils, first in small groups and then building up towards teaching whole classes. Thus a large part of their course was school-based. Teachers in the school, designated as 'mentors' worked daily with the interns. They were visited periodically by tutors from the university to enable a three- way evaluation (intern, mentor and tutor) of the intern's progress. Seminars took place both in school and in university led by mentors or tutors as appropriate. Internship was organized as a partnership between the university and the schools. A partnership committee steered the programme. Groups of tutors and mentors met periodically to design, review and evaluate the course. Through such meetings, teachers were drawn into the educative community and learned processes and skills of mentoring (Hagger & McIntyre, 2002).

Teacher Expertise, Teacher Learning and Teacher Education

The idea that schools and experienced teachers should play a significant role in teacher education has been supported by research on the nature of teacher expertise and the process of teacher learning. Research on teachers' classroom thinking has suggested that teachers' classroom actions are based on personal judgements made in particular circumstances (for example, Calderhead, 1987). Studies of 'expert teachers' showed that teacher expertise is shaped by conditions of classrooms and schools. In reviewing the research on teacher expertise, Hagger & McIntyre conclude,

> Teaching expertise ... is so complex, so individual and so much concerned with making decisions about what to do in specific situations that it can only be adequately understood in terms of particular teachers acting in particular circumstances. (2002, p. 487).

Other research has shown that teachers learn about teaching from personal experiences with parents and teachers, on the job from their own practice, and from the practice of their colleagues in school. Thus the content and context of teachers' experiences and the presence of professional support and a collegial culture in school are critical factors in learning to teach (Feiman-Nemser, 1983).

These research findings support the view that both pre-service and in-service programmes need to incorporate the realities of the school, include time for classroom practice and school experience, provide professional support to learn from practice, and the opportunity to learn from expert teachers who can guide the development of individual teacher learners in a mentoring process.

Studies investigating the impact of Professional Development School programmes showed that the trainee teachers were satisfied with their learning with the clinical teachers, were perceived by others to be better prepared, and were more effective with students (Bickel et al, 1987; Goodlad

& Sirotnik, 1988; Darling-Hammond, 2000; Teitel, 2001). These studies also identify several challenges to university–school partnerships for teacher education. These include a strong cultural and structural difference between the two institutions, difficulties in establishing and maintaining collaboration, and the low value placed on teacher education in both universities and schools. They suggest that organizational changes at both the university and the school were essential to sustain teachers' learning and to enable the use of the new knowledge in practice.

Implementation and Outcomes

The initial vision of the IED was inspired by the experiences and research findings described above. Thus IED was deliberately built within the campus of the Sultan Mohammed Shah Aga Khan Schools complex (including primary, secondary and higher secondary schools), and these were expected to be the laboratory schools, much like the Professional Development Schools in the USA. They would provide the real context to develop, test, refine and exemplify effective teaching practices through collaborative research and to provide a clinical setting for the professional development of in-service teachers who would be visiting the IED. The campus was to serve as both an academic centre, part of the AKU, and a Professional Development Centre (PDC).[1]

However, unlike the PDS in the USA and internship partnerships in the United Kingdom, the IED could not assume ready availability in Pakistan of teachers who could model the exemplary practices and new approaches to teaching, which the IED wished to introduce in schools. Such teachers had to be educated through an extensive programme, starting with M.Ed. studies as described above. Teachers were selected for this programme from the schools which accepted a partnership role with the IED. The programme was conducted mainly at the university and by university faculty, although with opportunities for classroom and school experience. Courses in the programme were both academically and professionally oriented with a focus on theory and research as well as on school-based practice and reflection.

During school-based experiences, however, the M.Ed. course participants and faculty from the university were perceived (by themselves and others) as people with knowledge rather than people who were there to learn from the school or from the teachers in whose classes they practised. Even when school staff (the graduates of the M.Ed. programme) taught university courses, such as the Visiting Teacher Programme (VTP), it was knowledge and expertise acquired at the university rather than their experience acquired at the school which qualified them to do so. Moreover, they worked under the supervision of the university faculty rather than 'with' the university faculty. These perceptions and practices raised issues of power, status and ownership and, shaped the nature of collaboration between IED and schools during this initial period. The university was the more powerful of the two in terms of formal knowledge, availability of resources and its affiliation with high status universities in the West. The schools were more powerful in their ownership of the teachers including the PDTs and the Visiting Teachers (VTs) who depended on schools for their jobs. Tensions arose in cases where the schools felt that their own status and power over the PDTs were being threatened or when the new knowledge from the university was not able simply and quickly to meet the schools' needs. An immediate response from some schools was to stop sending their best teachers for IED programmes. A different response from some other schools and systems was to resist sending IED graduates back to teach in university-based programmes. This response was actually an indication of IED's success in that the schools and school systems became less passive and more demanding as they began to understand the process of change being initiated by IED and to build their own structures for professional development.

An Evolutionary Process Promoting Change

Those who have studied school–university collaboration in other contexts suggest that university–school partnerships or collaboration are desirable and beneficial but difficult to implement (Darling-Hammond, 1994; Ginsberg & Rhodes, 2003; Dallmer, 2004). Goodlad & Sirotnik (1988) identified three conditions for symbiotic partnership: dissimilarity between or among the partners; mutual satisfaction of self-interest; and sufficient selflessness on the part of each member to assure the satisfaction of self-interest on the part of all members. Looking at the IED experience of collaboration with schools, we can see that, in the initial phase, the IED–school relationship met some but not all of the above conditions. As noted, IED and schools were different in their resources. IED had the strength of explicit, formal, theoretical and new knowledge about best practice in teaching and teacher education, primarily obtained in and from research and practice in western contexts. The schools had the strength of experiential knowledge which was implicit, informal and contextual. However, initially, not enough attention could be given to bringing the two together. A committee, with members from school systems, set up to advise the IED Director, neither succeeded nor endured. A head teachers' forum that was set up in the very first year of IED operations could have participated in collaborative leadership of the programmes but became a place of learning for the head teachers rather than a place for mutual sharing. While university knowledge was judged, both by the schools and IED, to be more significant and of a higher status, it was not always most relevant to achieving schools' self-interest. The schools recognized the need for change but their self-interest lay in maintaining practices that helped them complete the syllabus and obtain good examination results, thus satisfying the systems' demands and fulfilling parents' expectations.

Some of these tensions were reflected in the work of the M.Ed. course participants and IED graduates with schools. Although both course participants and graduates saw themselves as *mentors* working to support teachers in schools, their experience suggests that teachers associate authority and power with them as representatives of the university and/or the management and therefore as *evaluators* of teachers' work (Halai, 1998, 2002). Since these graduates were introducing new ideas, they did indeed challenge both the teachers' autonomy and the value of their prior experience, and they exposed gaps in teachers' subject knowledge. This was not helpful in promoting trust and collaboration or in readily converting teachers into reflective practitioners.

Another challenge to collaboration was the involvement of the PDTs in the delivery of VT programmes at the university-based Professional Development Centre. While, the schools had agreed, through an initial collaboration agreement, that the returning graduates (the PDTs) would be available, for several months a year, to teach programmes at the PDCs, a number of problems arose once this arrangement was put into practice. These best teachers in the schools (who had already been away for two years) would have periods out of school (each of several months) for another three years. Being away for several months at a time, meant that the school could not use them consistently as teachers or school-based teacher educators. Thus, from the perspective of the school, the partnership served university interests in delivering 'its programmes' and the individual PDTs' interests by providing them with the opportunity to work at a university as teacher educators. It did not serve the schools' interests since the PDTs were not available to the school full time and even when they were present in school they identified more with the university than with the school.

IED's interests were also determined by its external funding arrangements. Funding contracts with external development agencies required IED and its PDC to educate a large number of teachers from across a variety of school systems. The urgency to meet these targets and the differences between school and IED interests, as discussed above, made it difficult to engage in the kind of partnerships envisaged in some of the concepts derived from Professional Development Schools.

In addressing such challenges, IED's partnership with schools and school systems has survived and evolved over time. IED and its Professional Development Centre do not work exactly as envisaged in the models which inspired their establishment. Instead they have responded to the sociocultural context in which they are located, to their own needs, the needs of the individual teachers, the schools, and the school systems with which they have been associated.

Learning, Teaching and Development

Concepts and Issues

A major theoretical building block of the model proposed by the first task force was that of *reflection* as a central element of the developmental process.

The task force envisaged development of reflective teachers who would actively develop their teaching through reflective processes. Such conceptualization is rooted in theory and research over some decades relating to teachers' thinking and development of thinking and its relationship to professional practice in teaching and learning. We look first at some of the theory and research in this area and then relate this to issues in IED practice.

Teacher Thinking and Critical Reflection

Clark & Peterson (1986), with reference to Shulman's work (for example, Shulman, 1987), talk about the teacher as a thoughtful professional. Cooney (1984) talks about teachers' implicit theories of teaching and learning which influence their teaching decisions and classroom acts. Elbaz (1990) writes about the importance of encouraging the expression of teachers' own voice in order to 'redress an imbalance which had in the past given us knowledge of teaching from the outside only.' Smyth (1987) claims that it is only by exercising and intellectualizing their voice, through a critical approach to teaching, that teachers will be empowered in their own profession. These references chart a progression from recognizing teachers as thoughtful professionals to acknowledging the importance of teachers' overt expression of their thinking in a critical form. Smyth writes,

> Put simply, to act reflectively about teaching is to actively pursue the possibility that existing practices may effectively be challenged, and in the light of evidence about their efficacy, replaced by alternatives. Reflection, critical awareness or enlightenment on its own is insufficient – it must be accompanied by action. (Smyth, 1991, p. 44-45)

Smyth suggests that being critical involves more than a reflective approach to teaching, it requires action. Kemmis (1985) sees the reflective process itself as demanding action. He argues:

> We are inclined to think of reflection as something quiet and personal. My argument here is that reflection is action-oriented, social and political. Its product is praxis (informed, committed action) the most eloquent and socially significant form of human action. (p. 141)

Dewey (1933) wrote about reflection as involving action in response to a perceived problem: 'Demand for the solution of a perplexity is the steadying and guiding factor in the entire process of reflection' (p. 14). From these notions, teaching development can be seen as a form of critical reflection in which 'informed, committed action' is a fundamental characteristic. This is a theoretical ideal, and we shall see shortly how such an ideal relates to issues in practice.

Active Inquiry and Professional Growth

Critical reflection, as conceptualized above, can be translated into notions of *inquiry* in professional practice. *Informed, committed action* can be translated, practically, into inquiry approaches that are explicit in learning and teaching. Research shows that inquiry approaches facilitate knowledge development at all levels and influence communities within schools, educational localities and the educational establishment (for example, Hamilton, 1998; Wells, 2001). When such inquiry is conducted in a systematic manner and its results made public, it becomes research (Stenhouse, 1984). The kinds of research involved may vary from practitioner-research (insider research) designed to enhance practice, to more formal research designed to enhance knowledge in a generalized sense (outsider research). The rhetoric in teacher-research projects often suggests, implicitly if not explicitly, that these projects lead to better teaching. However, it is very hard for teachers on their own to undertake research since it is a very different activity from teaching (McIntyre, 1997). This is despite the fact that some teachers see their practice itself (of planning, teaching and reflecting on teaching) as a research process (Jaworski, 1998). Thus, an important question is how do teachers start to become inquiring professionals?

Schön's writing about the development of professional knowledge through reflective practice is now well known (Schön 1983, 1987). As teachers engage in research or inquiry, ask questions about their practice and explore aspects of practice, their knowledge develops. In Schön's theory, *reflection* and *action* are fundamentally linked in three stages: reflection-on-action, reflection-for-action and reflection-in-action. One interpretation of his use of these terms is that reflection on and for action by a teacher looking critically at what has happened in practice and planning for future practice leads to an enhanced awareness of issues and a theorising of concerns such that in moments of choice and decision-making in the classroom the teacher is able to make informed decisions in a moment of action.

The better informed the decisions, the more likely they are to contribute to enhanced learning for pupils. Such a theory accords with Mason's (2001) 'discipline of noticing', in which 'noticing-in-the-moment' leads to informed action in the classroom. As teachers become more aware of issues in their teaching, through reflection *on* practice, they become more able to notice issues as they arise in the classroom and respond there and then. Eraut questions whether teachers have the time in such classroom moments to reflect critically and act accordingly, and asks for more evidence of such practice (Eraut, 1994, 1995). However, some research conceptualizes the possibility for reflection-in-action and has provided examples from real classroom situations (for example, Jaworski, 1994, 1998). We need to be clearer about how such cycles of reflection and action *become* part of teachers' activity, particularly in relation to sociocultural settings which perhaps do not easily facilitate such ways of thinking.

Research shows that real opportunities for teachers' critically reflective engagement are unlikely to arise without support and encouragement (for example, Vulliamy & Webb, 1992; Atkinson, 1994; Jaworski, 1994). Support can be of many forms, but one form involves collaboration between teachers, educators and researchers in a variety of ways, as has become increasingly evident in the IED model. However, the intention of support, and good will in setting up support systems, does not ensure outcomes of the sort envisioned in theory.

From Conceptualization to Implementation

Based on theoretical perspectives identified above, *critical reflection* was from the start a key concept in IED operations. From the *Reconceptualization* module held at the beginning of 1994 in the first M.Ed. programme, through to modules in mathematics, science, English and social studies, reflection has been a cornerstone of the didactics of the M.Ed. course, and of course participants' growing theoretical understanding of learning and teaching activity in a range of subject areas. This has been seen practically in CPs' collective reviewing of a day's activity so as to address their own learning, in writing reflective journals at all stages of their course, and in learning to engage with critical issues. For example, CPs have reflected critically on forms of educational practice in which they had previously engaged as students and teachers. These included:

- repressive teacher actions such as physical punishment if the student had not responded in the way a teacher had expected;
- direct instruction in which they had to follow exactly the teacher's or the textbook's methods; and
- rote learning to reproduce exactly the answers required in an examination.

Course participants engaged in, and learned to value new practices in their various subject areas within the M.Ed. programme. These included inquiry approaches to learning and teaching mathematics, use of everyday materials in science and ways to address critical issues in social studies. They identified ways in which such approaches were more beneficial to students' learning than their own student experiences had been (see Chapter 4). In modules on teacher development and classroom change, they theorized reflection and related it to their didactic discussions. One danger that manifested itself as an outcome of implementation of conceptual development was that old practices translated as 'bad' and new practices as 'good'. Time was needed to accommodate the new thinking to deeper understandings of old practices. In the immediacy of relating new to old, as they visited schools and worked with pupils and teachers, some CPs developed an elitist attitude towards the existing practice of other teachers. In terms of Schön's three kinds of reflection, the CPs learned to engage in reflection *on* practice and reflection *for* practice, but reflection *in* practice was more elusive. They were unable to scrutinize their own thinking and action in sufficient depth and in relation to the theoretical perspectives they were starting to appreciate.

Early Outcomes from Implementation of Concepts

Practices *in* the M.Ed. programme encouraged CPs' reflection *on* their own learning, and where practices involved work with school pupils CPs also reflected *on* pupils' learning. Such practices contributed to the field-focused nature of the programme. CPs worked with pupils in an IED context or a school context determined by practicalities such as the time of year that contact with pupils was needed, or the nature of contact. If CPs needed to work with pupils during the school vacation, then some pupils were invited to the IED to make this possible. Sometimes it was possible to take 30 CPs into a small number of school classrooms, or a laboratory, where they worked in groups of two or three with four or five pupils. Such activities resulted in considerable learning for CPs which was articulated and consolidated in post-activity reflection, namely, reflection *on* practice. When CPs were in school working with teachers, or teaching lessons themselves, the same was true. However, periods in school were necessarily of short duration; relationships between CPs and pupils or teachers were correspondingly superficial, and CPs' engagement with or responsibility for the curriculum or other aspects of the systemic milieu was minimal. Considerable thought and energy was therefore required to forge relationships that allowed fruitful work in a very short time, and this militated against recognition of issues in practice, let alone action on recognized issues. Thus the CPs were never in a situation where they had to think in depth about issues in teaching as faced by the regular teachers.

Research shows us, also, that reflection *in* practice requires a deep engagement with issues of practice, that may be difficult for the inexperienced practitioner grappling with the demands of new practices (Calderhead & Shorrock, 1997; Jaworski & Gellert, 2003). Even for experienced practitioners, a deep or critical engagement with issues is not always a 'natural' state of everyday practice (Brown & McIntyre, 1993). Some kind of activity needs to promote such engagement and associated reflection. In this respect IED programmes have drawn on action research models as a basis for encouraging critical engagement with issues (Carr & Kemmis, 1986; McNiff, 1993). Many of the M.Ed. modules included an action research project, or theoretical work on action research. Course participants undertook very small-scale action research in other teachers' classrooms. Their understandings of the action-research cycles and of the processes, practice and issues of action research were at a naive level so that their focus remained on the exigencies of practice, rather than at the meta-level of issues arising. Thus interpretation in the M.Ed. programme of concepts of critical reflection and action research led to recognition of the complexities of translating theory into practice, both in systemic and conceptual terms.

Elements of the Evolutionary Process and their Associated Issues

Complexity here is a key concept whose recognition is an outcome of programme implementation. CPs coming from educationally limited starting points were introduced to new theories and perspectives, experienced new practices and had to put into practice themselves what they experienced. They were expected to reflect on their own activity and thinking, the associated practical outcomes and their relationships to sociocultural practices in settings where such thinking was not necessarily a part.

One part of this complex scene involved the pedagogical processes used by course leaders to promote learning at a number of levels: the learning of CPs themselves, CPs' promotion of pupils' learning and, less directly, CPs' facilitation of teachers' learning. One clear example of such pedagogical processes was the use of *cooperative learning* as a way to develop learning through interactivity and group dynamics in classrooms. Another was the use of *everyday materials* in science or in mathematics to promote conceptual thinking. Use of cooperative learning and everyday materials can be seen both as a set of strategies for organizing classroom activity, and as an example of interpreting philosophical positions on learning, based in sociocultural learning theory. Both philosophy and strategies were manifested in a range of modules where they took different forms and used different terms according to the experience and preferred terminology of the module leaders (see Chapter 4). It became clear, through reflective activity – both oral and in writing – that CPs perceived value for themselves in the activities they experienced, talking about activity in terms to which they had been introduced in respective modules. However, for CPs, the strategies took on an importance that seemed unrelated to their philosophical basis. Thus, CPs' planning for classroom activity with pupils might involve *group work*, the *jigsaw* strategy, or *homemade materials* without actually being specific on learning goals or ways in which such strategies were designed to address learning goals. Observation of these issues challenged module leaders to critique their own practices through which such terminology was introduced and concepts developed. We needed to rethink our implementation of the theories to which we were committed within the sociocultural frame in which we worked.

In the above paragraphs we have been talking largely about CPs' learning as part of the M.Ed. course. While our remarks here should not be seen to undervalue the learning and transformation which did take place for most of the CPs, problematic aspects of this learning became most evident when the CPs as graduates, now PDTs began to work in schools, fulfilling the learning cycle that was the driving force of the M.Ed. programme. As has been explained in earlier chapters, the growth of PDTs was far from painless:

PDTs faced problems in lack of acceptance or understanding in their school, by fellow teachers or head teachers, lack of role definition; trying to follow theoretical principles without the practical grounding or support for experimentation; concern about personal qualities or qualifications to deal with situations and issues. At the same time they were expected to offer courses for visiting teachers (VTs) at the IED, building on their knowledge of the M.Ed. programme.

We see here a complex microcosm of a more global situation. What was experienced here by CPs/PDTs in their learning process, guided by module leaders, the IED faculty, can be seen in the traditional approaches to learning and teaching that CPs criticized from their own experience; in the classrooms of partnership schools in which they worked with pupils and teachers; in the university seminar rooms in which they worked with IED faculty. In all such situations, in and beyond IED settings, learners are confronted with new experience leading to new knowledge, and to the assimilation and accommodation of such knowledge within sociocultural settings that limit the very processes that promote workable know-how. In conceptualizing reflection in action, the IED faculty sought modes of activity in which CPs would engage to promote desired learning. However, learning outcomes were not always what had been envisioned, and the promoters needed themselves to ask critical questions about the processes in which they had engaged.

Coming back to our earlier discussions of partnerships and collaboration, the PDT re-entering the field could be seen as a key character in systemic linkages, for example between school/school system and the AKU-IED. Bringing the wealth of new knowledge, or know-how, from the M.Ed. course (albeit with limitations as expressed above) the PDT had to adjust to a familiar 'old' system, while living with all the recent experiences from the 'new'. But, fitting into the new system had made it difficult to return to the old, since customs and expectations are so different. We can see from Razia Mohammad's doctoral research the difficulties that VTs found in returning to their classrooms and being teachers again while simultaneously accommodating their recent learning (Chapter 13; Mohammad, 2002). For PDTs, a longer time away from school and a greater awareness of educational issues and practices made it both less possible *just* to return to school culture and custom, and difficult to carve a new path for themselves due to insecurity or non-transferability of knowledge. Where teams of PDTs and VTs were able to work together and reflect on their experiences in doing so alongside IED faculty, there was more evidence of success. See for example the team activity in the Northern Areas (recounted in Chapter 12) and the mentoring programme in Baluchistan (Chapter 6). However, some teams were less coordinated than the cases reported in Chapters 6 and 12; their relationships with schools were of a short duration and on a one-off basis. In these cases, there was less overall satisfaction with the impact of the team on the school or schools with which PDTs worked.

We saw earlier something of power relationships and their influence on systemic collaboration and partnership. PDTs were expected to operate differentially and simultaneously in two different systems. Their teaching of courses for VTs bound them to the IED system, whereas their return to school demanded a re-acculturation to the school system. Mohammad (2002) makes clear some of the constraining factors in the school system: excessive correcting of 'copies' (exercise books), for example, or, in certain schools, lack of care for pupils' well-being or respect for their thinking and development; teaching that was largely teacher-centred, depending heavily on mandated texts and working towards the strict formality of examinations; teachers doing a job to earn an often meagre salary on which their family depended and therefore subject to the idiosyncrasies of head teachers who had to maintain the system.

Head teachers had a responsibility to maintain the system, but the courses for head teachers at the IED challenged many aspects of this system. Some came to see possibilities for change within seemingly inflexible structures, but nevertheless acknowledged difficulties in sustaining change (Chapter 9). These difficulties related to factors in the educational system and in society. Thus, head teachers taking part in IED programmes become also key characters in systemic linkage. Power relationships here are diversely related to knowledge and flexibility in systems. Where, as one CP put it, 'knowledge is power', those with more overt theoretical knowledge and practical know-how might be seen to have greater power – certainly in the sense that they are able to deal with abstract concepts and conceptualize alternatives. However, these qualities are not necessarily power-yielding as we see from experience, evaluation and research in IED programmes.

Engeström (for example, in Engeström, 1998), speaking from an activity theory perspective based on the work of Leont'ev, uses a triangular frame to capture mediational factors in an educational system (see Figure 10). Here the lower part of the triangle deals with factors often ignored (or hidden) in considerations of educational development. In IED collaborations, operation within the various systems involves deep layers of knowledge rooted in sociosystemic activity in which, to use Engeström's terms, the rules of operation and interaction, the community relationships, and the division of labour differ greatly from one system to another (Engeström, 1998).

For example, we might regard an activity system in which the PDT is the *subject*, with their *object* being certain goals deriving from their IED activity. Action plans, and so forth might be seen as *mediating artefacts* (see Chapter 3). If we consider only the top triangle, it is as if we consider only the tip of the iceberg. The lower triangles relating rules, community and division of labour can be seen as the 'hidden curriculum' which nevertheless influences and constrains what PDTs can achieve. This hidden curriculum involves rules of activity within the school and IED systems, intersecting communities within IED, school and society, and division of labour in terms of who takes responsibility or reports to whom at different levels, all seriously influence and constrain what is possible. These 'hidden' factors are extremely powerful in determining what the PDT can do and achieve. We can apply the triangular frame to the head teacher as subject in a similar way. The rules, community and division of labour that underpin in fundamental ways the activity of these participants cannot be ignored in developmental processes and practices as we have seen.

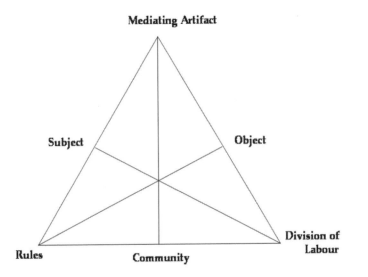

Figure 10. The mediational structure of an activity system (from Engeström, 1998).

There seems, potentially, to be some sort of clash between knowledge and systems. While knowledge developed through activity with philosophical groundings in reflection, collaboration and critical inquiry might be seen to confer power to act differentially, the inertial effects of school, society and culture militate against broader development. Thus we see embryos of achievement where developmental progress is in evidence, but these seem to be outweighed by systemic inertia. A key question seems to be how knowledge in different parts of the system interrelates in terms of human knowing, group or individual.

Assessing the Impact of IED and Moving Forward

The IED model of educational development was based on the assumption that a critical mass of professionally developed individuals (both teachers and managers) can bring about change in schools. In this chapter we have discussed many of the issues and challenges to this model. However, we now comment on what has been achieved and what lessons we can learn about teacher development and school change in developing countries from the IED experience.

Overall, the IED experiment is a success story of an institution being able to bring new ideas and adapt them to particular sociosystemic contexts in an evolutionary developmental process. In this process of reflection and adaptation, the IED programmes have become more field-based, and more flexible, providing time and opportunity to engage in reflection on action. Participants in the Certificate and Diploma programmes, for example, spend up to a full academic year in practising new knowledge learnt at IED in their own classrooms where they are supported by PDTs and IED faculty who visit and mentor them. The M.Ed. programme has been adapted over the years so that the course participants have more choices than were available in early years. CPs can now choose from a number of elective courses and opt either to carry out a dissertation or develop and implement a small-scale practical education project to complete the M.Ed. requirements. The participants can also elect to graduate with a specialization in teacher education or in educational management. This is an important possibility since many of the graduates of the programme go on to take on management positions from where they can affect the rigid systemic context we have been discussing in the last section.

IED has increased in its 'university-ness'. It is increasingly engaged in the development of, and experimentation with, educational programmes and in scholarship. However, at the same time it remains committed to the work in schools and its partnerships. Unlike other universities, IED maintains a continuing and active contact with its graduates, particularly the PDTs, and with schools in a variety of ways including the field-based course work and school-based research. In the process of evolution IED has realized that its partnerships with other institutions are desirable yet complex and demand flexibility in defining the terms of partnership. In the partnership with schools, for example, a key difficulty in implementing change was that while the individuals, who participated in IED's programmes, had changed there was no corresponding change in the school structures and systems – the 'inertia' we mentioned above. Such change has now begun to happen. We cite a few examples below.

Several private-not-for-profit collaborating schools have undertaken curricular reform and academic restructuring. The PDTs and other teachers who attended IED programmes have participated and taken leadership roles. Since the reform process is owned by the school system teachers are supported to change traditional teaching practices and introduce many of the teaching approaches and values promoted in the IED programmes. As one such school system encounters problems in introducing and sustaining change in classroom practice, it is beginning to formulate research questions and to invite IED to collaborate in and support research in the system's schools.

Another school has established a professional development centre associated with the school and offers professional development programmes for its own teachers and for teachers of its school network. Some of these programmes are offered in collaboration with IED and supported and supervised by its faculty but nevertheless held in the school. There is active support and much less resistance to classroom implementation of new teaching strategies introduced in these programmes because they are initiated by the school itself. A similar initiative has been introduced in an IED collaborating school in Bangladesh (Chapter 11) which has set up a very active school-based professional development programme.

Government education systems in Pakistan have been IED partners from the very beginning of IED activities and have sent teachers from the system to various IED programmes. However, the government is now beginning to take the initiative to try out new approaches and develop new structures. Thus, for example, one provincial government has become interested in establishing a professional development centre for in-service teacher education. The idea is that several of the PDTs from the government sector would develop the programmes offered by this centre. Another provincial government has invited IED to use the school-based approach to teacher education for a large number of teachers across the province. In the process of achieving this, the government seems open to changing policies and structures for in-service teacher education in the province.

As these developments have come about, IEDs' role and expectations of itself and schools have, quite naturally, changed. As discussed earlier, a number of constraints, not least the funding arrangements required for large-scale interventions, would not allow IED to engage directly in school improvement work and invest in close collaboration with individual schools as envisaged in the initial inspiration for the IED model, the Professional Development School. Instead, the IED has taken on the varied roles of consultant, adviser, supporter and collaborator with the systems while it continues to educate teachers, teacher educators and educational managers to lead change in these systems. The tensions of power and territory which were apparent in the early years have dissipated where schools and systems have developed expertise (primarily through IED involvement), become more confident, introduced new academic and professional development structures and taken on ownership of change. It is clear that IED has succeeded in raising awareness in these schools and systems, with some acknowledgement of teachers as professionals. It has also contributed to building school-based expertise and to promoting a culture of professional collaboration for school improvement in many of the schools it worked with.

The need to assess the impact of the IED model is keenly recognized. Several in-depth case studies of schools from various systems and regions in which IED has made an input have been started by IED faculty to identify impact and extract the stories of personal and institutional change. Initial analysis from some of the cases underscores the immense complexity of the process but also shows the possibilities. These studies of the IED model will add very significantly to our knowledge about the nature and process of partnership and change in schools and school systems and add to the rather limited literature on school improvement and change in developing countries. In doing so, it will also contribute to the theory of educational change which is at the moment primarily based on the experience and evidence in the context of the western countries.

Note

[1] Since these times, the IED has grown to encompass a second PDC in the Northern Areas of Pakistan, a third in Chiltral in the North West Frontier province of Pakistan, and a fourth in Eastern Africa. At the time of writing, a fourth PDC in central Asia is in the planning phase, as is a second IED in Dar es Salaam, East Africa.

References

AKU-IED (1991) *A Proposal of the AKU Board of Trustees*. Unpublished first Task Force report. Karachi@AKU-IED.

Atkinson, S. (1994) Rethinking the Principles and Practice of Action Research: the tensions for the teacher-researcher, *Educational Action Research*, 2(3), pp. 383-399.

Bickel, W., Stanley, D., Johnston, J., Lemahieu, P., Saltrick, D. & Young, J. (1987) Clinical Teachers at the Schenley Teacher Centre: Teacher Professionalism and Educational Reform, *Journal of Staff Development*, 8(2).

Brown, S. & McIntyre, D. (1993) *Making Sense of Teaching*. Buckingham: Open University Press.

Calderhead, J. (1987) *Exploring Teachers' Thinking*. London: Cassell.

Calderhead, J. & Shorrock, S.B. (1997) *Understanding Teacher Education*. London: Falmer Press.

Carr, W. & Kemmis, S. (1986) *Becoming Critical: education, knowledge and action research*. London: Falmer Press.

Clark, C.M. & Peterson, P.L. (1986) Teacher's Thought Processes, in M. Wittrock (Ed.) *Handbook of Research on Teaching*, pp. 255-296, New York: Macmillan.

Cooney, T.J. (1984) The Contribution of Theory to Mathematics Teacher Education, in H.G. Steiner (Ed.) *Theory of Mathematics Education (TME)*. Bielefeld: Universität Bielefeld, IDM.

Dallmer, D. (2004) Collaborative Relationships in Teacher Education: a personal narrative of conflicting roles, *Curriculum Inquiry*, 34(1), pp. 29-46.

Darling-Hammond, L. (Ed.) (1994) *Professional Development Schools: Schools for Developing a Profession*. New York: Teachers College Press.

Darling-Hammond, L. (2000) How Teacher Education Matters, *Journal of Teacher Education*, 51(3), pp. 166-173.

Dewey, J. (1933) *How We Think.* London: D.C. Heath.

Elbaz, F. (1990) Knowledge and Discourse: the evolution of research on teacher thinking, in C. Day, M. Pope & P. Denicolo (Eds) *Insights into Teachers' Thinking and Practice.* London: Falmer Press.

Engeström, Y. (1998) Reorganising the Motivational Sphere of Classroom Culture: an activity-theoretical analysis of planning in a teacher team, in F. Seeger, J. Voigt & U. Waschesio (Eds) *The Culture of the Mathematics Classroom.* Cambridge: Cambridge University Press.

Eraut, M. (1994) *Developing Professional Knowledge and Competence.* London: Falmer Press.

Eraut, M. (1995) Schön Shock: a case for reframing reflection-in-action?, *Teachers and Teaching: Theory and Practice,* 1(1), pp. 19-22.

Feiman-Nemser, S. (1983) Learning to Teach, in L. Shulman & G. Sykes (Eds) *Handbook of Teaching and Policy,* pp.150-170. New York: Longman.

Goodlad, J.I. (1990) *Teachers for Our Nation's Schools.* San Francisco: Jossey-Bass.

Goodlad, J.I. & Sirotnik, K.A. (Eds) (1988) *School-University Partnerships in Action: concepts, cases and concerns.* New York: Teachers College Press.

Ginsberg, R. & Rhodes, L.K. (2003) University Faculty in Partner Schools, *Journal of Teacher Education,* 54(2), pp. 150-162.

Hagger, H. & McIntyre, D. (2000) What Can Research Tell Us about Teacher Education? *Oxford Review of Education,* 26(3&4), pp. 483-494.

Halai, A. (1998) Mentor, Mentee, and Mathematics: a story of professional development, *Journal of Mathematics Teacher Education,* 1(3), pp. 295-315.

Halai, A. (2002) Mentoring In-service Teacher: issues of role diversity. Paper presented at the School Improvement Conference, Uganda, November.

Hamilton, M.L. (1998) *Reconceptualising Teaching Practice: self study in teacher education.* London: Falmer Press.

Holmes Group (1986) *Tomorrow's Teachers: a report of the Holmes Group.* East Lansing, MI: Holmes Group, Inc.

Jaworski, B. (1994) *Investigating Mathematics Teaching: a constructivist enquiry.* London: Falmer Press.

Jaworski, B. (1998) Mathematics teacher research: process practice and the development of teaching, *Journal of Mathematics Teacher Education,* 1(1), pp. 3-31.

Jaworski, B. & Gellert, U. (2003) Educating New Mathematics Teachers: integrating theory and practice, and the role of practising teachers, in A.J. Bishop, M.A. Clements, C. Keitel, J. Kilpatrick, & F.K.S. Leung (Eds) *Second International Handbook of Mathematics Education.* Dordrecht: Kluwer.

Kemmis, S. (1985) Action Research and the Politics of Reflection, in D. Boud, R. Keogh & D. Walker (Eds) *Reflection: turning experience into learning.* London: Kogan Page.

Mason, J. (2001) *Researching Your Own Classroom Practice: from noticing to reflection.* London: Routledge Falmer.

McIntyre, D. (1997) The Profession of Educational Research, *British Educational Research Journal*, 23(2), pp. 127-140.

McNiff, J. (1993) Teaching as Learning: an action research approach. London: Routledge.

Mohammad, R.F. (2002) From Theory to Practice: an understanding of the implementation of in-service mathematics teachers' learning from university into the classroom in Pakistan. Unpublished D.Phil. thesis, University of Oxford, Oxford.

Schön D.A. (1983) *The Reflective Practitioner*. London: Temple Smith.

Schön D.A. (1987) *Educating the Reflective Practitioner*. Oxford: Jossey-Bass.

Shulman, L.S. (1987) Knowledge and Teaching: foundations of the New Reform, *Harvard Educational Review*, 57(1), pp. 1-23.

Smyth, J. (1987) Transforming Teaching by Intellectualising the Work of Teachers, in J. Smyth (Ed.) *Educating Teachers*. London: Falmer Press.

Smyth, J. (1991) *Teachers as Collaborative Learners*. Buckingham: Open University Press.

Stenhouse, L. (1984) Evaluating Curriculum Evaluation, in C. Adleman (Ed.) *The Politics and Ethics of Evaluation*. London: Croom Helm.

Teitel, L. (2001) An Assessment Framework for Professional Development Schools, Going beyond the Leap of Faith, *Journal of Teacher Education*, 52(1), pp. 57-69.

Vulliamy, G. & Webb, R. (1992) The Influence of Teacher Research: process or product? *Educational Review*, 44(1), pp. 41-58.

Wells, G. (Ed.) (2001) *Action, Talk and Text: learning and teaching through inquiry*. New York: Teachers College Press.

List of Acronyms

ADISM	Advanced Diploma in School Management
AKDN	Aga Khan Development Network
AKES	Aga Khan Education Services
AKES,P	Aga Khan Education Services, Pakistan
AKF	The Aga Khan Foundation
AKS, D	Aga Khan School, Dhaka
AKU-IED	The Aga Khan University – Institute for Educational Development
APT	The Association of Primary Teachers
ASSET	Association of Social Studies Educators and Teachers
CE:ELM	Certificate Course in Educational Leadership and Management
CEC	Commission of European Communities
CEM	Certificate in Educational Management
CEP	Certificate in Education Programme
CIDA	Canadian International Development Agency
CPs	Class Participants
CTs	Clinical Teachers
DD	Deputy Director
DFID	Department for International Development
EPCK	Enhancing Pedagogical Content Knowledge
FBTDP	Field Based Teacher Development Programme
H.H.	His Highness the Aga Khan
IED	Institute for Educational Development
IPD	Institute for Professional Development
LEAP	Learning Enhancement and Achievement Programme
MAP	Mathematics Association of Pakistan
MBAR	Mountainous Badakhshan Autonomous Region
MoU	Memorandum of Understanding
MTRC	Mobile Training Resource Centre
NGO	Non-governmental Organisation
NORAD	Norwegian Agency for Development Cooperation
OISE-UT	Ontario Institute for Studies in Education, University of Toronto
OUDES	Oxford University Department of Educational Studies
PAIE	Pakistan Association of Inclusive Education

PDC	Professional Development Centre
PDCN	Professional Development Centre, North
PDT	Professional Development Teacher
PED	Primary Education Directorate
PEDP	Primary Education Development Project
PITE	Provincial Institute for Teacher Education
PREL	Pacific Resources for Educational and Learning briefing paper
PTMP	Primary Teachers Mentoring Programme
PU	Partner Universities
SAP	Science Association of Pakistan
SDP	School Development Programme
SHADE	School Heads Association of Pakistan
SHAP	School Health Action Plan
SIC	School Improvement Centre
SIP	School Improvement Programme
SMS	Sultan Mohamed Shah
SPELT	Society of Pakistan English Language Teachers
TDMP	Teacher Development and Management Plan
TLRT	Teacher Learning Resource Team
TTSU	Teacher Training Support Unit
UN	United Nations
UNDP	United Nations Development Programme
UNESCO	United Nations Educational, Scientific and Cultural Organization
UPE	Universal Primary Education
VT	Visiting Teachers
VTP	Visiting Teachers Programme
WHO	World Health Organisation
WSIP	Whole School Improvement Programme

Notes on Contributors

Takbir Ali grew up in a remote, but legendarily beautiful valley in the Northern Areas of Pakistan. He earned a Masters in Education (Teacher Education) from AKU-IED. He is currently a Ph.D. candidate at the University of Toronto in Canada. He worked at the Professional Development Centre in the Northern Areas as a Professional Development Teacher and later became part of its core faculty.

Zubeda Bana has been Academic Manager for Regional Coordination at the Ismaili Tariqah and Religious Education Board for Pakistan since February 2003. Prior to this she was at AKU-IED as a Senior Instructor in educational management. She has extensive experience in teacher education in Sindh, Balochistan, North West Frontier Province, Northern Pakistan and East Africa.

Yasmeen Bano is currently working as an academic manager in the Education Office, South Aga Khan Education Service, Pakistan. She started her teaching career at the Aga Khan Boys' Secondary School, Kharadhar in 1985 and worked there as the Head of Science and then the Deputy Head until 1996. Yasmeen completed her M.Ed. at the AKU-IED in 1998.

Sultan Mahmud Bhuiyan is a Professional Development Teacher (PDT) at the Aga Khan Education Service, Bangladesh (AKES, B). He has been conducting in-service professional development programs for the teachers since 1998 in Bangladesh and Pakistan. Currently he is also a Ph.D. research (Fellow) in Bangladesh.

Sadia Muzzaffar Bhutta is an Instructor at AKU-IED. Currently she is reading for a Ph.D. degree (2002-05) at the University of Oxford, Department of Educational Studies. She is a graduate of the M.Ed. programme at AKU-IED and also holds a Master's degree in Educational Research Methodology from Pakistan and the United Kingdom (UK).

Bernadette L. Dean is an Assistant Professor and Head of Academic and Student Affairs at AKU-IED. She has teaching and research interests in social studies education/citizenship, curriculum, teaching and learning and action research. Her publications include social studies textbooks for primary schools and various articles and book chapters.

Iffat Farah joined AKU-IED in 1994 and is currently Professor of Education. She has a Ph.D. in Education from the University of

Pennsylvania, USA and a Master's degree in applied linguistics from the University of Kent, UK. She is currently Associate Professor and Head, Research & Policy Studies at AKU-IED.

Anjum Halai graduated from the first M.Ed. programme at AKU-IED and obtained a doctorate in Mathematics Education from Oxford University, UK. She is currently Assistant Professor at AKU-IED. Anjum was a founding member and first chairperson of the Mathematics Association of Pakistan, which plays a key role in providing a platform for continuous professional development of mathematics teachers.

Nelofer Halai earned a Ph.D. from the University of Toronto in Canada. She is an associate professor at AKU-IED. Her research interests lie in two broad areas – science education and teaching of research. She has been teaching research methods to M.Ed. students for more than three years.

Rana Hussain is a senior instructor at AKU-IED. She has a special interest in primary education and brings with her a vast experience of working in schools in the capacity of teacher, teacher educator and manager of primary schools.

Shahida Jawed is a head teacher of a girls' school in Karachi. She began her career as a science teacher and graduated from the first Masters in Education programe offered at AKU-IED. Since her graduation she has initiated and participated in many school improvement programmes including the establishment of a professional development centre in her school.

Barbara Jaworski is Professor of Mathematics Education at Agder University College, Norway. She was a Reader at the University of Oxford during the time that this book was written. She is Editor-in-Chief of the *Journal of Mathematics Teacher Education*.

Gulzar Kanji was educated in Tanzania and Uganda. She has worked as primary school teacher, head teacher, local authority inspector and Her Majesty's Inspector in the UK. She worked as Project Director of a school improvement project in Kampala, Uganda. From 1998 to 2001 she was Associate Professor at AKU-IED and established the Professional Development Centre in Gilgit. She continues to work at AKU-IED as visiting faculty.

Anil Khamis is lecturer and course coordinator for the M.A. in Education and International Development at the Institute of Education, University of London. He was Assistant Professor at AKU-IED from 1998-2000.

Tashmin Kassam-Khamis was awarded her Ph.D. in 1996 in Nutritional Sciences from King's College London. From 1997 to 2001 she worked as Assistant Professor at AKU-IED and was Principal Investigator of the Health Action Schools action research project, funded by Save the Children (UK). Currently Tashmin heads the Child-to-Child Trust (UK).

Firdousali Lalwani graduated from the M.Ed. programme at IED. He has been associated with the Ismaili Tariqah and Religious Education Board and with AKU-IED as a Professional Development Teacher. He has been involved in the development, implementation and evaluation of a number of human resource development programmes.

Rakhshinda Mehar is a graduate of the M.Ed. programme at AKU-IED and has worked for several years as a PDT at the Professional Development Centre in Karachi. She has vast experience of teaching and teacher education. She has taught in and coordinated many certificate in education programmes at AKU-IED.

Muhammad Memon joined AKU-IED in December 1993 and is now a Professor and Head of Programmes. He has played a significant role in introducing educational leadership and management as a field of studies in Pakistan. He has conducted a number of research studies in the area of educational leadership and organizational learning and has served as a member of various committees and task forces on reforming education in the public sector of Pakistan.

Razia Fakir Mohammed started her career as a secondary school mathematics teacher in an Aga Khan School in Karachi. After completing an M.Ed. from AKU-IED she worked as a Professional Development Teacher in the AKES schools. Since 1998 she has been a senior instructor at AKU-IED.

Gulgunchamo Naimova is a Professional Development Teacher from Badakshan in Tajikistan. She started her career as an English language teacher. Since 1998 she has been working with the Aga Khan Education Service, Tajikistan, conducting professional development courses for the teachers at the Aga Khan Lycée in Khorog. Currently she is working at AKU-IED and is involved in the Educational Development Projects of AKU-IED for Tajikistan and Afghanistan.

Sadrudin Pardhan joined AKU-IED in April 1993. He is currently Professor and Director of Outreach Programmes and Activities at AKU-IED. He has been associated with AKU-IED since its start up in July 1993. His major areas of interest are science education, teacher education and institutional development.

Richard Pring M.A. (Oxon), Ph.D. (London), Hon.D.Litt. (Kent), Emeritus Professor of Green College, Oxford, Director of the Department of Educational Studies, University of Oxford (1989-2003), presently Lead Director, Nuffield Review of Education and Training. Recent books: *Philosophy of Educational Research*, (Continuum, 2000); *Philosophy of Education: Aims, Theory, Common Sense and Research* (Continuum, 2004).

Jane Frances Akinyi Rarieya is a graduate of the M.Ed. programme at AKU-IED. She has worked as a teacher educator in the East African Region and Pakistan conducting in-service courses for teachers and participating in school improvement projects in Tanzania and Kenya. She is currently a Senior Instructor at AKU-IED and a Ph.D. candidate at the University of Keele, UK.

Fauzia Shamim is an Associate Professor at AKU-IED. She holds a Ph.D. from the University of Leeds, UK in TESOL and has extensive experience of teaching English and of teacher education in a variety of settings both in Pakistan and the UK.

Tim Simkins is Professor of Education Management at Sheffield Hallam University, UK. He has more than 25 years' experience of teaching and researching leadership and management in education. He is a former Chair of the British Educational Leadership Management and Administration Society. He has designed, managed and contributed to the wide range of continuing professional development programmes for education leaders and managers in the UK and overseas and has acted as a consultant to a number of international development agencies in the designing and evaluation of management development programmes.

Charles Sisum is Senior Lecturer in Continuing Professional Development at Bath Spa University College, UK. He was teaching leadership and management in education at Sheffield Hallam University when this chapter was written. Charles has extensive experience of providing professional development for school leaders both within the UK and overseas.

Dennis Thiessen is a Professor and the Chair in the Curriculum, Teaching and Learning at the Ontario Institute for Studies in Education of the University of Toronto.

Fred Tukahirwa is Education Programme Officer at Aga Khan Education Service, Uganda. He received his M.Ed. from AKU-IED. He has been a teacher in primary and secondary schools and continues to work as Teacher Educator in AKES schools in Uganda.